Witchcraft in Early Modern Europe

PROBLEMS IN EUROPEAN CIVILIZATION SERIES

General Editor
Merry E. Wiesner

A witch brews up a storm, sinking a ship and killing all on board, from Olaus Magnus's *Historia de gentibus Septentrionalibus (History of the Northern People)*, a huge survey of Swedish customs, folklore, and traditions first published in 1555. Witch trials frequently included accusations of harm caused through manipulating weather, such as hail, floods, drought, or storms. *(From Olaus Magnus's* Historia de gentibus Septentrionalibus, *Rome, 1555. Print provided by Glasgow University, Department of Special Collections.)*

Witchcraft in Early Modern Europe

Edited with an introduction by

Merry E. Wiesner

University of Wisconsin–Milwaukee

Houghton Mifflin Company   Boston   New York

Publisher: Patricia A. Coryell
Senior Sponsoring Editor: Nancy Blaine
Senior Development Editor: Jeffrey Greene
Associate Project Editor: Deborah Berkman
Associate Manufacturing Buyer: Susan Brooks
Senior Art and Design Coordinator: Jill Haber
Senior Photo Editor: Jennifer Meyer Dare
Composition Buyer: Chuck Dutton
Senior Marketing Manager: Katherine Bates
Marketing Assistant: Lauren Bussard

Cover image: Witches burnt in Derneburg in 1555 (coloured engraving)
by German School (16th century)
Credit: © Bibliotheque des Arts

Printed in the U.S.A.

Library of Congress Control Number: 2006924895

ISBN-10: 0-618-47480-3
ISBN-13: 978-0-618-47480-6

123456789-EB-09 08 07 06

Contents

Preface

During the sixteenth and seventeenth centuries, hundreds of thousands of people were investigated and tried, and tens of thousands executed, for witchcraft in Europe. These witch hunts are both fascinating and challenging. Most people in Europe believed in witches for centuries before this era and many continued to do so for long afterwards. Other than a handful of cases, however, only during these two centuries were there large-scale hunts and mass executions. Why?

This question has puzzled people since the time of the witch hunts themselves, and many different answers have been proposed. Learned authorities at the time, some of who were themselves hunting or trying witches, suggested that the flourishing of witchcraft and magic was a sign of the coming end of the world. The devil, they wrote, was more active and violent because he knows the last days are coming; he thus seeks out more people to do his bidding, and more people are tempted because of the moral decay that prophecy foretold would precede the apocalypse. Human agents could not stop this, but they were to resist the forces of darkness and work to rid their societies of evil as much as possible.

By the eighteenth century, this explanation had been turned on its head. The "forces of darkness," wrote Enlightenment philosophers, were the authorities who had persecuted generally harmless people for witchcraft, not the witches themselves. The witch hunts were the most extreme example of the misguided and irrational nature of religion, they asserted, particularly that of the Catholic Church and its Inquisition, whose power was slowly loosened with the advent of science and reason. Nineteenth-century historians generally ignored the witch hunts in their story of the political, economic, and intellectual changes of what they increasingly saw as the beginning of the "modern" era. Witch-beliefs were an unfortunate remnant of a "medieval" past, and had little to do with the rise of capitalism, the development of the nation-state, the Protestant and Catholic Reformations, and other changes that were truly important. Because witchcraft had no objective reality, they noted, it was not really the proper subject for historians, or at most an aberration worthy of only the briefest mention.

The twentieth century demonstrated just how powerful ideas with no objective reality could be, and the last half of the century saw hundreds of studies of the witch hunts; this interest shows no signs of abating in the twenty-first century. As historians have delved into actual records of trials and the writings of those concerned with witches, they have discovered that many earlier ideas about the witch hunts—some of which continue to shape popular understanding, and are now repeated endlessly on various websites—are simply wrong. The most intense period of witch-hunting was not the Middle Ages, but the late sixteenth and early seventeenth centuries, clearly part of modern times. Protestants were just as active in hunting witches as were Catholics, and skeptics about the power of witches included people from all Christian denominations. The Inquisition—whether Spanish, Portuguese or Roman—actually tried relatively few witches and executed only a small number. Economic changes, including the development of capitalism, did play a role in many hunts. Rulers intent on creating nation-states were, in fact, often very avid witch-hunters, and one—James I and VI of England and Scotland—even wrote a treatise on demonology. The authors of other important works on witchcraft included leading political philosophers and scientists, who saw the power of witches as part of the natural world they were seeking to understand and explain. This research has made clear that the witch hunts were not marginal events involving ill-educated villagers and fanatical clergy, but a central part of this era.

This volume addresses four of the major themes in recent studies of the witch hunts. Part I explores the intellectual foundations for early modern European witchcraft, particularly the works of learned demonologists. Part II focuses on political, economic, and social contexts, the broader framework within which witch hunts operated. Part III looks at the process of witch hunts, which began with an accusation, led often (but not always) to a trial, and sometimes ended in a wave of mass persecutions generally termed a "panic." Part IV presents several different approaches historians have taken when looking at connections between gender and witchcraft as they have tried to understand why about three-quarters of those accused, tried, and executed were women.

All of the selections in this volume were first published within the last twenty years, and some within the last two. They thus represent the very newest in research on the witch hunts, and many of them explicitly test ideas that were developed in the 1970s, when academic research on witchcraft saw its first high point. The selections include some that focus on areas where witch-hunting was most intense, such as eastern France and the Holy Roman Empire, and others on areas where there were few hunts, such as Norway and Italy. Some selections come from articles in journals and some from books, including several enormous recent studies that have proved especially influential, such as Stuart Clark's *Thinking with Demons*, Robin Briggs' *Witches and Neighbors*, and Wolfgang Behringer's *Witchcraft Persecutions in Bavaria*. The authors include scholars from the United States, England, Scotland, Norway, Germany, Hungary, and Australia, for research on the witch hunts is truly an international enterprise.

I am less of a specialist on the witch hunts than are the authors in this volume, and I owe a debt of gratitude to them, and many others, who have helped my understanding of the ways in which a mythology about evil forces can lead people to carry out unspeakable acts. I have enjoyed conversations with Gerhild Williams, Brian Levack, and Lyndal Roper for more years than I care to remember, and over a shorter period with Charles Zika and Diane Purkiss. Discussions with scholars of witchcraft whose work is not in this volume, including William Monter, Richard Golden, David Harley, Edmund Kern, Erik Midelfort, Jens-Christian Johansen, Susanna Burghartz, David Sabean, and the late Sigrid Brauner, have been very important. Finally, I would like to thank Nancy Blaine at Houghton Mifflin for suggesting both that I prepare this book, and take over as the editor of this series. Both tasks have been more interesting, though slower in their realization, than I imagined.

Merry E. Wiesner

Series Editor's Preface to Instructors

There are many ways to date ourselves as teachers and scholars of history: the questions that we regard as essential to ask about any historical development, the theorists whose words we quote and whose names appear in our footnotes, the price of the books purchased for courses that are on our shelves. Looking over my own shelves, it struck me that another way we could be dated was by the color of the oldest books we owned in this series, which used to be published by D.C. Heath. I first used a "Heath series" book—green and white, as I recall—when I was a freshman in college in a modern European history course. That book, by Dwight E. Lee on the Munich crisis, has long since disappeared, but several Heath books that I acquired later as an undergraduate are still on my shelves. Those that I used in graduate school, including ones on the Renaissance and Reformation, are also there, as well as several that I assigned to my students when I first started teaching or have used in the years since. Of course, as with any system of historical periodization, this method of dating a historian is flawed and open to misinterpretation. When a colleague retired, he gave me some of his even older Heath series books, in red and black, which had actually appeared when I was still in elementary and junior high school, so that a glance at my shelves might make me seem ready for retirement.

The longevity of this series, despite its changing cover design and its transition from D.C. Heath to Houghton Mifflin, could serve as an indication of several things. One might be that historians are conservative, unwilling to change the way they approach the past or teach about it. The rest of the books on my shelves suggest that this is not the case, however, for many of the them discuss topics that were unheard of as subjects of historical investigation when I took that course as a freshman thirty years ago: memory, masculinity, visual culture, and sexuality.

Another way to account for the longevity of this series is that several generations of teachers have found it a useful way for their students to approach historical subjects. As teachers, one of the first issues we confront in any course is what materials we will assign our students to read. (This is often, in fact, the very first thing we must decide, for we have to order books months before the class begins.) We may include a textbook to provide an overview of the subject matter covered in the course, and often have a number from which to choose. We may use a reader of original sources, or several sources in their entirety, because we feel that it is important for our students to hear the voices of people of the past directly. We may add a novel from the period, for fictional works often give one details and insights that do not emerge from other types of sources. We may direct our students to visual materials, either in books or on the Web, for artifacts, objects, and art can give one access to aspects of life never mentioned in written sources.

Along with these types of assignments, we may also choose to assign books such as those in this series, which present the ideas and opinions of scholars on a particular topic. Textbooks are, of course, written by scholars with definite opinions, but they are designed to present material in a relatively bland manner. They may suggest areas about which there is historical debate (often couched in phrases such as "scholars disagree about . . . ") but do not participate in those debates themselves. By contrast, the books in this series highlight points of dispute and cover topics and developments about which historians often disagree vehemently. Students who are used to the textbook approach to history may be surprised at the range of opinion on certain matters, but we hope that the selections in each of these volumes will allow readers to understand why there is such a diversity. Each volume covers several issues of interpretive debate and highlights newer research directions.

Variety of interpretation in history is sometimes portrayed as a recent development, but the age of this series in its many cover styles indicates that this account is not accurate. Historians have long realized that historical sources are produced by particular individuals with particular interests and biases that consciously and unconsciously shape their content. They have also long—one is tempted to say "always"—recognized that different people approach the past differently, making choices about which topics to study, which sources to use, which developments and individuals to highlight. This diversity in both sources and methodologies is part of what makes history exciting for those of us who study it, for new materials and new approaches allow us to see things that have never been seen before, in the same way that astronomers find new stars with better tools and new ways of looking at the universe.

The variety and innovation that is an essential part of good historical scholarship allow this series both to continue and to change. Some of the volumes now being prepared have the same titles as those I read as an undergraduate, but the scholarship on that topic has changed so much in the last several decades that they had to be completely redone, not simply revised. Some of the volumes now in print examine topics that were rarely covered in undergraduate courses when the series began publication, and a few former volumes are no longer in print as the topics they investigated now show up rarely. We endeavor to keep the series up-to-date and welcome suggestions about volumes that would prove helpful for teaching undergraduate and graduate courses. You can contact us at http://college.hmco.com.

Merry E. Wiesner

Series Editor's Preface to Students

History is often presented as facts marching along a timeline, and historical research viewed as the unearthing of information so that more facts can be placed on the timeline. Like geologists in caves, or physicists using elaborate microscopes, historians discover new bits of data that allow them to recover more of the past.

To some degree this is an accurate model. Like laboratory scientists, historians do conduct primary research, using materials in archives, libraries, and many other places to discover new things about the past. Over the last thirty years, for example, the timeline of history has changed from a story that was largely political and military to one that includes the experiences of women, peasants, slaves, children, and workers. Even the political and military story has changed, and now includes the experiences of ordinary soldiers and minority groups, rather than simply those of generals, rulers, and political elites. This expansion of the timeline has come in part through intensive research in original sources, which has vastly increased what we know about people of the past.

However, original research is only part of what historians do, in the same way that laboratory or field research is only part of science. Historical and scientific information is useless until someone tries to make sense of what is happening—tries to explain why and how things developed the way they did. In making these analyses and conclusions, however, both historians and scientists often come to disagree vehemently about the underlying reasons for what they have observed or discovered and sometimes about the observations themselves. Certain elements of those observations are irrefutable—a substance either caught fire or it did not, a person lived and died or he or she did not—but many more of them are open to debate: Was the event (whether historical or scientific) significant? Why and how did it happen? Under what circumstances might it not have happened? What factors influenced the way that it happened? What larger consequences did it have?

The books in this series focus on just those types of questions. They take one particular event or development in European history, and present the analyses of a number of historians and other authors regarding this issue. In some cases the authors may disagree about what actually happened—in the same way that eyewitnesses of a traffic accident or crime may all see different things—but more often they disagree about the interpretation. Was the Renaissance a continuation of earlier ideas, or did it represent a new way of looking at the world? Was nineteenth-century European imperialism primarily political and economic in its origins and impact, or were cultural and intellectual factors more significant? Was ancient Athens a democracy worthy of emulation, an expansionary state seeking to swallow its neighbors, or both? Within each volume there are often more specific points of debate, which add complexity to the main question and introduce you to further points of disagreement.

Each of the volumes begins with an introduction by the editor, which you should read carefully before you turn to the selections themselves. This introduction sets out the *historical* context of the issue, adding depth to what you may have learned in a textbook account or other reading and also explains the *historiographical* context, that is, how historians (including those excerpted in the volume) have viewed the issue over time. Each volume also includes a timeline of events and several reference maps that situate the issue chronologically and geographically. These may be more detailed than the timelines and maps in your textbook, and consulting them as you read will help deepen your understanding of the selections.

Some of the volumes in the series include historical analyses that are more than a century old, and all include writings stretching over several decades. The editors include this chronological range not only to allow you to see that interpretations change, but also to see how lines of argument and analysis develop. Every historian approaching an issue depends not only on his or her own original research, but also on the secondary analyses of those who have gone before, which he or she then accepts, rejects, modifies, or adapts. Thus, within the book as a whole, or within each section, the selections are generally arranged in chronological order. Reading them in the order they are presented will allow you to get a better sense of the historiographical development and to make comparisons among the selections more easily and appropriately.

The description of the scholarly process noted above is somewhat misleading, for in both science and history, research and analysis are not sequential but simultaneous. Historians do not wander around archives looking for interesting bits of information, but turn to their sources with specific questions in mind, questions that have often been developed by reading earlier historians. These questions shape where they will look, what they will pay attention to, and therefore what conclusions they will make. Thus the fact that we now know so much more about women, peasants, or workers than we did several decades ago did not result primarily from sources on these people suddenly appearing where there had been none, but from historians going back to the same archives and libraries that had yielded information on kings and generals with new questions in mind. The same is true of science, of course. Scientists examining an issue begin with a hypothesis and then test it through the accumulation of information, reaching a conclusion that leads to further hypotheses.

In both history and science, one's hypotheses can sometimes be so powerful that one simply cannot see what the sources or experiments show, which is one reason there is always opportunity for more research or a reanalysis of data. A scholar's analysis may also be shaped by many other factors, and in this volume the editor may have provided you with information about individual authors, such as their national origin, intellectual background, or philosophical perspective, if these factors are judged important to your understanding of their writings or points of view. You might be tempted to view certain of these factors as creating "bias" on the part of an author and thus reduce the value of his or her analysis. It is important to recognize, however, that every historian or commentator has a particular point of view and writes at a particular historical moment. Very often what scholars view as complete objectivity on their own part is seen as subjective bias by those who disagree. The central aim of this series over its forty plus years of publication has been to help students understand how and why the analyses and judgments of historians have differed and changed over time—to see that scholarly controversy is at the heart of the historical enterprise. The instructor in your course may have provided you with detailed directions for using this book, but here are some basic questions that you can ask yourself as you read the selections:

- What is the author's central argument?
- What evidence does the author put forward to support this argument?
- What is the significance of the author's argument?
- What other interpretation might there be of the evidence that the author presents?
- How does each author's argument intersect with the others in the chapter? In the rest of the book?
- How convincing do you find the author's interpretation?

These questions are exactly the same as those professional historians ask themselves, and in analyzing and comparing the selections in this book, you, too, are engaged in the business of historical interpretation.

Merry E. Wiesner

Chronology

1324–1325	Trial of Dame Alice Kytler in Ireland, first with charges of ritual demonic magic and devil worship as well as *maleficia*
1420s–1430s	Trials in France and Switzerland first include charges of nightflying to orgiastic sabbats
1486	First publication of *Malleus Maleficarum* (last early modern edition 1669)
1542, 1563, 1604	Witchcraft statutes passed by English Parliament
1563	Witchcraft statute passed by Scottish Parliament
1563	First publication of Johann Weyer's *On the Tricks of Devils*, questioning whether women could ever make demonic pacts
1580–1650	Height of European witch hunt
1580	First publication of Jean Bodin's *The Demon-mania of Witches*
1585–1593	Witch hunt in Trier, Germany, where accused witches name about 1500 accomplices, resulting in between 500 and 1000 executions
1590s	First publication of Nicolas Rémy's *Three Books of Demonolatry* and Martin del Rio's *Six Books of Disquisitions on Magic*, major demonological treatises
1597	Publication of King James VI of Scotland's *Daemonologie*, urging the severe punishment of witches

Introduction

Nearly all pre-modern societies believe in witchcraft and make some attempts to control witches, who are understood to be people who have contact with supernatural powers and use them for evil purposes. Only in early modern central and northern Europe and the English colony in Massachusetts, however, did these beliefs lead to wide-scale hunts and mass executions. Because so many records have been lost or destroyed, it is difficult to make an estimate for all of Europe, but most scholars agree that during the sixteenth and seventeenth centuries somewhere between 100,000 and 200,000 people were officially tried and between 40,000 and 60,000 were executed. Given the much smaller size of the European population in comparison with today, these are enormous numbers.

This dramatic upsurge in witch trials, often labeled the "Great Witch Hunt" or the "Witch Craze," has been the subject of a huge number of studies during the last thirty years, and a variety of explanations have been suggested. Some scholars have chosen to emphasize intellectual and cultural factors: During the late Middle Ages, Christian philosophers and theologians developed a new idea about the most important characteristics of a witch. Until that period in Europe, as in most cultures throughout the world, a witch was a person who used magical forces to do evil deeds (*maleficia*). One was a witch, therefore, because of what one *did*, causing injuries or harm to animals and people. This notion of witchcraft continued in Europe, but to it was added a demonological component. Educated Christian thinkers in some parts of Europe began to view the essence of witchcraft as making a pact with the devil, a pact that required the witch to do the devil's bidding. Witches were no longer simply people who used magical power to get what they wanted, but people used by the devil to do what *he* wanted. (The devil is always described and portrayed visually as male.) Witchcraft was thus not a question of what one *did*, but of what one *was*, and proving that a witch had committed *maleficia* was no longer necessary for conviction.

Gradually this demonological or Satanic idea of witchcraft was fleshed out, and witches were thought to engage in wild sexual orgies with the devil, fly through the night to meetings called sabbats which parodied the mass, and steal communion wafers and unbaptized babies to use in their rituals. Some demonological theorists also claimed that

1

witches were organized in an international conspiracy to overthrow Christianity, with a hierarchy modeled on the hierarchy of angels and archangels constructed by Christian philosophers to give order to God's assistants. Witchcraft was thus spiritualized, and witches became the ultimate heretics, enemies of God.

Learned ideas gradually began to infiltrate popular understanding of what it meant to be a witch. Illustrated pamphlets and broadsides portrayed witches riding on pitchforks to sabbats where they engaged in anti-Christian acts such as spitting on the communion host and sexual relations with demons. Though witch trials were secret, executions were not; they were public spectacles witnessed by huge crowds, with the list of charges read out for all to hear. By the late sixteenth century, popular denunciations for witchcraft in many parts of Europe involved at least some parts of the demonic conception of witchcraft. Conversely, popular understandings of witchcraft also shaped demonology; charges such as witches entering cellars and storerooms to steal food and wine emerge first in local accusations, and then later show up in formal demonological treatises.

Though witch trials died down somewhat during the first decades after the Protestant Reformation when Protestants and Catholics were busy fighting each other, they picked up again more strongly than ever about 1560. Protestants rejected many Catholic teachings, but not demonology. Protestants may have felt even more at the mercy of witches than Catholics; they rejected rituals such as exorcism, which Catholics believed could counter the power of a witch. The Protestant and Catholic Reformations may have contributed to the spread of demonological ideas among wider groups of the population, for both Catholics and Protestants increased their religious instruction of lay people during the sixteenth century, and demonological ideas were a key part of such teaching.

Part I of this reader explores the intellectual foundations for early modern European witchcraft, and includes four selections that focus in particular on the works of demonologists. Stuart Clark analyzes ways in which witchcraft beliefs and concepts of demonology held by European intellectuals fitted rationally with their ideas about science, history, religion, and politics. Charles Zika investigates ways in which popular charms and traditional folkloric beliefs were gradually "theologized," and increasingly understood as invisible operations possible only through diabolic power rather than visible phenomena carried out by spirits or humans. Gerhild Scholz Williams discusses the writings of one particular witch-hunter, the French magistrate Pierre de Lancre, sent to investigate witchcraft in the Basque-speaking Labourt area of southern France, which he found more ungodly, disorderly, and disturbing than reports coming back to Europe about the residents of the New World. Walter Stephens looks more closely at one aspect of witchcraft theory, the great concern with demonstrating that demons and their actions were *real*, and that demons had actual bodies when they interacted with witches.

While many historians have focused on demonology and related intellectual developments, others have highlighted the importance of political, economic, and social factors. The great witch hunts occurred at a time when monarchs in western and northern Europe were consolidating royal power, creating what would become nation-states out of more decentralized feudal territories. Even in areas where nation-states were not developing, such as the Holy Roman Empire in central Europe, rulers of smaller territories were consolidating their holds and determined to prove their power vis-à-vis both their neighbors and their subjects. Witches represented both a real internal enemy and a symbol of hostility to the ruler and the community.

In terms of the economy, Europe entered a period of dramatic inflation during the sixteenth century and continued to be subject to periodic famines resulting from bad harvests. This was also a time when people were moving around more than they had in the previous centuries, when war, religious conflict, the commercialization of agriculture, enclosure, and the lure of new jobs in the cities meant that villages were being uprooted and the number of vagrants and transients increased. These changes led to a sense of unsettledness and uncertainty in values, and in many places a greater gap between rich and poor. Because most people accused of witchcraft came from the poorest level of society, economic factors may have played a role in witch accusations.

Social factors are also important in understanding the development of the witch-craze. Though there were "witch-hunters" who came into areas specifically to hunt witches, most witch trials began with an accusation of *maleficia* in a village or town. Individuals accused someone they knew of using magic to spoil food, make children ill, kill animals, raise a hailstorm, or do other types of harm. Local studies have shown that kinship stresses often played a role in these initial accusations, for tensions over property, stepchildren, or the public behavior of a relative or in-law were very common in early modern families. Household or neighborhood antagonisms might also lead to an accusation, particularly those between people who knew each other's lives intimately, such as servants and their employers.

Part II of this reader focuses on political, economic, and social contexts. Brian Levack tests theories that link the upsurge in witch persecutions with the rise of the nation-state, focussing particularly on Scotland, but also providing some comparative discussion of other states of Europe. J. T. Swain investigates the role that economic factors played in several very well-documented cases of witchcraft in Pendle Forest, a part of Lancashire in England that was undergoing significant economic change in the early seventeenth century. Gábor Klaniczay uses cases from Hungary to assess the strengths and weaknesses of several explanations that link social tensions with witch persecutions. Robin Briggs takes us into the intimate realm of family relationships, using cases from the Lorraine in eastern France to explore the ways that hostilities between husbands and wives, or between stepmothers and stepchildren, or between family members at a wedding, could become potent forces in witch accusations.

All of the historians who explore the political, social, and economic contexts of witchcraft, and many who focus on demonology, also investigate actual trials. Their primary sources are court records of various types, which can be both disturbing in their details and frustrating in their incompleteness. Records of arrests and questioning may never indicate the ultimate outcome, or suspects are not completely identified, making it difficult to tell exactly who they are, or records from some years are missing or destroyed, so that it is impossible to trace patterns. Thousands of trial records do survive, however, some of them numbering many pages. Based on such local records, historians now distinguish between two types of hunts, the isolated case or small hunt involving one or only a few suspects and the mass hunt, where the accused could number in the hundreds. Large-scale hunts have often been called "witch panics," though some historians are now avoiding that expression, as well as the expression "witch-craze" because both imply that witch-hunting was an emotional outburst or a bizarre aberration. Recent research has made clear that witch-hunting was generally carried out in a systematic manner using methods understood to be legal, and that ideas about witchcraft formed an integral part of the general intellectual life of early modern Europe.

Most large-scale hunts were the outgrowths of smaller investigations, in which the circle of suspects brought in for questioning simply continued to grow unchecked. Some were also the result of legal authorities rounding up a group of suspects together, and then receiving further denunciations. They often occurred after some type of climatic disaster, such as an unusually cold and wet summer, and came in waves. Large hunts spread in southern Germany and eastern France in the 1570s, 1590s, 1610s, and 1660s, the last spreading as far north as Sweden. In large-scale trials a wider variety of suspects were taken in—wealthier people, children, a greater proportion of men. Mass hunts tended to end when it became clear to legal authorities, or to the community itself, that the people being questioned or executed were not what they understood witches to be, or that the scope of accusations defied credulity. Some from their community might be in league with Satan, but not this type of person and not as many as this.

Part III looks at different types of trials from various parts of Europe, both single cases and mass hunts. Wolfgang Behringer investigates witchcraft cases in southeastern Germany—the area that is now the state of Bavaria—particularly the wave of mass persecutions that swept through this area during the years around 1590. Robert Walinski-Kiehl focuses on several trials from the late 1620s in central Germany involving one particular type of witch—the child witch; one of these was a mass hunt and one involved only one suspect. Julian Goodare looks at the Scottish witchcraft panic of 1597, a year in which Scotland saw famine, plague, and violent riots against King James VI, who himself served as an investigator at several trials. Thor Hall analyzes a case involving one woman in the years around 1620 in southeastern Norway, far away from the heartland of witch persecutions.

Though Norway was far from the main centers of witch persecution, the trial examined by Hall was typical in many ways of European witch trials as a whole, beginning with the gender of the accused. About 80 percent of those questioned, tried, and executed for witchcraft in Europe after 1500 were women. The reasons for this are complex: women were viewed as weaker and so more likely to give in to the Devil's charms or use scolding and cursing to get what they wanted; they had more contact with areas of life in which bad things happened unexpectedly, such as preparing food or caring for new mothers, children, and animals; they were associated with nature, disorder, and the body, all of which were linked with the demonic.

The first person accused in many trials, especially in the German heartland of the witch-craze, often closely fit the Halloween and Hollywood stereotype of a witch: female, old, poor, and in some way peculiar looking or acting. She was seen as motivated by envy and malice and accused of riding through the air to a sabbat where she had sex with the devil (though usually on a goat or pitchfork rather than a broom). She consorted with an animal familiar—often a dog rather than a black cat—and tempted children with sweets and delicacies, just like the evil stepmother in Snow White or the witch in Hansel and Gretel.

Misogyny (and agism) clearly played a role in shaping the witch hunts, but the story is more complicated than simply male control of women. In Finland and Estonia about half of those prosecuted for witchcraft cases were male, and in Iceland and Muscovite Russia the vast majority of those prosecuted were men charged with sorcery or harming animals. Negative ideas about women were just as prevalent in these areas, however, and in areas that saw few trials, such as southern Europe, as in areas where most witches were women. In areas where women predominate as witches, they also figure very prominently among accusers and witnesses. Women gained economic and social security by conforming to the standard of the good wife and mother, and by confronting women who deviated from it. Witch accusations often grew out of all-female settings, such as household kitchens or celebrations after childbirth, and expressed women's fears and concerns about the health of their children or their ability to provide acceptable food for their families.

Part IV of this reader presents several different approaches historians have taken when looking at connections between gender and witchcraft. Hans Peter Broedel traces ways in which the *Malleus Maleficarum*, the influential guide to identifying and trying witches written in the 1480s, built on and extended earlier notions of the sexual connections between women and demons. Lyndal Roper evaluates accusations against lying-in maids, the older women who took care of women and their infants right after childbirth, in Augsburg, a German city that saw sporadic trials, but never a mass hunt. Diane Purkiss explores women's ideas about witchcraft as they emerge in trial records and printed pamphlets in England. Sally Scully analyzes the multiple trials of two half-sisters charged with magical practices in Venice, where such cases were heard by the Roman Inquisition.

Just as there were regional differences in the gender balance among accused witches, there were great regional variations in the outcome of accusations. In Spain, Portugal, and much of Italy, all cases of witchcraft were handled by the Spanish, Portuguese, or Roman Inquisitions, which continued to make a distinction between ritual magic and diabolic witchcraft. If there was no evidence the suspect had worshipped the devil or used Christian objects such as crucifixes or communion hosts, the case was most often simply dismissed. In Europe north of the Alps and Pyrenees the initial accusation might also be dismissed if the judges regarded the evidence as questionable. Areas in which the learned stereotype of witchcraft as a devil-worshipping international conspiracy was never fully accepted, including England, the northern Netherlands, and Scandinavia, had a more restricted use of torture and few mass hunts. Torture and demonology were linked, as torture was generally used primarily to find out a witch's accomplices and learn the details of the demonic pact; it was employed most by those convinced of the reality of massive numbers of witches and in turn led to the denunciation of as many other people as the judges thought necessary, for torture was stopped only when the accused supplied what the judges thought was a sufficient number of names.

In the sixteenth and early seventeenth centuries, the vast majority of judges and other members of the learned elite firmly believed in the threat posed by witches, but there were a few skeptics. The German physician Johann Weyer (1515–1588) and the English gentleman Reginald Scot (1538?–1599) questioned whether witches could ever do harm, make a pact with the devil, or engage in the wild activities attributed to them. In 1631, the Jesuit theologian Frederick Spee (1591–1635) questioned whether secret denunciations were valid or torture would ever yield a truthful confession. Such doubts gradually spread among the same type of religious and legal authorities who had so vigorously persecuted witches, and they increasingly regarded the dangers posed by the people brought before them as implausible. Older women accused by their neighbors or who thought themselves witches were more likely to be regarded as deluded or mentally defective, meriting pity rather than persecution. These intellectual changes resulted in the demand for much clearer evidence and a decreased use of torture, which in turn led to fewer accusations. By the end of the sixteenth century, prosecutions for witchcraft were already difficult in the Netherlands and the area under the jurisdiction of the Parlement of Paris; the last official execution for witchcraft in England was in 1682, the same year that trials for witchcraft were prohibited in France.

Skepticism about the extent of witches' powers or the possibility that the type of people normally accused of witchcraft could have such powers slowly grew into doubts about the reality of witchcraft in general. Such views emerged first in the writings of those who criticized the power of clergy, such as the English scholar John Wagstaffe (1633–1677), who published *The Question of Witchcraft Debated* in 1669. Wagstaffe and others who expressed similar opinions were charged with being "atheists," as doubts about witchcraft or demonic power seemed to many to suggest doubts about divine power as well. Skeptical attitudes slowly spread, however, as increasing numbers of middle- and upper-class people expected religion and politics to be "reasonable," or saw witchcraft as a purely theological matter and not something for secular judges. People with at least some education gradually became convinced that natural explanations should be sought for things that had been attributed to the supernatural. Creating a godly society ceased to be the chief aim of governments, and in some parts of Europe, district and national judges fined local pastors or bailiffs for arresting and torturing accused witches.

By the eighteenth century other countries in Europe followed the lead of France and forbade prosecutions for witchcraft—England in 1736, Austria in 1755, and Hungary in 1768. Sporadic trials continued into the late eighteenth century in other areas, but even in the Holy Roman Empire they were rare; the last execution for witchcraft in the Empire was in 1775. At the popular level, belief in the power of witches often continued, but this was now sneered at by the elite as superstition, and people ceased to bring formal accusations when they knew they would simply be dismissed. This did not mean an end to demands for death to witches, however; lynchings for witchcraft or sorcery have been recorded in Europe within the last few decades, and as recently as 1998, calls for the pardon of a woman convicted of pretending to be a witch made headlines in London.

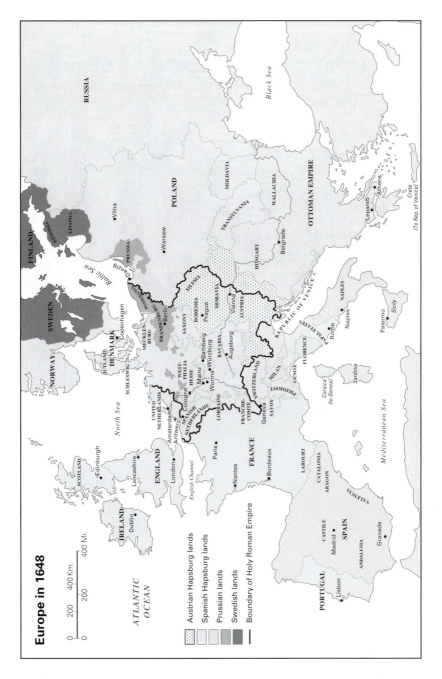

Europe in 1648

RUSSIA

Black Sea

FINLAND

NORWAY

SWEDEN

•Vilna

POLAND

MOLDAVIA

WALLACHIA

OTTOMAN EMPIRE

LIVONIA

ESTONIA

Baltic Sea

Danzig

Copenhagen

DENMARK

JUTLAND

SCHLESWIG

PRUSSIA

•Warsaw

SILESIA

BOHEMIA

MORAVIA

•Prague

TRANSYLVANIA

HUNGARY

•Belgrade

Athens

Lepanto

Crete (To Rep. of Venice)

MECKLEN-BURG

BRANDENBURG

POMERANIA

•Berlin

SAXONY

AUSTRIA

•Vienna

BAVARIA

•Augsburg

HESSE

WEST-PHALIA

•Bamberg

•Würzburg

•Mainz

•Worms

Cologne•

UNITED NETHERLANDS

Amsterdam•

Antwerp•

SPANISH NETHERLANDS

LORRAINE

FRANCHE-COMTÉ

SWITZERLAND

Geneva•

SAVOY

PIEDMONT

MILAN

GENOA

FLORENCE

REPUBLIC OF VENICE

PAPAL STATES

•Rome

NAPLES

•Naples

Palermo

Sicily

Corsica (to Genoa)

Sardinia

North Sea

SCOTLAND

•Edinburgh

ENGLAND

Lancashire•

London•

IRELAND

Dublin•

English Channel

•Paris

FRANCE

•Nantes

•Bordeaux

LABOURT

CATALONIA

ARAGON

VALENCIA

CASTILE

Madrid•

SPAIN

ANDALUSIA

Granada•

PORTUGAL

Lisbon•

Mediterranean Sea

ATLANTIC OCEAN

0   200   400 Km.

0   200   400 Mi.

Austrian Hapsburg lands

Spanish Hapsburg lands

Prussian lands

Swedish lands

Boundary of Holy Roman Empire

Satan marks a male witch, while other well-dressed female and male witches gather in front of him. This woodcut illustration appeared in Francesco Maria Guazzo's *Compendium Maleficarum (Compendium of Witches)*, a demonological treatise first published in Milan in 1608. Guazzo's treatise included many of the standard charges against witches, including night flying, insensitivity to pain, and the murder of children. *(From R. P. Gauccius'* Compendium Maleficarum, *Milan, 1626. Print courtesy www.geocities.com/pagantheology/woodcuts.html)*

I Intellectual Foundations and Demonology

Ideas about the activities of the devil, demons, and witches can be found in many types of writings from the fifteenth through the seventeenth centuries—Biblical commentary, chronicles, almanacs, legal treatises, sermons, medical essays, scientific works, political theory, doctoral dissertations. They appear in their purest form in the hundreds of works specifically dealing with witchcraft and demonology that were penned—and then very often published—by learned men. Demonology was not written in a vacuum, however, nor by authors sitting in scholarly seclusion. Most of the authors of demonological works also wrote other things, and many were active as pastors, officials, university professors, lawyers, physicians, and even a few rulers. Some were also witch-hunters, judges, or officials involved in actual trials. They brought their ideas with them to the trials, framing questions based on their readings, and then used their experiences as the basis for their demonology. The fact that their questions often elicited the same or similar answers over broad geographic areas fueled the idea that witchcraft was an international conspiracy.

Historians in the nineteenth and much of the twentieth century who analyzed demonology generally regarded belief in witchcraft as an aberration when it appeared in the writings of highly learned men such as the political theorist Jean Bodin. They viewed such beliefs either as remnants of earlier ways of viewing the world that intelligent men like Bodin had not yet been able to shake, or as marginal to intellectuals' main concerns. Surely such people could not really have accepted the idea that thousands of people made pacts with the devil, through which they gained powers to harm their neighbors? More recently, however, intellectual historians have increasingly focused on connections and correspondences between witchcraft and other ideas held by educated Europeans. They have explored demonology as an intellectual system that made sense to those who accepted it, and been less concerned with highlighting the contrast between beliefs in witchcraft and an objective reality beyond those beliefs. Such studies have been part of the "linguistic turn" in history, in which greater attention is paid to texts, language, and visual images—what is generally called "discourse"—than to events, individuals, or groups.

Stuart Clark has been a major voice in studies of the discourse of demonology, and a brief excerpt from his massive *Thinking with Demons: The Idea of Witchcraft in Early Modern Europe* is the first selection in this section. For this book, Clark read essentially all of the demonological works that were published in Europe from the fifteenth century through the early eighteenth, and hundreds of other writings as well. He analyzes ways in which witchcraft beliefs held by European intellectuals fitted rationally with their ideas about science, history, religion, and politics. He notes that learned authors may actually have been *more* convinced of the strength of witches' powers and their links to Satan than their less learned neighbors. The title of his book captures his primary point: witchcraft was an *idea,* not simply a matter of belief, and demons were something that helped people to think about a variety of matters. He takes the idea of "thinking with" from the French anthropologist Claude Lévi-Strauss, who, when studying the function of totem animals in many cultures, commented that "animals are good to think with."

The second selection in this section, Charles Zika's "The Devil's Hoodwink: Seeing and Believing in the World of Sixteenth-Century Witchcraft," narrows the focus from all of demonological literature to one work, a short treatise titled *The Devil's Hoodwink (Dess Teuffels Nebelkappen),* written by the German Lutheran pastor Paulus Frisius and published in 1583. In his many articles and books on early modern witchcraft, Zika has emphasized the visual, looking at the ways in which woodcuts, engravings, paintings, and other types of visual representations of witches both shaped and were shaped by ideas expressed in words. Here he looks at the way one author used a visual metaphor drawn from folklore, the hoodwink, a magical hood that made its wearer invisible, to discuss the illusions and deceit of the devil. Operating through witches or directly, the devil could make the visible invisible and the invisible visible, making it difficult for anyone to tell what was real or not real. Interpreting reality was, for Frisius, the job of learned theologians and political authorities, not everyday people, whose abilities were no match for the devil's trickery. Zika thus sees this short treatise, like much longer works of demonology, as part of the move by clerical and secular authorities to control access to spiritual power by "theologizing" traditional folkloric beliefs and transforming them into diabolic actions. Most Protestant writers on witchcraft, including Frisius, were pastors, and viewed witchcraft as a challenge to the moral and spiritual health of their congregations. They saw both witchcraft and popular magical practices such as fortune-telling as examples of doubt about God's power and providence. Protestant demonology—and witch-hunting—were part of what Clark, Zika, and others term the "reforming impulse," one of the many ways learned pastors sought to change popular belief and practice in a broad religious agenda.

The reforming impulse was not limited to Protestants, for Catholic authorities also sought to change popular belief and practice, and Catholic writers produced a steady stream of demonological works. In the third selection in this section, *Defining Dominion: The Discourses of Magic and Witchcraft in Early Modern France and Germany,* Gerhild Scholz Williams, a scholar of literature, analyzes the writings of the Catholic French magistrate Pierre de Lancre, sent in the early seventeenth century to investigate witchcraft in the Basque-speaking Labourd area of southern France. Lancre was even more culturally distant from the people he was charged to investigate than were Protestant pastors such as Frisius, for the residents of the Labourd spoke a language he could understand only through interpreters and engaged in practices that he found as foreign as any reports from the New World. Lancre asserts, in fact, that there is an actual link between witchcraft and European discoveries, for it was the arrival of missionaries in the Americas that prompted Satan and his demons to return to Europe, accompanying Basque fishing ships straight to the Labourt. Everyone in this ungodly area was likely to fall into Satan's snare, argued Lancre, who questioned children as well as adult men and women, and eventually executed priests as well as lay people. He "came to the Labourt firmly convinced of the reality of witches and of their real transport to the sabbath," Williams notes, and "left the area just as certain of these phenomena," despite—or perhaps because of—his close observation of the people and their customs.

Williams, Zika, and Clark all accept that the demonologists they write about thought that witchcraft was real, but in the final selection in this section, taken from *Demon Lovers: Witchcraft, Sex, and the Crisis of Belief,* Walter Stevens provides a very different interpretation. He argues that the dramatic upsurge in accusations of witchcraft and development of demonological theory resulted not from certainty about the reality of witchcraft, but from growing skepticism. In the late Middle Ages, Stevens asserts, highly-learned churchmen, lawyers, and officials increasingly doubted the reality of the supernatural order, divine as well as demonic. This "crisis of belief" led them to search desperately for proof of the physical existence of demons, for which interactions between human and demonic bodies were the best verification. While Zika, Clark, and Williams see attempts by learned theorists to define the reality of witchcraft primarily in the context of their desire to exert control over others, Stevens sees them primarily as attempts to control and negate their own skepticism as they wrestled with "problems of being and knowledge" and doubts about "God's existence and presence in the world." He agrees with the other three authors, however, in seeing demonological theory as a central part of Christian theology during this period, and not the realm of "fanatics and obscurantist crackpots."

Stuart Clark

Thinking with Demons: The Idea of Witchcraft in Early Modern Europe

By the early 1980s modern studies of most aspects of [witchcraft] were fast appearing but no sustained attempt had yet been made to reconsider the views of the many intellectuals—clergymen, theologians, lawyers, physicians, natural philosophers, and the like—who published books about it at the time. Many of these so-called demonologists advocated the prosecution of witches and could plausibly be said to have influenced the trials that took place. . . .

. . . Witchcraft theory was not, however, written in isolation and ought not to be read in that way. Another of the features of research that it seemed worthwhile to challenge was the tendency to regard the topic as somehow peculiar and historically unassimilable. I made the further assumption, therefore, that a body of ideas that survived for nearly 300 years must have made some kind of sense and that this probably lay in its coherence with ideas about other things. I was influenced, in particular, by a remark of Alasdair MacIntyre's (also put to use by Robert Bartlett in his book on medieval ordeals): "To say that a belief is rational is to talk about how it stands in relation to other beliefs." It soon became apparent that demonology was a case in point, and that witchcraft beliefs at this level were sustained by a whole range of other intellectual commitments. This is because the theoretical arguments clustered around particular issues: whether it was possible or not for witchcraft to happen as a real phenomenon in the natural world, why it was afflicting Europe at a particular time, what kinds of sins it involved and how clergymen should counteract them, and why rulers and magistrates should act to rid the world of the threat. In effect, demonology was a composite subject consisting of discussions about the workings of nature, the processes of history, the maintenance of religious purity, and the nature of political authority and order. Inevitably, its authors took up particular intellectual positions in relation to these four major topics of early modern thought. Quite simply, their views about witchcraft depended on concepts and arguments drawn from the scientific, historical, religious, and political debates of their time. Equally, by theorizing about witches, they made important contributions to these same debates; the relationships I shall be exploring were very much complementary ones. In many cases, indeed, the subject of witchcraft seems to have been used as a means for thinking through problems that originated elsewhere and that had little or nothing to do with the legal prosecution of witches; hence my adoption of the somewhat Lévi-Straussian title *Thinking with Demons* to convey this sense of demonology as an intellectual resource.

So seamlessly does demonology merge with these other debates—so much do they cease to *be* other debates—that I would like to propose, not the death of the author, but the dissolution of the "demonologist." Although I started out by adopting this traditional label, I was soon forced to recognize that it had misleading implications. I rapidly discovered that there was too much demonology embedded in early modern books— books of all kinds and on many subjects—for it to be attributed to one kind of writer. More seriously, the inference seemed to be that those who wrote about witchcraft were somehow interested in it to the exclusion of anything else; this was their speciality, and an aberrant one at that. But for the vast majority it was not. They had many of the other typical—one might even say ordinary—intellectual interests and affiliations of their age. They were primarily theologians, jurists, philosophers, or whatever, who, in the course of some intellectual or moral project, felt it necessary to turn to the subject to see how it related to their wider concerns. If we go on calling them "demonologists," we run the risk of setting them apart from these more general pursuits—indeed, from precisely the things that help us understand why they were interested in witchcraft at all and how they could believe in its reality. Of course, as a subject, "demonology" too was not just concerned with witchcraft; it embraced discussions of magic, of superstition, and, not unnaturally, of demons themselves. . . .

Witchcraft and Science

No two things could be further apart, seemingly, than demonology and science. Yet between the fifteenth and the eighteenth centuries—leaving some very considerable moral issues aside—the questions that dominated learned discussions of witchcraft concerned its very possibility as a genuine occurrence in the physical world. Demonology was the study of a natural order in which the existence of demonic actions and effects was, largely, presupposed. But there were still matters of detail to discuss. Could devils and witches really achieve all the effects that were commonly attributed to them? Could witches, for example, be transported, with or without their bodies, to sabbats? Were their alleged sexual exploits with devils true or false and, if true, could they lead to the birth of offspring? Could witches transform themselves, or others, into animals? More mundanely, could they cause storms by incantations and rites, or bring illnesses merely by looking at their victims or cursing them? . . . [T]hese, and a cluster of related questions, were debated over and over again in literally hundreds of texts. They were particularly prominent in the earlier period, when witchcraft theory was influenced heavily by the *Canon episcopi*, a ninth-century canon that attributed night flying and the sabbat to demonic illusion. Nevertheless, these same questions provided the main agenda for the literature of witchcraft throughout its history, and they explain why the style and tone adopted by its authors often seem just as interrogative — indeed, just as inquisitorial — as the legal investigations into witchcraft themselves must often have been. The important point is that the whole dispute centred on whether, as a matter of fact, certain physical events could actually take place in the real world. This meant asking which laws of cause and effect they obeyed, and which they infringed. . . . [I]t is hard to deny that the form of the discussion, at least, was broadly, but genuinely, scientific.

But so were the matters themselves. Almost instinctively, modern science refers the deeds of devils and witches to a realm of "supernature" wholly beyond natural laws; the only way to account for them naturalistically today is by complete redescription. As C. S. Lewis wrote, "such creatures are not part of the subject matter of *'natural* philosophy'; if real, they fall under pneumatology, and, if unreal, under morbid psychology." This means that demonology, like astrology or alchemy, has invariably been regarded as an "occult" or "pseudo" science and, therefore, incompatible with scientific insight and progress. Usually, reasons other than those intrinsic to it have been sought for its popularity and longevity; it was the product, so it has been said, of lingering superstition, of irrationality, or, worse still, of collective derangement. But the history (as well as the anthropology) of science shows that the perceived boundary between nature and supernature, if it is established at all, is local to cultures, and that it shifts according to tastes and interests. The one now generally in force among the tribes of the West is only as old as the scientific production that goes with it. Before "Enlightenment" and the coming of the "new" science, things were different, metaphysically speaking, and nature was thought to have other limits. In fact, the ontology of the demonic was entirely the reverse of today's. In early modern Europe it was virtually the unanimous opinion of the educated that devils, and, *a fortiori*, witches, not merely existed in nature but acted according to its laws. They were thought to do so reluctantly and (as well shall see) with a good many unusual, or "preternatural" manipulations of phenomena, yet they were always regarded as being inside the general category of the natural. Devils, wrote one typical witchcraft theorist, "cannot advance natural things without natural causes being present"; witches, he deduced, could do nothing "that surmounts the forces of nature." It was what was natural about their alleged behaviour that made it a physical possibility and, thus believable; what was unnatural was deemed to be impossible and delusory. These were matters of principle for writers on witchcraft; for them, *not* to accept them was superstitious and irrational. . . .

Witchcraft and History

. . . Sooner or later, witchcraft theorists . . . could scarcely evade the additional matter of why the devil and his agents were so much more active in their own age than in any other. "What is the reason," ran a chapter heading in Franciscus Agricola's *Gründtlicher Bericht*, "why so many Magicians, Sorceresses and Witches are discovered in these our times? "Why," wrote Hermann Samson from Riga, "are there so many Magicians in this present age?" James VI of Scotland ended his *Daemonologie* wondering why "divellishe practises . . . were never so rife in these partes, as they are now." Pierre de Lancre asked not merely about the number of contemporary magicians and witches but when precisely they had first infiltrated France. For many others, discussion of this further aspect of the subject—let us call it the dimension of witchcraft as event—was a vital, even indispensable, ingredient of successful demonology. . . .

. . . [H]ere, as elsewhere, their view of witchcraft was bound up with the wider intellectual interests of Europeans. On the one hand, we shall find that early modern demonology depended for its categories of historical speculation on one of the dominant historiographical models of the period. Its writers shared their notions of agency and causation, of change and periodization, and of the overall shape and morality of the historical process with the general practitioners of Christian or, as it might be termed, "Augustinian" history-writing. In particular, they were preoccupied with one of its central themes—the eschatological reading of current affairs. On the other hand, demonology itself offered opportunities for confirming and refining this historiography. The evidence of events of witchcraft alone reinforced the binary division of Augustine's world-history as a dramatic struggle between antithetical moral forces, with (what Claude-Gilbert Dubois called) its "dichotomous design . . . founded on opposition, of which the outcome is made certain by the victory of one group over the other." Evidence of their acceleration gave precision to the idea that the denouement was near, made the placing of present time at the end of history a more exact matter, and aided greatly with the identification of the Antichrist. In this sense, the phenomenon of witchcraft helped substantially to focus an entire historiographical paradigm.

The intellectual traffic was thus two-way; witchcraft writers depended on a theology of history (in which the devil had, in any case, a primordial and constitutive role) and at the same time contributed to its elaboration. The result was an apocalyptic interpretation of witchcraft. . . .

Witchcraft and Religion

It might well seem perverse to distinguish "religion" as a separate feature of European witchcraft beliefs. If the devil of traditional Christianity was not a religious entity, then he was nothing. Demonology in all its manifestations was not merely saturated with religious values; it was inconceivable without them. They lay deep in its conceptual structure and, more overtly, in the patterns of thought and language of those who wrote about witchcraft. Demonic actions were defined in contrast to divine ones and the vices of (female) witches in contrast to the virtues of their godly (male) contemporaries. Demonism was only physically possible at all thanks to a particular theology of nature, and it was eventually made physically impossible by a different one. Its place in history—indeed, its historical role—was determined (so it was thought) by biblical prophecy and uncovered by eschatological enquiry. . . .

Yet it is equally obvious that "religion" is not exhausted by high-level metaphysics and ethics, or by its influence on natural, historical, and political philosophy. What is striking about books on witchcraft and magic from the early modern period is how many of them were produced either by clergymen or by those who trained or advised clergymen. The questions these authors addressed were largely to do with the problems of piety arising from the personal good fortune or (more usually) misfortune of parishioners, where the last thing that was needed was complicated metaphysics or philosophy: how should lay people try to prevent or respond to their afflictions, including *maleficium*; what sorts of preservatives or remedies should they use and who should they consult for them; what was the difference between allowable (godly) and forbidden (demonic) practices in this area; what was the nature of the sins that might be committed and how might these be punished? Such texts were aimed first and foremost at clerical practice, and their religiosity was the religiosity of churches. Their tone was homiletic and evangelical, rather than intellectual and theoretical, the intention being to guide both the pastoral efforts of the clergy and, through them, the patterns of lay behaviour. They ran parallel, in this sense, to discussions of such things as sexual behavior and the regulation of families, observance of the sabbath, the evils of drinking and dancing, and other issues of lay morality.

Many of these texts originated as sermons and some retained this form in print. Others were composed as dialogues to improve their didactic impact. Here, the continuity between specialist discussions and a more general literature was complete. Those who chose to concentrate on this kind of evangelical demonology surrounded their notions of "witchcraft," "magic," and "superstition" with a theological orthodoxy available to them in religious dogmatics, in casuistry, and in biblical commentary. One senses a faithful transposition of the ideas taught in countless faculties of theology into the writings of their clerical graduates. Conversely, the same topics received constant attention from the dogmatists and casuists themselves. Between the fifteenth and eighteenth centuries, an enormous number of discussions of these transgressions can be found in the manuals of advice addressed to penitents and confessors, in the books of rules written for inquisitors, in expositions of the Decalogue, in both catechetical texts and guides to how to benefit from them, and, of course, in sermons. . . .

. . . There was never such a thing as "mere" witchcraft in early modern Europe—some essential, unmodified residue lying beyond particular versions of it and intelligible without recourse to them. Like any use of language, "witchcraft" only meant what it meant in particular cultural settings—"language-games," as it were—and nowhere is this more true than in its reflection of, and its capacity to convey, religious meanings.

Nor was the connection an unimportant one, either for demonology or for reformation thought and practice, whether Protestant or Catholic. . . . [W]itchcraft, magic, and superstition were allied to the foremost theological preoccupations of the age—divine sovereignty, human faith, religious therapies, the pure conscience. Their eradication was thus a reformers' priority. . . .

. . . [T]his clerical perception stemmed not from literalness in witchcraft matters but from an overwhelmingly spiritualized reading of the sin. Even if it is conceded that their preoccupations were with the demonic elements in witchcraft (and in magic and superstition too), it should not be assumed that all clerics sensationalized these elements by dwelling for example on the lurid details of the witches' sabbat. The texts . . . whether Protestant or Catholic, whether English or Continental, are notable for the way they internalized virtually all the traditional ingredients of witchcraft, turning them into spiritual problems. . . . In this way, the devil became an evangelical enemy, and witchcraft a branch of idolatry. . . .

Witchcraft and Politics

. . . The logical closure of the ideal argument was a call to action. At this point authors asked practical questions about what concrete steps should be taken to rid the world of witchcraft, who should undertake them, and how they should proceed. . . .

. . . [T]he central preoccupation was the role of the magistrate in the fight against a crime. Ritual act, natural phenomenon, historical event, offence against God—witchcraft now became a social sin, a violation of laws, and a threat to civil order. The duty of magistrates (it was mostly argued) was to protect the community by using the full weight of their office to eradicate those responsible. "Policy" demanded the punishment of witches, wrote the Englishman John Gaule in 1646, "because they disturb her peace."

Although there has never been the slightest obscurity about this particular element in demonology, there have been few attempts to understand the general assumptions which inspired it. Yet there is no such thing as a presuppositionless call for change: "The world of practical experience is a world of judgements, not of mere actions, volitions, feelings, intuitions, instincts or opinions." In describing witchcraft as a social evil authors necessarily invoked a conception of the social order, an idea of *communitas*. In addressing magistrates they committed themselves to views about authority and about the general desirability of certain forms of rulership. In asking for the implementation of punishment they appealed to notions of justice and the requirements of divine, natural, and positive law. In all this, and in demanding and justifying action in the public domain, they spoke what can only be termed the language of politics. . . .

. . . This is not to say that demonology merely mirrored routine political sentiments; although, to recognize the extent that it did is, as I have argued in other contexts, to begin to acknowledge its intellectual probity. As we have found in every other area of the subject, there was a mutually reinforcing relationship of ideas. In talking about authority witchcraft authors adopted one of the dominant political vocabularies of the period; in resorting to St Paul, in speaking of magistracy as a divine stewardship or ministry, and in deriving all their models of action from the Old Testament, they shared what has been called, crudely but not unhelpfully, the "descending" theory of government. Indeed, witchcraft was only the crime it was, and the duty to punish it could only be seen as religious, in those areas of political culture that were very largely committed to theocratic principles and where authority was inherently sacred. It was (I shall argue) precisely because there was a mystical dimension to politics that there was a political dimension to magic; both were modifications of the same world of thought.

In reverse, demonology was itself capable of enunciating theocratic political ideals with unusual, even unique, force. The proposal that demonic power could be nullified by the authority of the godly ruler made the magistrate and the witch adversaries of a very special kind; in effect, it made witchcraft prosecutions a critical test of political legitimacy. In the rituals of the trial-room, but also in the symbolism of royal court festivals, demons and witches became the perfect antagonists of those who claimed power by divine right, since their defeat could only result from supernatural, not physical superiority. The defendants in the North Berwick witchcraft trials, accused of treasonable *maleficium* by James VI, asked the devil why "all the devellerie culd do na harm to the King, as it did till others dyvers." The reply they received is epigraphic: "Il est un home de Dieu." But as well as morally antipathetic, magistrates and witches were morally equivalent; their symmetry was as important as their opposition. "Those appointed to judge witches," wrote the anthropologist and historian Julio Caro Baroja in a memorable phrase, "were sometimes akin to the people they were trying to destroy: at heart they were inverted sorcerers." In early modern mythography it was usual to trace both the arts of government and the arts of magic to the god Jupiter. An act of justice against witches, remarked Martín Del Río, brought together the servants of God and the servants of the devil. . . .

To some extent, then, we are dealing with witchcraft as a property conferred on individuals according to the principles (some might say the prejudices) of a specific kind of political society. Its identity as a crime was subject to judgements about conformity and deviance made by those with broadly theocratic conceptions of rulership and the systems of legal control in which these judgements were embodied. As one contemporary put it, if the prince was a divine figure on earth, "it must of necessitie follow, that . . . his lawes should have a taste and resemblance of Gods laws also," amongst which were those given to Moses to combat witchcraft. . . .

. . . [W]itch-hating (if not witch-hunting) was entailed by a certain concept of rulership and not merely contingent upon the general desire to strengthen government and streamline obedience to it. [This] kind of political authority . . . was an authority before which it was *necessary* that demons and witches should give way; this, indeed, was one of its defining aspects. . . .

If demonology appealed finally to the ordering power of the magistrate, this is because it was premissed on a vision of disorder in human affairs. Writers who closed their texts by demanding legal action against witches often opened them by evoking the chaos and disruption that witchcraft either caused or reflected. This established the mood of what they said in between, but it also dictated the kind of political intervention they ultimately sought. The vehemence with which witches were denounced in print stemmed directly, it seems, from the sense of appalling social and material crisis that many early modern authors genuinely felt. More important, the type of magistracy these authors invoked, with its supernatural attributes, bore an intrinsic, rather than merely pragmatic, relationship to the situation they diagnosed; the latter was of such seriousness that only political thaumaturgy could cope with it. To some modern eyes, the diagnosis itself has appeared exaggerated, simplistic, and untypical—just the thing that witch hunters might be expected to say. But they said nothing that cannot be found in other depictions of disorder from the same period. In this, as always, they were orthodox, not exotic. What is important, in any case, is the character, the force, and the political implications of their perception, not its accuracy or inaccuracy as a matter of report.

This needs emphasizing even in the face of analyses, conducted largely from the perspective of the sociology of deviance, that have seemed, in effect, to corroborate the link between disorder and witch trials. The suggestion is that, between the fifteenth and the seventeenth centuries, Europe *did* go through a series of changes of such magnitude and relative rapidity that the real lives of its peoples were indeed marked by fundamental dislocation. So traumatized were they by this experience that they readily resorted to prosecuting witches, as a way of explaining the problems and assuaging the anxieties that actually beset them. There are many things wrong with this argument in its usual form, including the lack of any historical particularity or rigour; if anything is exaggerated and simplistic, this surely is. But what matters for the moment is the lack of sufficient attention to the conceptual link between the experience of disorder and the punitive attitude to witches. Instead, this link is established causally, in terms of law-like generalizations concerning the creation of deviants and scapegoats (of whatever kinds) in societies objectively under stress.

The reasons why *witches* were held responsible for disorder, or deemed to be symptomatic of it, were, nevertheless, to do with beliefs; or, if we prefer, with assumptions, attitudes, fears, prejudices, or whatever. And these can only be reached if, once again, the perceptions of those involved are accorded the necessary referential autonomy. Attacks on witchcraft were not the incidental products of social trauma, products that, from a causal point of view, could have taken a quite different form. On the contrary, the very notion of witchcraft was inseparable from how disorder was often conceived and experienced—experienced . . . as the inversion of hierarchical values, or the troubling of nature's normal processes, or the heralding of apocalyptic events, or the consequences of idolatry and sin. In such categorizations, demonism was always already implicated and witches were not far behind.

Charles Zika

The Devil's Hoodwink: Seeing and Believing in the World of Sixteenth-Century Witchcraft

The history of Christianity and of Western culture in general, is fraught with tension between visible and invisible worlds. The sensible world is regarded as a shadow or reflection of the invisible reality; the ignorant are described as those blinded to the reality which underlies the apparent; as pilgrims in this world we see as though through a glass darkly; whereas some may come to see the truth, that truth may be no more than mirage or illusion. Such common metaphors are heavily dependent on images of seeing, blindness and light, metaphors which have become deeply embedded in the history of Christian culture. The eyes and the act of seeing are more representative of the senses and that which is seen or visible is representative of the sensible world as a whole.

It is not surprising therefore that in the fifteenth and sixteenth centuries, when theologians and intellectuals were engaged in a large-scale reformulation of the relationship between the sensible world of human experience and the eternal realms of the divine, a religious discourse would develop around the status of material sacred objects and also around the nature of visual perception. Late medieval religiosity was fundamentally a religion of seeing. The cult was organised around sacred images and relics to which the gaze as well as the entreaties of suppliants were directed. Religious devotion was increasingly expressed through a ritual of group spectacle, and was affirmed either through direct visions of the divine and saints or through visible manifestations of their active presence through miracles. Religious knowledge was communicated as

Charles Zika, *No Gods Except Me: Orthodoxy and Religious Practice in Europe 1200–1600*, ed. C. Zika. Melbourne: History Department, University of Melbourne, 1991 [Melbourne University History Monographs, no. 14.] Reprinted with permission.

much through the visual representations of the sacred lives of Christ, Mary or the saints, as through the audible word of preachers' sermons.

For many sixteenth-century Protestants these images and the cults they spawned were perceived as idols and idolatry. The mass in particular, which had been restructured during the later medieval period into a ritual which reached its climax with the visible presentation of the Christian God in the elevation of the host, before the host-god was eaten, was nothing short of blasphemous sacrilege for the reformers. As Protestants stressed the separation between spirit and flesh, soul and body, man and God, material objects such as images or the physical relics of the saints could no longer be regarded as suitable sites for sacred power and divine energy. They were now ridiculed as nothing but wood and stone, of no more worth than animal bones. But for Catholics too, the scope of a visible and sensible religious experience was being more diligently circumscribed and supervised. Religious visions were increasingly met with scepticism and rituals involving sacred objects were carefully scrutinised for their orthodoxy and kept firmly within clerical control. . . .

The religious discourse about eyes, vision and images, the relationship between visible and invisible worlds, is also carried through in the increasingly systematised literature of witchcraft and demonology of the later fifteenth and sixteenth centuries. But while this discourse served to widen the gap between the human and divine, partly in an attempt by clerical and lay experts to ensure control over religious practices, it also served to narrow the gap between the human and the demonic. The theological and legal phenomenon of witchcraft, which had been gradually constituted through the theoretical systematisations of fifteenth- and sixteenth-century theorists and the legal decisions of the courts, needs to be carefully differentiated from the sorcery practices which had been an integral part of European culture for centuries beforehand. Witchcraft was premised on the belief in a special relationship between the person accused of witchcraft and the devil. It was argued that the witch acquired special powers from the devil, which would enable her or him to do evil (*maleficium*, malefice) in society. This was the result of a pact between witch and devil, consummated through sexual intercourse and other forms of exchange. Through witchcraft, humans and devils were joined physically, psychologically and strategically, sexual partners and active collaborators in a program of evil destruction on earth.

One of the main concerns of witchcraft theorists, therefore, was to explain the basis for the behaviour of those men and women traditionally called sorcerers, witches, cunning folk, diviners and so on. Their power could not be easily reconciled with the normal workings of nature, nor did it depend on rituals which lay within the control of the church. Nor could these theorists accept that the individuals themselves possessed marvellous powers. Any wonders which they could perform, argued the theorists, such as harm done to fellow villagers, animals or crops, or claims of night-flying or shape-shifting, were to be attributed either to an imagination influenced by the devil or to the direct operation of diabolical power. The evil power certainly did not rest with the women or men themselves. Their power was a diabolical power. They were puppets, decoys and conduits for the world behind the world.

While this theologisation of the powers attributed to traditional sorcery ensured a heightened sense of the operations of the demonic in the world, it also emphasized that those operations were invisible. For explaining, the social power of those who acted as healers, diviners and matchmakers, those who wreaked vengeance and harm on the community, or who removed the charms and curses which stemmed from others, allowed theologians entry into broad realms of personal and social experience, over which they previously had little control. Defining a wide range of social practices as "witchcraft," as "superstition" or as "magic," located these actions within the realms of God and devil, realms in which the theologian could justifiably claim expertise and thereby exercise control.

This transformation of local sorcery practices constitutes an important part of that broader reform of popular culture, which historians of the last two decades have recognised as fundamental to the change which characterises sixteenth-century society, and have variously described as an acculturation of local practice, the colonising of minds, the christianising and civilising of society or the establishment of social discipline and control. The sixteenth century marked the beginnings of European hegemony not only over the cultures of the indigenous peoples of the new European worlds, but also over the local cultures of the old. It was a hegemony which sought to encompass those worlds geographically, politically and also culturally, to carefully inscribe those cultures within the parameters and definitions of the European past and present. Within Europe, just as outside it, the processes of collecting local and regional folklores and customs, setting them in print and disseminating them to a European-wide audience had begun. And hand in hand with this early interest in local cultures and their ethnographies came the theologisation of those cultures through the literature of witchcraft and superstition. The emphasis on religiously and morally purified communities in the sixteenth-century Reformations could not help but give weight to this cause. Gradually the power of rituals and words was subsumed under the strategems of the devil, and the folklores of sacred places, propitious times and sympathetic action were subverted by a religious economy of temptation, faith and apostasy.

All these issues are raised in a short and quite remarkable treatise which is the subject of this paper. The work is entitled *Dess Teuffels Nebelkappen* or *The Devil's Hoodwink*. It was written by a certain Paulus Frisius and published in Frankfurt in 1583. Quite surprisingly the work has received virtually no attention from modern scholarship. Yet it warrants close examination and analysis for the way it appropriates an image from traditional folklore, the *Nebelkappe*, in order to present a theologised and diabolical understanding of the operations of witchcraft. . . .

The Devil's Hoodwink and Folklore

. . . *Nebelkappen*, literally translated as "hoodwinking," derives from *Nebelkappe*, which means a hood or cowl, a capuche, a large hat, even a cloak of mist. *Nebelkappe* probably derives from *Nebel* (mist), which shrouds the summits of mountains and makes them invisible; and in Germanic legend, was the name given to a cloak or large hood or cowl worn by dwarfs to make them invisible. From the fifteenth century in particular, the term is found in German literature to refer to large capuche-like hoods worn by foreigners, and especially Italians (called *Venediger* or *Walen*), who lived in the mountains and searched for gold. If disturbed at their work, they were reported as donning their hoods in order to make themselves invisible; or standing on their cloaks in order to be able to fly through the air to their home in Italy.

Folklorists have related these magical hoods to the hats and helmets worn by figures from Germanic and classical legend, such as Hermes, Perseus, Odin and Wodan. As well as controlling weather and wind, these hoods were principally used to achieve invisibility and anonymity. This was the case not only for dwarfs, but also for spirits and demons. Just as dwarfs were reported as flying through the air, veiled in a fog which rendered them invisible, and allowed them to do such harm as destroying pea crops, stealing children, collecting food and taking part in banquets, so were spirits and demons.

Many legends recount the methods humans use to gain the powers associated with these magical hoods. The power of the hoods could function, for instance, in reverse. By putting on a dwarf's hood one could make the invisible dwarfs visible again; or by accidentally knocking the hood off invisible spirits, these spirits would automatically become visible. Alternately, if one stood at the crossroads on Christmas eve and drew a magic circle, one could then demand a *Nebelkappe* from the spirit which appeared. One could also use the hood to trick the devil. On Christmas eve, when the priest transformed bread and wine into the body and blood of Christ, the devil was said to take off his hood and hang it outside the church on the church door. Whoever grabbed it, could use it to become invisible.

Invisibility, then, was associated with the various spirits and creatures who disappeared into the air, travelled through the air or operated in the darkness of night. Pacts with the devil were also often said to bring invisibility, and the familiars who accompanied witches were claimed as the instruments by which witches could achieve it. This was especially the case with toads which often feature in the witchcraft literature and also in visual representations. The Luzerne chronicler, Johann Frund, for instance, writes of a trial of witches in Wallis in Switzerland in 1428, in which toads were used to make the witches invisible. . . .

Frisius' text drew upon and exploited all these levels of meaning in articulating the webs of deception within which the acts and perceptions of witchcraft were caught. "Hoodwink," in sixteenth-century English, was also used to mean covering the eyes with a hood or blindfolding, and only gradually took on the metaphoric meaning of deceit, with which we largely associate it today. Deceive, delude, illude, beguile, kid, bamboozle, dupe, swindle, diddle are only some of the analogues of the verb listed by Roget in his *Thesaurus*. But *Nebelkappe* in sixteenth-century German referred to blinding as both instrument and effect, and the effect referred both to those who wore the hood and to those who acted as observers. The hood was worn in order to ensure either anonymity or invisibility, or conversely, to make visible what was invisible. Depending on the perspective from which the actions were observed, different actors could be understood as deceived or suffering from delusion. And then to link the *Nebelkappen* with the devil, the father of lies, was only to make more dense the web of duplicity and illusion. . . .

. . . [T]he fundamental shape of his text does not differ all that much from the work of his predecessors and followers. He structures the work according to five systematic questions which are commonly raised in such treatises. But what differentiates this work is that these questions largely become subordinate to the stories of the devil's power which are used to make sense of everyday human experience. The use of such *exempla* is common to the formulation of witchcraft theory from the earliest period, and in sixteenth-century Germany receives extra emphasis through its relationship to the new genre of "devil books." Whether witches exist, what witches can do, whether the power of witches depends on the objects they use, whether witches should be punished with their life, and whether witches have sexual relations with the devil and bear his children—are the five questions posed. But in Frisius' work they are usually answered with only cursory reference to theological or philosophical argument. It is the stories and reports of mysterious deeds and wonderful claims which receive primary attention. Some of these stories seem to be drawn from contemporary folklore, while others are drawn from earlier ecclesiastical authorities, such as Augustine, Cassian and Vincent of Beauvais, or more recent authorities such as Erasmus Sarcerius. Frisius takes on the role of the preacher, welding together accounts of common experience. He uses common cultural experience to display the compact between the witch and devil. His task is to make the invisible diabolical world more real than the world of sense experience. The reality of the world behind the world is to be made visible by recourse to the devil's hoodwink. . . .

Frisius' work is part of the second wave of demonological and witchcraft treaties which helped shape European social, political, religious and judicial thought and practice in the second half of the sixteenth century. These treatises both developed and challenged the theories about witchcraft which had been systematised in the first wave of treatises at the turn of the sixteenth century, on the basis of the long history of late medieval theological, philosophical and judicial speculation and sorcery trials. . . .

A key element in this understanding of witchcraft, which placed much greater stress on the role of the devil and was to influence later writers as Frisius, was the capacity of the devil to create illusion and deception. . . .

Frisius' emphasis on the role of the devil in earthly affairs must have also been related to the heightened sense of diabolical power which was disseminated through the German territories by the new literary genre of the "devil books" (*Teufelbücher*) in the second half of the sixteenth century. The first of these books appeared in 1552, and during the 1560s fourteen first editions and seventy reprints were issued, adding up to about 100,000 volumes in total. The following two decades saw approximately 100,000 further copies and fifteen new editions. Even though some of this literature merely moralised social and personal vices such as swearing, drinking and dancing, it is difficult to believe that it did not lead to an increasingly demonised sense of the world. It has been argued that this literature helped disseminate religious precepts and assure social and political control. And there can be no doubt that it helped make the ground receptive for notions of diabolical delusion, especially in the region of the middle Rhine, to which audience Frisius' work seems especially directed. Frankfurt am Main, where *Dess Teuffels Nebelkappen* was printed and Frisius' dedication was written, was the principal centre for the dissemination of this devil literature. . . .

The most intensive attacks on witchcraft throughout the Hessian territories after the death of Philip in 1567 occurred in [the] County of Upper Katzenelnbogen under the rule of Landgrave George. In June 1582 several women were condemned and burnt as witches in Darmstadt, and in August of the same year ten more witches were burnt, including a boy of 17 and a girl of 13. In the same year, George issued a criminal code for his territory, the first within Hesse to stipulate specific punishments for witchcraft. The ordinance described witchcraft as an ungodly vice which "at the present time has spread almost everywhere among women." In 1586 the consequences of such an order were being felt throughout the county. In that year at least thirty women were brought to trial for witchcraft: seventeen were burnt as witches, seven were exiled, five fled and one died either through suicide or torture.

Frisius' work of 1583, therefore, was dedicated to a prince who had shown himself, and was to continue to show himself, zealous in his determination to root out witchcraft. One wonders, then, why Frisius felt he needed to give George his support and encouragement. Frisius might have considered it necessary in view of the pressures exerted on George by the rather less zealous policies of his two brothers, or by the quite varied theological and legal opinions which were being publicly voiced within Hesse just at this time. . . .

But why did Frisius adopt this particular metaphor [the *Nebelkappe*] to describe what numerous contemporary and earlier writers had described as the deceit, trickery, illusions of the devil? My suggestion is that such a metaphor acquired cultural power and acceptance because of its capacity to be linked with other contemporary and traditional discourses constructed around the metaphors of seeing and believing. One such discourse was that of the blindness of the Jews. Diabolical blinding had been traditionally employed to explain the marginalisation of Jews within Christian society. The female figure of blindfolded *Synagoga*, which adorned numerous late medieval churches, was a visible and public testimony and reminder of the failure of the Jews to recognise their Messiah. With a veil or blindfold covering her eyes, and sometimes holding a broken standard which served as a contrast to the victorious *Ecclesia*, *Synagoga* was a permanent sign of Jewish blindness and stubbornness, which had led Jews to murder their unrecognised saviour. Given the close association between Jews, sorcery and magic in the cultural thought and political persecution of the fifteenth and sixteenth centuries, such a conceptual and cultural link between the metaphor of the devil's hoodwink and blindfolded *Synagoga* seems likely, at least on an unconscious level.

But another, more pertinent discourse was that of the blindness of folly. Frisius' *Nebelkappe* seems to relate directly to the *Narrenkappe*, the fool's hood or cap, which served as the most visible and powerful sign of the presence of folly in the literature and visual representation of the sixteenth century. To have the fool's cap, with its bells and asses' ears, placed on one's head, was to be turned into a fool, to be fooled. The fool's cap not only pointed to the presence or act of a fool, it also signified someone being fooled. This image, which was extremely popular at every level of sixteenth-century German culture and was critical to that culture's moralising discourses, paralleled the reform agenda of demonological literature. By the sixteenth century folly had come to represent the inversion of proper order, the time when the bodily and social worlds were turned upside down; it was the world and time of carnival, when the lower became higher, when the lower body was given control over the head, when the instinctual, the sensual and the sexual were crowned king and given free rein. The *Narrenkappe* represented the victory of the senses, the submission to the power and deceits of lust. And the *Nebelkappe*, as we've already seen, also represented the deceits of the devil, and was often associated with licentiousness and the failure to control sexuality. . . .

Frisius was clearly engaged in a discourse which was very current not only within the German territories of the 1580s but within learned circles in Hesse. A cultural and political climate had been created in which the existence and activities of witches were being taken very seriously and there was little doubt about the need to apply imperial law in cases involving witchcraft. Differences nevertheless did exist, over whether those accused of witchcraft caused actual physical harm, and whether they actually engaged in the deeds they claimed they did. Given the range of different views expressed and the different uses to which the same discourse was put, it may be possible that Frisius felt that a dedication to George would stiffen his resolve in the eradication of witches from his territory and counteract some of the other views which kept alive the doubts of his confessionally like-minded brother Ludwig. But it is clear that Frisius' interpretation of witchcraft also helped resolve some fundamental tensions in witchcraft theory. By defining witchcraft in terms of the devil's hoodwink, Frisius could accommodate notions of the devil's critical role in any sorcery (and through the devil, assert God's ultimate providential control), but it also allowed considerable flexibility in making judgements about particular cases. In this way ultimate expertise in interpreting reality lay squarely with those who understood the behaviour of the devil, the pastors and theologians. Secondly, and most importantly, the use of the devil's hoodwink tended to move the emphasis of witchcraft accusations away from the sorcery effects or the evil power of the witch towards the conditions by which witches became the objects of the devil's attention and were implicated in his deceits. . . .

Frisius' adoption of the devil's hoodwink as the metaphor to explain the operations of witches alerts us, therefore, to the manner in which so much of the demonological literature of the sixteenth century needs to be understood, in Stuart Clark's recent phrase, as a "pastoral demonology." The search for witches, the articulation of theories of witchcraft and demonology, was not a cultural byway, but was central to the formulation of such strategies. It involved an attack on contemporary magical and folk practices and beliefs, on the one hand, by theologising those beliefs and locating them within a theological framework which identified them with the work of the devil; and it involved an attack on sexual and social behaviour which did not conform to the moral requirements of the agencies of church and state. In a very practical way this demonological literature registered the need for increased surveillance over the intimate lives and behaviour of the general population, in line with all those impulses generated by the sixteenth-century Reformations.

The cosmic struggle between God and his church against the devil and his agents the witches, the theological premise upon which the whole strategy to eradicate witchcraft was based, was a struggle about establishing an approved perception of the relationship between visible and invisible worlds and of the authorities who could recognise them. The attacks against these diabolical forces were also attacks on the sensible world and those who placed their faith in it. The attempts to colonise and christianise sixteenth-century European societies, to have them surrender their control over minds and bodies, involved a surrender in the belief in what one could see and an acceptance of what one could not. Seen and unseen worlds had been very confused and poorly demarcated before the sixteenth century. The sixteenth-century discourse which asserted their radical separation, stressed at the same time the overwhelming presence and influence of the unseen in the world of the seen. An analysis of the devil's hoodwink shows that this discourse was as much about who could see, as about what could be seen.

Gerhild Scholz Williams

Defining Dominion: The Discourses of Magic and Witchcraft in Early Modern France and Germany

The French magistrate Pierre de Lancre lived and worked in Bordeaux, the city of his birth, around the turn of the century. . . .

. . . In 1583 he joined the Bordeaux parliament as a magistrate. In 1609 King Henry IV of France appointed him head of a commission to investigate the activities of witches in the Labourt, the Basque region of France. Situated in the extreme southwest corner of France, which bordered on Spain and Navarra, the Labourt had approximately thirty thousand inhabitants. According to Lancre, most of these people engaged in

Gerhild Williams, *Defining Dominion: The Discourses of Magic and Witchcraft in Early Modern France and Germany.* Copyright © 1995 by The University of Michigan Press. Reprinted with permission.

active satanic associations and practices. During the course of a visit that lasted until December 5, 1609, Lancre by his own account led investigations against forty-six suspected witches, among them twelve priests, and thirty-five informants. His report notes that three priests and eight witches were actually burned. In 1612 the Spanish inquisitor Salazar, who was occupied with the same problem on the Spanish side of the border, reported eighty persons burned as witches in the Labourt. During that year Lancre published a report on his extraordinary four-month stay in the Labourt, the *Tableau de l'inconstance de mauvais anges et demons, ou il est amplement traicté des sorciers et de la sorcelerie,* the *Tableau* for short. Lancre based his book on the original trial records. Since these records were destroyed during the eighteenth century, Lancre's report has to this day assumed the authority of an authentic witness to the persecutions. . . .

Closely scrutinizing the Labourt, which to him was a foreign culture, Lancre produced a report that went beyond the established parameters on witchcraft indictments and warnings. The reasons for this departure are twofold: Lancre's account is clearly more politically motivated than comparable tracts of the period; and his authorial posture, that of a man encountering a strange culture and an unfamiliar people, has much in common with contemporary reports of travels to the New World. Descriptions of exotica from across the ocean supplied Lancre with a rhetoric that familiarized the unfamiliar, the rhetoric needed to articulate the combination of strangeness and fear that marked his encounter with the Labourdins. His descriptions of the religious, demonological, and judicial aspects of the magic/witchcraft phenomenon were guided by the investigative gaze of a bureaucrat with strong anthropological interests. His depictions of the Labourdins and their unfamiliar language and customs oscillate between amazement at their strange behavior, on the one hand, and on the other, authoritative pronouncements about people who were, like him, subjects of the king of France and bound by monarchic law.

Lancre was a product of elite French culture—he was raised and educated at the court and the university—and his social and economic distance from the people whose deliverance from satanic magic was entrusted to him could not have been greater. He found to his utter amazement that these people, not unlike the natives of the New World, adored Satan and his demons and practiced rituals that would have been as incomprehensible to him as those of faraway peoples, had it not been for his previous knowledge of demons and witches. Worse yet, since Christian missionaries had been successful in spreading God's word among the natives, Satan and his demons had been forced to leave their hiding places in the Americas and to return to Europe, specifically to the Labourt, in large numbers. Lancre cites travelers who had seen them flying across the sky:

> Travelers coming in search of wine in this city of Bordeaux assured us that on their way they saw great numbers of demons appearing as horrific human beings passing through France. This is the reason why the number of sorcerers is so great in the Labourt.

It had been reported from overseas that the natives sought access to their demon-divinities by inhaling the smoke of a plant they called *cohoba*. . . . "Having remained a certain time in an ecstatic state, they rise all lost and crazed, telling marvels about their false gods that they call Cemis, just like our witches when they return from the sabbath." From what Lancre could observe, the Labourdins practiced similar customs. They smoked tobacco, which seemed to put them into a trance; when they awoke, they reported having flown across the sea to distant shores in the company of many of their friends and having delighted in strange and wonderful experiences. Lancre believed in the reality of such transports. But he also saw the poverty of the people who smoked those weeds, and he offered yet another, more sober explanation for such indulgence. He noted that the herbal smoke quieted hunger pangs and that the imagined travel to distant and happier shores might merely have been a fanciful escape from the misery and poverty of daily life. . . .

Contemplating his experiences months later, Lancre not only committed to writing a wealth of impressions about the Labourt, its people, and their customs; he also conceived his book as an explanation of, and an apologia for, his relentless—and, judging by the many appeals to the French crown made against him—questionable legal practices exercised in governing the prosecutions of the Labourt witches and their priestly coconspirators. Lancre came to the Labourt firmly convinced of the reality of witches and of their real transport to the sabbath. It seems that he left the area just as certain of these phenomena. In spite of his remarkably keen ethnographic eye, his tract remains to the very last line a fierce indictment of all those whom he considered lenient or in any way skeptical about witchcraft accusations. . . .

The experiential realism of Lancre's report combines the physical proximity of the observer to the object of his interest with the distance of the prosecutor. It unites his horror at a people misguided by devilish pro-clivities with his sense of social order and government agency. His work thus evidences both the rapture of the male onlooker and the fanaticism of one committed to the eradication of sin. In spite of the skepticism articulated throughout the century by many educated men in Italy, Spain, France, and Germany, the coherent depiction of the magical world—real witches dancing at a real sabbath and representing a real threat to the community—controlled Lancre's gaze and that of like-minded men as they attempted to identify the members of the witches' sect. The discursive virulence of his language, which so shocks contem-porary readers, was to a large extent prompted by the passionate and, by all appearances, intra-European dispute about the reality of the witch phenomenon. The violence of this debate dominated Lancre's thoughts and actions as he struggled for mastery over the strange behavior of the Labourdins and over the chaos that such behavior represented. . . .

Once at his destination, Lancre encountered a rebelliously free people whose culture and language were so foreign to him that the only discourse available to capture the flavor of this otherness was that of the New World discoveries:

> The Indians, as the letters written from this country report, adore the gods of the sky, as they call them and the devils, but they make images of the devils from feathers of wildly diverse colors: undoubtedly, that is to signify their *inconstancy and mutability* marked by the feathers and by their many colors.

Comparisons to the natives of the New World and other peoples at the periphery of the known world abound in this text. . . .

. . . Lancre's book must be considered one of the most compelling reports of the period to describe Europe's encounter with the witch as, to adopt Céard's phrase, "the inside other." Characterized by great lin-guistic and cultural diversity, the Labourt was, according to Lancre, a perfect playground for Satan and an exceptionally fitting meeting place for the witches' sabbath. The remoteness of the mountain villages and towns allowed the witches to travel through the regions with great speed. And after fear had been transported across the French/Spanish border by those who fled from Lancre's prosecution, inquisitorial practice helped the craze to flourish and spread.

Lancre's eagerness to prosecute was seriously hampered by his in-ability to speak Basque. In his effort to alleviate this problem, he hired a translator/interpreter. . . .

Nevertheless, Lancre was troubled, to the point of constant anxiety, by the possibility that a translator might alter the message of the accused in a number of ways, intentionally or unintentionally. An interpreter could either translate the words incorrectly, or he could distort them for reasons of ignorance or through a desire to take sides in the dispute. Translators, Lancre believed, must be . . . "true echoes that remain perpetually silent if no one speaks . . . since it is necessary for them to speak only if someone is talking, and they should never vary even a little bit the words spoken to them."

The persistent threat to linguistic and epistemological transparency, the risk that distortions would be brought to the text by unreliable translator-go-betweens or court witnesses, were increased substantially by the special nature of witch inquests. The uncertainty and inconstancy of Satan and his associates continually disturbed and discredited the judicial process. Lancre's persistent return to the question of whether language was capable of representing truth in a world fraught with uncertainty underscores the fear implicit in his writing that discursive imprecision, and the opacity potentially present in all utterances, could and did encourage the intellectual skepticism that led to judicial leniency. . . .

. . .[H]e was unable to escape the mental seduction of the people's almost pagan sense of freedom, which he registered with a mixture of amazement and dread. The dichotomy between these " . . . poor suffering and burdened people" and their apparent haughtiness; between their unwillingness to bend to the discipline of work and the arrogance with which they made titles out of their tiny landholdings—calling each other "dame" and "sieur" and affecting an air of proud nobility—astonished Lancre. Their insouciance toward all social conventions as he knew them likewise unnerved him. In his eyes, they affected nobility where they had only poverty, freedom where there was satanic enslavement. He could not tolerate this undoing of his world.

Lancre's perceptive description was by no means class-blind. He made little secret of the fact that the otherness so captivating to him was exhibited only by the women of the lower classes. The manners of the Basque aristocracy, male and female, were familiar to him; since they spent much time in the company of their French equals and were educated at French schools, their language and their comportment conformed to the rules of French courtliness. What he observed in the Labourt was vastly different. He spoke with wonder of the "menu peuple" [small people], of the women's carelessly free way of life. He was struck by the specialness of their beauty, whose crowning glory, quite literally, was the unique quality of their hair. Giving voice to visual impressions, he described with the intensity of a lover's praise the women's tresses falling over their shoulders and seductively covering their faces, making their eyes shine with extraordinary brilliance:

> . . . their hair flowing over their shoulders and complementing their eyes, so that they appear much more beautiful in their simplicity. . . . Their beautiful hair gives them such a great advantage, makes them so irresistible, that the sun shining its rays on this cluster of hair as on a cloud, the burst of light is so violent and forms as brilliant streaks as occur in the sky when one witnesses the birth of Iris; from which comes their fascination with eyes, as dangerous in love as in witchcraft, although among them it is a sign of virginity to wear one's hair freely.

This beauty was deceptive. Lancre knew that hair was always a potential tool of bewitchment; one of the first and most profoundly intimidating gestures in most witch interrogations was the shearing of head and body hair. He had read that Kramer and Bodin urged judges to avoid looking into the eyes of a suspected witch for fear that she might inspire leniency merely by the power of her gaze. . . .

Living in their counterparadise, the Labourdins, true children of a Basque Eve, grew only one fruit in any quantity, the apple. With this fruit of transgression, they seduced the children of Adam: ". . . they eat with abandon this fruit of transgression, which caused the trespass against God's commandment and ignore the prohibition made to our first father." Small wonder, then, that living in the inhospitable mountains and swimming with lascivious abandon in the inconstant and dangerous sea, these ". . . girls and young fishermen" lent their ears as willingly to the seductions of men as to those of Satan. In the grottos by the ocean and on the high, inaccessible mountains, they found ready hideaways for their sexual pleasures. Lancre watched them returning from their diversions and observed how they regaled each other with what he presumed to be tales of their exploits, for they were laughing and dancing about in careless abandon. As the outsider, the learned city dweller, he was convinced that it made little difference to the obvious amusement and gaiety of these women and girls whether they told about their erotic exploits at some village feast or at the witches' sabbath.

It seemed to matter even less to the priests in whose care the souls of these women had been entrusted. Negligent yet arrogant servants of the church, the priests seemed to join the sabbath celebrations of their flock as readily as if they were leading them in Sunday mass. Contrary to the accepted practice, which allowed only males to handle the implements of worship or approach the altar and view the elevation of the host, the *benedictes,* as the women were called, carried the chalice and ornaments during mass and generally attended to the ritual needs of church services and, by implication, of the church servants. Their intimacy with priests was as remarkable as their persecution as witches was inevitable: ". . . they were permitted to view the elevation of the host, or one gave them permission to draw the veil or the curtain, and one also conceded that they do the responses." Lancre's suspicions became convictions: witchcraft in the Labourt was not only a family but also a community affair; there was no haven for the innocent, not even the church, and no person was secure, not even the smallest child. Lancre was convinced that of the thirty thousand Labourdins, the majority, if not all, had sworn allegiance to Satan. . . .

The Basque people were indeed as foreign to Lancre as any of the people across the ocean or in the far corners of Europe. When he did not condemn their sensuality and their lust for life, he scrutinized them as if they were children. His reaction was not unlike the early discoverers, who had similar reactions to the New World natives. Columbus's letters to the Spanish sovereigns and Las Casas's defense of the natives made equally effective use of the image of the child—negatively interpreted as irresponsible and sexually permissive, or positively valued as innocent, easily exploited, and grievously mistreated. . . .

During Lancre's stay in the Labourt, the number of children who accused their elders of taking them to the sabbath had grown steadily. . . . Lancre mentioned that as many as five hundred children, once even two thousand, had been part of the proceedings in the later stages of his work. At the height of the craze, there was hardly a village in the region where panic-stricken parents were not moved to demand the execution of suspected witches who had allegedly taken their children to Satan. They tied the children to their beds or endeavored to keep them awake, terrified that once the children closed their eyes, even for an instant, they would be unable to resist satanic abduction. Or parents brought them to church in the vain hope of seeking protection. . . .

. . . The child-witch craze . . . brought much suffering to the children: many were severely punished, some even burned at the stake.

In the end, Lancre's tract returns to the severity of judgment and the pervasiveness of the threat of adult witch activity. Italy, Germany, and Spain needed the inquisition to prosecute their heretics and their witches. In the name of royal majesty, Lancre strove to punish these people with the full weight of the law behind him. He was not entirely successful. "Making justice" meant more to him than prosecuting individuals accused of practicing witchcraft; his work had broader implications. Commenting on the two priests who were burned for their satanic activities, he declared:

> It is very dangerous that a priest be pardoned of sorcery, magic, and similar crimes, even one who is in charge of souls. For this clemency is ill conceived and very dangerous *for the republic*, and especially for a country as infected as the Labourt.

The results of leniency were *atheisme, heresie, idolatrie*. Satan and his minions wanted more than to destroy souls; they wanted to annihilate the society of Christian men and women.

Walter Stevens

Demon Lovers: Witchcraft, Sex, and the Crisis of Belief

After 1400, Western witchcraft mythology insistently repeats that witchcraft is a combination of *maleficia* and *corporeal interaction with incarnate devils*. In a definition of *witchcraft* from 1505, the individual crimes imputed to witches are all familiar, but there is a strikingly insistent repetition of the words *corpus, res corporales, corporaliter*. This litany underscores at every turn that these crimes were committed through the interaction of human and demonic *bodies.*

The arena par excellence of human interaction with demons was the Sabbat, or "witches' dance," or "witches' game." Accused witches . . . allegedly met the Devil (or a devil) for the first time when they were alone and vulnerable to discouragement or lust. But devils and witches had a social life as well. They supposedly gathered at immense meetings, often by the thousands. The most sordidly fascinating aspects of witchcraft mythology concern this mass meeting of witches and devils, where they engaged in a wide variety of shockingly perverse activities. According to Francesco Maria Guazzo, a theorist of the early seventeenth century, witches denied the Christian faith and withdrew their allegiance from God; they repudiated their baptism and their godparents and accepted a new name from the Devil. They gave their clothes, blood, and children to the Devil and begged him to inscribe their names in the "book of death"; they vowed to strangle or suffocate a child in his honor once or twice a month; they allowed themselves to be branded or marked by the Devil; and they repudiated the church's sacraments. . . .

Like the rest of the activities at the Sabbat, demonic copulation served to *anthropomorphize demons.* Sabbatic evidence demonstrated that real *human* interaction was possible between witches and devils. The idea of bodily contact organizes the whole concept of the Sabbat. There, the sexual orgies and other activities were supervised by Satan himself, to whom witches paid homage through a variety of degrading and disgusting rituals involving bodily contact. At times, Satan appeared in the guise of a relatively normal human being. At other times, he appeared in animal form. And sometimes his body showed a mixture of human, animal, and even inanimate characteristics. Whatever his physical form, Satan always interacted with his devotees in a strictly human and corporeal fashion: he distributed money and food, oversaw a sexual orgy, and beat or berated witches who displeased him. The Devil's rewards and punishments resembled those that a human tyrant might have meted out, not the unmistakably superhuman actions of a god, even a pagan one. He did not change people's nature or annihilate them, as Greco-Roman gods were supposed to do. Because his rewards and punishments were overwhelmingly corporeal and evil, he offered a striking moral contrast to God, the angels, and the saints; but, most important, *he behaved exactly like a human being.*

There was no defeatism or despair behind theorists' enthusiastic descriptions of the hordes attending Satan's meeting. The Sabbat was literally "hell on earth." It amounted to a transferral of Satan's court from the invisible realm of spirit to the sphere of bodily interaction; and it was *visitable*. It provided evidence that intimate contact with demons was available on a large scale, often involving thousands of people at once, for witches had to testify that they had seen each other there. Large-scale witch panics happened when such testimony—rather than evidence of *maleficia*—was systematically demanded by judges. . . .

Not only were fantasies of the Sabbat driven by the satisfaction of discovering human enemies; they also provided the exhilarating confirmation that suprahuman or supernatural enemies were *real*. . . . Modern readers have generally reacted to the representation of women's bodies and sexuality in witchcraft literature without noticing how these topics reacted to portrayals of demons' sexuality and corporeality. This bizarre topic is completely foreign to the Western view of the world since at least 1800. Yet it is crucial to understanding the motives that drove literate European men to construct the myth of witchcraft crimes.

Demonic corporeality and sexuality are not even "hidden" topics; they have been staring us in the face all along, in what we know about the peculiarities of European witchcraft between 1400 and 1700. Witchcraft in this period differed from witchcraft in other cultures—including the culture of European intellectuals and churchmen before 1400—in its twofold emphasis on *maleficia* and demonolatry. *Maleficia*, or acts of harmful magic, are the basis for any definition of witchcraft around the world; but demonolatry, the intentional worship of and subservience to demons, is peculiar to early-modern European witchcraft. Summarizing the relevant scholarship, Brian Levack asserts that "many individuals tried for witchcraft were not accused of performing any *maleficia* at all; their crime was simply worshipping the Devil. Whenever large witch-hunts took place, those persons who were implicated by confessing witches were almost always accused simply of attending the sabbath, not of practicing specific acts of magic." And sexual relations with demons were conceptualized as the most common expression of demonolatry or "demonomania," as the jurist Jean Bodin called it in the late sixteenth century. Sexual submission to demons was defined as a ritual act, demonstrating the witch's servitude, in both body and soul, to the demonic familiar and to Satan, the archenemy of God. This sexual slavery was allegedly undertaken eagerly by the novice witch, but she—or he—was often portrayed as enduring it with regret and even loathing after the initial trysts.

Sex with demons was only one aspect of a more general European fixation on *physical interaction with demons*. Demons, appearing in human or animal form, required their human devotees to worship them "in person." They demanded formal contractual agreements or "pacts" with humans; one "sold his soul to the devil" as if selling a horse or a field. Most dramatically, demons required that humans engage in outlandish, orgiastic sex with them. Strangely, while scholars of witchcraft have devoted much time to cataloging the great variety of such corporeal interactions between demons and humans, they have overlooked the significance of corporeal interaction itself. What would it have meant in 1430 or 1680 to assert that humans could interact with demons in the same way in which they interacted with other humans? What was the cultural and philosophical meaning of *commerce, association*, or *fellowship* between human society and the society of hell? Thus far, only the moral dimension of these concepts has interested scholars. But there are compelling reasons to suspect that moral condemnation of human-demon interaction was often a facade, an alibi for preoccupations of another sort entirely. . . .

For a long time, the demonological concerns of interrogators were probably incomprehensible to ordinary farmers, shopkeepers, and parents: "Illiterate peasants could not fully understand the sophisticated theories of the demonologists, . . . monks and theologians. Their concern with, and fear of witchcraft centered on the witch's ability to cause harm by occult means, not her relationship with the Devil." Of course, many individuals may have had witch-hunting motivations that stemmed from both sources: an inquisitor, for instance, could have been born in a peasant environment where witches were blamed for agricultural and interpersonal disasters. Eventually, the common people adopted the elite concern with demons, being educated into it through sermons, and solemn pageantry of trials and executions, and, eventually, their own literacy. . . .

The possibility of having unmistakable contact with demons through sex was anything but unproblematic between 1400 and 1700. Sex with demons was a highly complex idea. It had evolved very slowly within the literature culture since about 1150, and it had to overcome philosophical, physiological, and theological objections of tremendous weight and variety. In a nutshell, the objections had one source: Western Christian theologians had proclaimed for centuries that angels and demons are "pure spirits" and as such have no bodies at all.

This doctrine raises crucial questions: How is it possible to have sex with a being that has no real body? How can one do so with the firm conviction that one's partner is fully human? Why did defendants recognize their mistake *immediately* after consummation? More important, from the standpoint of witchcraft interrogations, what logic was served by *forcing* someone else to confess such experiences? . . .

Most of the interrogators who required such confessions would have known that demons were supposed to be purely spiritual. Thus, they appear to have enforced nonsensical, delusional confessions. Yet they presumed that the defendants were both sane and willful. Similar contradictions have traditionally been addressed, if at all, through speculation about the probable psychology of defendants, judges, or both. But here we would need to explain why defendants consistently made such confessions: Was postcoital depression and guilt so widespread that it made people "demonize" their sex partners? As for the interrogators, surely not every cleric had phobias about sex; not every married judge was a prude or an impotent voyeur.

Neither defendants nor interrogators were demonstrably insane, stupid, or neurotic; rather, their interactions took place within the confines of a great problem that was both complex and delicate. Although we cannot ascertain the preoccupations of individual interrogators in witch trials, we know that theoretical treatises about witchcraft had to create elaborate and often fragile explanations to resolve the contradictions between demonic incorporeality and demonic copulation. As time went on, these explanations depended increasingly on illustrations drawn from trials. Late-sixteenth- and early-seventeenth-century treatises are filled with confessions that are used to explain away the contradictions of demonic copulation.

Theorists and interrogators did not constitute a social class, but they shared fundamental assumptions based on literacy and theology. Their emphasis on demonic sexuality illustrates a profound difference between their mental world and that of defendants and accusers. After about 1200, the literate elite had less and less reason for uncomplicated belief in the reality of devils, angels, and the whole world of spirit; by 1400, the entire notion was demonstrably in crisis. Most, if not all, witchcraft theorists—and probably the majority of witchcraft interrogators—were interested in sexual and other corporeal relations between humans and demons because they were anxious to confirm the reality of the world of spirit. They considered the carnal knowledge of defendants their most valuable proof of that reality.

There are numerous indications that the elite exploited and misinterpreted common people's beliefs about the spirit world in an attempt to repair and rehabilitate their own. People who could not read and write were obviously unable to leave firsthand records of their beliefs about spirits: the descriptions that we have inherited were recorded by the literate and are probably tainted by literate presuppositions and anxieties. Nonetheless, it appears that, throughout the history of European witchcraft, the illiterate accusers and defendants in trials had a firmer, less complicated belief in the reality of spirits than did the literate elite who forced them to discuss spiritual reality. Fairies, elves, and other beings foreign to the biblical and theological tradition were probably mentioned initially by defendants or accusers, not interrogators.

Although we cannot know the realities of popular beliefs or precisely how those beliefs were distorted and exploited in trials, we know that witchcraft theorists assumed that common people believed more readily. Indeed, phrases like *for the witches firmly believe* occur with great frequency when witchcraft theorists discuss the nature of demons. This makes for a startling and shameful irony about European witch mythology. Although witchcraft treatises discuss *maleficium* in detail, their primary concern was the demonstration that demons are real. As a result, in the early treatises, *maleficium* was often invoked explicitly as a demonstration of demonic reality. . . .

Early Witchcraft Theory

There is a remarkable conceptual unity about demons and their human allies in early texts [about witchcraft]. The overt ethical and moralistic slant of these works defined witches and their immediate forerunners as hostile, aggressive assaulters of good Christians. The moralism was reinforced by defining witches as "demon lovers," the paramours of devils. Yet, despite reviling witches as *malefici* and *maleficae*, male and female "evildoers," the earliest witchcraft theorists were not primarily interested in witches' magical assaults on good people. Far more enthusiasm was reserved for witches' physical interactions with demons. Those interactions were imagined as fully corporeal and include sexual intercourse, conceptualized as a form of knowledge gathering.

The philosophical attention that the theologians lavished on this stereotype reveals that the real demon lovers, the persons who most ardently desired physical relationships with embodied devils, were the theologians themselves. Their desire for "carnal knowledge" of demons was not pornographic, but metaphysical. Their fantasy of witches' corporeal ravishment translated their own desire for an overwhelming intellectual conviction, one that would annihilate their involuntary resistance to the idea of demonic reality. . . .

To say that witchcraft theorists did not believe their theories is not to say that they thought like modern educated secular people. With two or three centuries of scientific thinking and rationalistic skepticism in his or her mental baggage, the modern educated layperson looks at elements of the mythology of witchcraft and thinks: "Such things cannot happen." Yet, at some point in the distant past, activities attributed to witches, and powers attributed to devils, must have commanded belief among literate Europeans. Before the twelfth century, writings about interactions between demons and humans sometimes betray no doubt. They are told straightforwardly, with a matter-of-fact attitude toward the possibility that such encounters could actually take place. These pre-twelfth-century writings are short on theory and demonstrate no apparent need for complicated explanations. There are no convoluted chains of proof, no attempts to head off the reader's skepticism with elaborate preemptive refutations. The internal logic of these writings seems to express a mental attitude to the effect that "this is how such things must happen, this is the most satisfactory explanation." It seems therefore quite safe to qualify such writings as expressions of belief.

The thirteenth century was a watershed in the history of Christian beliefs about spirits. David Keck has demonstrated that, "as late as 1200, scientific angelology . . . was still in its infancy. By contrast, fifty years later, both Aquinas and Bonaventure had developed thorough, systematic, comprehensive angelologies that addressed all of the major natural and metaphysical issues concerning angels." Because demons were defined as fallen angels, no discussion of angelology could ignore them. But the search for precision and certainty about a world that was invisible to humans generated significant perplexities and doubts. In this respect, witchcraft theory was a direct outgrowth of thirteenth-century angelology and demonology.

As thirteenth-century angelology evolved toward fifteenth-century demonology and witchcraft theory, literate discussions of the spirit world progressively accumulated the telltale signs of bad faith that were missing from the earlier literature. The luxuriant proofs of the 1400s and 1500s display neither belief nor rationalistic skepticism. Instead, they are saturated with an attitude best expressed as "these things cannot *not* be happening in the way in which I propose." The older, late-antique and early-medieval mentality had been "this must be true." The modern rationalist stance is "this cannot be true." The early-modern contention was "this cannot *not* be true." Witchcraft theorists often employed this very phraseology.

The early-modern attitude thus occupies an uncomfortable halfway point between belief and skepticism, an attempt to maintain belief while fighting off skepticism. The attitude of witchcraft theorists toward their theories was not belief but rather *resistance to skepticism*, a desperate attempt to maintain belief, and it betrays an uncommonly desperate *need to believe*. . . .

Interpretations of texts about witchcraft err to the degree that they do not stop to ask whether such elaborate theories are necessary in order to achieve the ends that witchcraft treatises ostensibly pursue. Was all this theological reasoning about spirits necessary if the primary goal of witchcraft theory was the social control of humans? Was such reasoning merely a demonstration of its authors' deeply held beliefs? Why was that necessary? . . .

Witchcraft theory became quite uniform. Its stereotypes and commonplaces crystallized, not just because theorists read each other, or because they read previous theologians, but also because there was a logic to the "cumulative concept" that appealed to most theorists. That logic is thoroughly implicated by the fundamental doctrines of Christianity concerning the nature of *spirit*. Anyone engaged in the prosecution of witches must have felt its attraction, whether he was familiar with formal witchcraft theory or not.

That logic, I argue, implied that the identification and persecution of witches was nothing less than a defense of fundamental Christian principles. Those principles remained central to Christianity from long before Martin Luther until long after the Council of Trent. They were

not moral or ethical questions about conduct, as we have been led to believe, but scientific problems of being and knowledge, concerning devils,
angels, the human soul, the truthfulness of the Bible, and the evidence
of God's existence and presence in the world. Witchcraft theory was far
more than a demonology. It was not an anomaly in the history of Western
Christianity. It was an expression of Christianity's deepest and truest logic,
although in oversimplified and neurotic form. Not that its practitioners
were usually treated as fanatics or obscurantist crackpots; they participated in the most vital, wide-ranging, and up-to-date philosophical and
scientific debates. . . .

. . . But skepticism was infectious; many later authors fought it
because they had internalized it, and it riddles their texts with clashing
logic and rhetoric. Witchcraft theory was an impassioned protest that
"these things cannot be imaginary!"

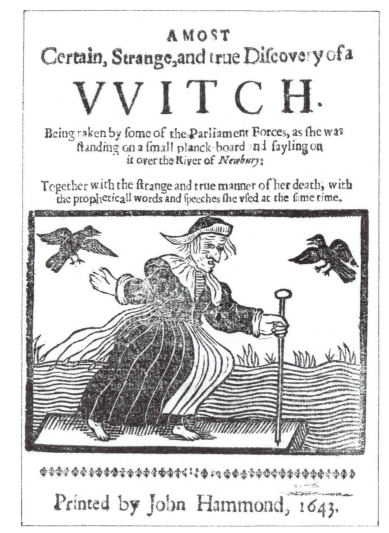

A MOST
Certain, Strange, and true Difcovery of a

VVITCH.

Being taken by fome of the Parliament Forces, as fhe was
ftanding on a fmall planck-board and fayling on
it over the River of *Newbury*;

Together with the ftrange and true manner of her death; with
the propheticall words and fpeeches fhe vfed at the fame time.

Printed by John Hammond, 1643.

Title page of an anonymous witchcraft pamphlet, published during the English Civil War,
which describes how a witch sailed over a river on a plank, and was later captured and
killed by Parliamentary forces. The words and actions of those accused of witchcraft were
sometimes interpreted as political prophecies, as in this pamphlet. (*Title page from pamphlet by John Hammond, "A Most Certain, Strange, and True Discovery of a Witch," quarto
(in AL—x.57). Print provided by Glasgow University, Department of Special Collections.*)

PART

II Political, Economic, and Social Contexts

Historians who explore the intellectual contexts of the witch trials have a wide range of written and visual sources at their disposal, and those who explore the political, economic, and social settings have even more. Some examine the debates surrounding the passing and enforcement of secular laws against witchcraft, such as the criminal code of the Holy Roman Empire from 1532 or the English and Scottish witchcraft statutes of 1563. They explore the ways in which rulers and their officials increased the size and scope of political institutions, including systems of taxation and government bureaucracies, and the complex relationship between the expansion of centralized power and a heightened concern about witchcraft.

Other scholars look at developments in legal procedure, using legal treatises and court records. They have particularly highlighted the change from an accusatorial legal procedure to an inquisitorial procedure. In the former, a suspect knew the accusers and the charges they had brought, and an accuser could in turn be liable for trial if the charges were not proven; in the latter, legal authorities themselves brought the case. According to many historians, this change made people much more willing to accuse others, for they never had to take personal responsibility for the accusation or face the accused's relatives. Inquisitorial procedure involved intense questioning of the suspect, often with torture; areas in Europe that did not make this change saw very few trials and almost no mass panics. Inquisitorial procedure came into Europe as part of the adoption of Roman law, which also (at least in theory) required the confession of a suspect before she or he could be executed. This had been designed as a way to keep innocent people from death, but in practice in some parts of Europe led to the adoption of ever more gruesome means of inquisitorial torture; torture was also used to get the names of additional suspects, as most lawyers trained in Roman law firmly believed that no witch could act alone.

The use of inquisitorial procedure did not always lead to witch hunts, however. The most famous Inquisitions in early modern Europe, those in Spain, Portugal, and Italy, were in fact very lenient in their treatment of those accused of witchcraft: the Inquisition in Spain executed only a handful of witches, the Portuguese Inquisition only one, and the Roman Inquisition (which had jurisdiction in much of Italy) none, though in each of these areas there were hundreds of cases. Inquisitors firmly believed in the power of the devil, but they doubted very much whether the people accused of doing *maleficia* had actually made a pact with the devil that gave them special powers. They viewed them not as diabolical devil-worshippers, but as superstitious and ignorant peasants who should be educated rather than executed. Because the Inquisitions played such a minor role in witch trials compared to other types of courts, none of the articles in this book focuses on them, and only one discusses southern Europe.

In "State-building and Witch Hunting in Early Modern Europe," the first article in this section, Brian Levack takes a closer look at the relationship between the rise of the centralized nation-state, including its use of inquisitorial procedure, and the witch hunts. He focuses particularly on Scotland, which has been seen as a key example of this relationship since the very influential book by Christina Larner, *Enemies of God: The Witch Hunt in Scotland,* published in 1981. In a later book, Larner also relates the political context of witch trials to religious developments, arguing that with the Reformation, Christianity became a political ideology. Rulers felt compelled to prove their piety and the depth of their religious commitment to their subjects and other rulers; they did this by fighting religious wars, and by cracking down on heretics and witches within their own borders. Witchcraft was thus used as a symbol of total evil, and total hostility to the community, the state, the church, and God.

Levack's article tests these assertions by exploring the specific circumstances surrounding the passage of the Scottish witchcraft statute, the use of inquisitorial torture, and the development of scepticism about the powers of witches. He finds local lower-level religious and secular officials were often more adamant in their desire to prosecute than were high-ranking advocates of stronger centralized power, and argues that officials cannot be considered as an undifferentiated group. Brief, comparative comments on France and Denmark also note the same pattern: more prosecutions and convictions at the local or provincial level, and fewer at the higher courts that were directed from the center.

The second article in this section, J. T. Swain's "The Lancashire Witch Trials of 1612 and 1634 and the Economics of Witchcraft," also tests several widely-known theories, in this case ones that link witchcraft and economic distress. Several historians of witchcraft in England, including Alan Macfarlane and Keith Thomas, identified cases in which the initial accusation came from people who had refused to help a fellow villager, and then blamed later misfortune on her anger or revenge; they have suggested that in such a scenario, witchcraft accusations were used as a way of assuaging guilt over uncharitable conduct. Swain analyzes several trials that originated in the Pendle Forest, an area of Lancashire in which patterns of landownership were changing and gaps between rich and poor growing greater, testing both the relationship between economic distress and witchtrials and the Macfarlane/Thomas model of the refusal of charity.

We move from the British Isles to Hungary with the third selection in this section, Gábor Klaniczay's "Witch-hunting in Hungary: Social or Cultural Tensions?" (To keep the article a manageable length, only the section dealing with social tensions has been included here.) Witch trials reached their peak in Hungary later than they did in western or central Europe, and combined ideas and procedures imported from outside with local traditions and practices. Like Swain, Klaniczay begins with the sociological explanation for witchcraft suggested by Keith Thomas and Alan Macfarlane—that witch accusations grew out of social conflict and a dissolution of neighborliness.

To this he adds an idea suggested by the German historian Wolfgang Behringer, that witch-hunting waves may correlate with famines, plagues, revolts, and other crises. He then looks at several quite different types of trial-series, two from urban milieus, two from the court of the prince of Transylvania, and one from the world of shepherds. As might be expected, social tensions were quite different in each of these social settings. Klaniczay also discovers that various other factors were clearly interwoven with social issues—religious differences, personal jealousy, the presence of ethnic outsiders, in this case German soldiers. His examples support the ideas of Thomas and Macfarlane about economic and neighborly tensions, but also suggest that these cannot be seen as definitive and sufficient causes. Similarly, witch trials in Hungary sometimes occurred during periods of crisis, as Behringer proposed, but some major crises, including peasant revolts and devastating plagues, saw no increase in witch trials.

The final selection in this section comes from Robin Briggs' major study, *Witches and Neighbors: The Social and Cultural Context of European Witchcraft.* Briggs is a historian of early modern France who spent many years researching all types of social and cultural tensions before he turned specifically to witchcraft. His book concentrates on cases from the Lorraine, the part of eastern France that saw the most witch trials. In contrast to the three previous selections, Briggs does not specifically evaluate the ideas of other individual historians, but certain key ideas underlie his approach: that witchcraft accusations arose in part from social tensions, that economic shortages exacerbated those tensions, and that emotions such as guilt and resentment played an important role. In the selection included here, from the chapter "Love and Hatred: Spouses and Kin," Briggs looks at how these issues played themselves out in the intimate circle of the family, where love and loyalty were often accompanied by hatred and hostility. Briggs presents examples of the varied ways in which husbands responded to an accusation of witchcraft against their wives, and also of the ways in which complicated family relationships—stepchildren, half-siblings, childless families, orphans—created even more possibilities for hostility and allegations.

Brian P. Levack

State-building and Witch Hunting in Early Modern Europe

During the last two decades a number of historians have attempted to establish a causal relationship between the great European witch hunt of the sixteenth and seventeenth centuries and the development of the modern state. These scholars have claimed that "the rise of the nation-state" is at the very least one of the secondary causes of the witch hunt; that the hunt resulted from the centralisation of royal power; that it is one reflection of the advance of public authority against "particularism"; that it is integrally related to the assertion of reason of state; and that it proceeds from an impulse towards both absolutism and state sovereignty. The general impression one gets from this line of argument is that witches were in a certain sense victims of the advance of that emerging leviathan, the centralised, bureaucratised, secularised modern state. The purpose of this chapter is to examine this line of argument and to suggest some limitations to it. It will also test some of these theories about the connection between state-building and witch hunting with reference to one country in which it is alleged that they are especially apparent, the kingdom of Scotland.

The argument consists of four separate but related strands. The first deals with judicial and administrative centralisation, which is incontestably one of the most salient features of state development. Here the argument is that the growth of the state involved the advance of central, i.e. royal, jurisdiction, as a result of which areas which had enjoyed a large measure of autonomy, especially those on the geographical periphery of royal domains, came within the ambit of central government control. The ideal after which rulers strove was "a centralized authority with a perfect bureaucracy, consisting of local official bodies that were merely executive powers." This attack on localism and particularism, so it is claimed, led

Brian P. Levack, "State-building and Witch Hunting in Early Modern Europe." Jonathan Barry, et al., eds. *Witchcraft in Early Modern Europe: Studies in Culture and Belief.* Copyright © 1996. Reprinted with the permission of Cambridge University Press.

to an increase in the prosecution of witches, as the state enforced witch-craft edicts from the central government and instructed local authorities about a crime they were ill prepared to prosecute. No matter where pros-ecutions occurred, they reflected the inexorable process by which the juggernaut of the state imposed its authority on subordinate units.

The second strand of the argument deals with both the officialisation of judicial power and its enhancement through new methods of repres-sion, especially judicial torture. The rise of large-scale witch hunting was facilitated by the adoption of inquisitorial procedure, according to which governmental officials conducted the entire legal process by themselves and used physical force to compel men suspected of secret crimes to con-fess. Inquisitorial procedure was improved during the fifteenth and six-teenth centuries, mainly by involving the state more and more in the initiation of cases, and by the seventeenth century it had become one of the main features of the absolutist state. When witches were subjected to this procedure they became entrapped in what is referred to as the state machine, from which, so it is argued, there was little hope of escape. It is interesting to note in this connection that the justification given for the exercise of these new judicial powers was the doctrine of "reason of state," which itself reflected the "secular rationality" of the early modern period.

The third strand of the argument deals with the efforts of the state to reform society and transform it into a godly community. This involved the disciplining of the population or the "acculturation of the rural world" that Robert Muchembled sees as one of the main characteristics of the absolutist state. This enterprise was undertaken by an entire hierarchy of officials, from the king down to the local judges and parish priests, all of whose authority the state was promoting. The prosecution of witches, according to this thesis, was just one part of this process of acculturation, one in which the state, usually with the assistance of the church, pursued the ultimate objective of destroying superstition, producing a more godly and homogeneous population, and promoting obedience to the "absolute king and to God."

The fourth part of the argument concerns the relationship between church and state. One of the main indications of the growing power of the state during the early modern period was that it effectively gained con-trol over, or at least secured the support of, the church. In terms of juris-diction, this meant either the assumption of control by secular authorities over matters previously entrusted to the church, or the use of ecclesiastic courts to provide effective support for secular tribunals. These changes, which took place throughout Europe in the sixteenth century, greatly facilitated the prosecution of witches. The state, with its almost unlimited judicial resources, was much more capable of conducting these prosecutions than the church had ever been. Even more important was the cooperation that developed between church and state, which was especially apparent in a crime of mixed jurisdiction like witchcraft. As that cooperation became more common, the crime of witchcraft was often viewed as treason against God on the one hand and an act of rebellion against the state on the other. The identification of secular and religious crime was deliberate: the state prosecuted witches, so it is argued, in order to legitimise new regimes through the pursuit of religious deviants.

It is not the purpose of this chapter to challenge all these propositions. There is much of value in the historical work that has just been summarised, and historians of witchcraft have used it to deepen our understanding of the phenomenon we are studying. It is, for example, incontestable that the secularisation of witchcraft prosecutions had a dramatic impact on the intensity of prosecutions and the number of executions. It is also incontestable that the use of inquisitorial procedure by temporal authorities facilitated numerous prosecutions that otherwise might have been unsuccessful. There is, however, a danger inherent in this line of thought that we shall view that state, and especially the monarchy and the central authorities that most clearly embodied and represented it, as the dynamic force in witchcraft prosecutions. Nothing could be further from the truth. The active, the dynamic force in most witchcraft prosecutions were local authorities, members of local elites who did whatever they could to gain the sanction of central authorities but who did not serve as their direct agents. The central officers of the state, moreover, did much more to restrain these local authorities than to abet them in their efforts to prosecute witches.

In order to illustrate this point, let us look closely at the Scottish situation. In many ways Scotland serves as the ideal test case for the process we are studying. The witch hunt in that country has been referred to as one of the major witch hunts in Europe, and the intensity of prosecutions was quite high, perhaps twelve times as great as in England, although it did not reach the level of some German states. While by no means one of the most powerful states of Europe, Scotland made sustained efforts throughout the sixteenth and seventeenth centuries to increase the power of the central government, and it is precisely this attempt to strengthen the state that lies at the centre of the argument that has been outlined above. The Scottish parliament proclaimed the imperial status of its monarchy even earlier than did England, and from the fifteenth century onwards its rulers aspired towards absolute power. Scotland also experienced a reception of Roman law and adopted at least some aspects of inquisitorial procedure. Torture was used as part of an effort to repress political dissent and to assist the state in prosecuting crime.

The links between this process of state development and witch hunting appear to be stronger in Scotland than in other European states. The prosecution of witches was secularised in Scotland at a fairly early date, and there was considerable cooperation between church and state in prosecuting the crime. James VI, the king of Scotland during one of the country's most intense periods of witch hunting, not only was a royal absolutist but also wrote a treatise that encouraged the prosecution of witches. There were many efforts made throughout this period to associate witchcraft with political dissent. Finally, and most important, the crime of witchcraft was, according to Christina Larner, centrally managed. It seems therefore that Scottish witchcraft prosecutions can easily be placed within a framework of political development. According to Larner, "The Scottish witch hunt spanned a period which began with the rise of the doctrine of the divine right of kings and ended with the decline of the doctrine of the godly state."

Our inquiry must begin with the passage of the Scottish witchcraft statute of 1563, the law upon which all secular prosecutions were based until its repeal in 1736. On the face of it, this, like other European witchcraft statutes, proclamations or edicts, was an attempt by the state to assume control of a crime that was prosecuted, if at all, under the jurisdiction of relatively impotent church courts. But the statute does not represent any such secular initiative. The witchcraft statute was adopted by a parliament that was under considerable pressure from the church to inaugurate a campaign of moral reform and establish a godly discipline. This pressure marked the beginning of a long campaign by the clergy to encourage secular Scottish authorities to prosecute witches. This pattern is worth noting; the history of witchcraft prosecutions in Scotland is much more the story of a reluctant central government responding to pressure from subordinate authorities, in this case the clergy, than the attempt of a developing state to discipline the population. . . .

But what about the procedures that were used to try those witches who were successfully prosecuted? Part of the argument that links witch-hunting to the growth of state power is the employment of inquisitorial procedure and the use of torture in the prosecution of witches. Both of these developments mark the officialisation and bureaucratisation of the judicial power as well as the replacement of private by public authority. With inquisitorial procedure the state assumes control over, if it does not also initiate, prosecutions, and through methods like torture it acquires the information that it needs successfully to prosecute dissenters and other enemies of the government. In many ways the advent of inquisitorial procedure is the quintessential expression of the new power of the state.

Now it is important to recognise that Scottish criminal procedure was only partially inquisitorial. Scotland never did away with the petty trial jury, for example, an institution that vanished in those countries where the state gained full control of the judicial process. Nevertheless, Scottish courts did employ many features of continental criminal procedure, such as the initiation of cases by information and the creation of a legal dossier, and therefore it is worthwhile to inquire whether those features of Scottish justice contributed to the intensification of witch hunting. A strong case can be made for the fact that they did not. The main consideration here is that anything resembling inquisitorial procedure was utilised only in the court of justiciary and on circuit, where trained judges could oversee the judicial process, and it was precisely in these tribunals that witch hunting was greatly restrained. The lord advocate, to be sure, did initiate cases that might not have otherwise reached the courtroom. But once the case began, the officialisation of the Scottish criminal process worked to the advantage of the witch, resulting in a surprisingly high percentage of acquittals, almost as high as in England. One reason for this was the fact that in these central trials the witch was often granted a defence counsel, a luxury denied to her southern English neighbour. . . .

It appears therefore that the growth of state power and the officialisation of the judicial process did very little to intensify witchcraft prosecutions in Scotland. Indeed, it was the *failure* of the state to control local authorities and to supervise local justice, that led to the great prosecutions of the seventeenth century. These local authorities figured how to use the power of the state to their advantage, mainly by obtaining commissions that entitled them to proceed. Once they started that procedure, however, they virtually ignored the rules regulating the administration of justice that the state had established, and illegally used one of the most terrifying instruments of state power, judicial torture, to secure convictions. . . .

Leaving Scotland for the moment, let us ask whether we can extend this argument regarding state power to other European countries. . . .

Crossing the channel to France, . . . it seems we might expect to find the strongest support for the "state thesis," if we may call it that. In France the prosecution of witches has been associated not only with "centralising absolutism" and an attack on particularism but with the efforts of the state to discipline the population. Robert Muchembled has seen witch hunting as part of a larger attack on popular culture that was conducted by agents of state and church and was inspired by both the Counter-Reformation and a programme of royal absolutism. Now if we consider the "state" to comprise all "natural rulers" from the king down through the hierarchy of provincial and local officials to parish priests and fathers within families, as Muchembled does, and if we consider absolutism to have entailed an assertion of power by all these authorities, then it is hard to deny that witchcraft prosecutions, which usually involved the exercise of power by elites over their inferiors, were the result of the rise of the absolutist state. The difficulty arises only when we attribute the inspiration of these witchcraft prosecutions to those royal officials who stood at the top of this hierarchy and when we see these trials as part of a policy of centralisation. It is true that most of those prosecutions took place in the peripheral regions of the kingdom, outside "royal" France, but it is difficult to see this as part of an effort to destroy particularism. Indeed, the main reason why prosecutions flourished in these outlying regions was the failure of the government to supervise the judicial process. Local elites in these areas, to be sure, did everything they could to use state power to their advantage, just as they did in Scotland, but they did not prosecute witches as part of some centrally managed or centrally inspired campaign. . . .

The important consideration for our purposes is the fact that the process of state-building, the process of controlling the periphery, indeed the process of establishing anything more than the most tenuous links between the centre and the periphery, had nothing to do with the encouragement of prosecutions and everything to do with its restraint. The effect of judicial centralisation in France was that the higher courts could monitor the actions of local judges, as they did frequently between 1580 and 1650, and even bring criminal charges against those who used abusive procedures in trying witches. It has been argued that one of the reasons for the high incidence of witchcraft prosecutions in the outlying regions of France was precisely the fact that they did *not* fit into the centralised judicial system of the absolute state and therefore did not have an automatic review or appeals process. . . .

The final country in this survey, Denmark, is especially relevant to our concerns, since that kingdom, like Scotland, had a monarch who developed a personal commitment to witch hunting. Christian IV (1588–1648), duly alarmed by a witch hunt that took the lives of eleven women in Køge in 1612, apparently was instrumental in the promulgation of the famous ordinance of 1617, which defined the crime of witchcraft for the first time and reserved the penalty of burning only to those who had made pacts with the devil. Since prosecutions increased dramatically after 1617, it is tempting to see them as the result of actions taken at the centre, especially since accompanying legislation against adultery and fornication suggests a broader policy of state-sponsored discipline. Once again, however, appearances are deceptive. Whatever the role of King Christian in these trials—and it has not been established that there was any at all—his government can certainly not be assigned responsibility for the hunt that occurred. Quite to the contrary, the impulse to witch-hunting came from below, from the district courts, whereas the role of the central government was to ensure the adherence to established procedures, and to guarantee that all convictions from the lower courts be appealed to the county courts and, if necessary, to the supreme court. It is instructive to note that just under 90 per cent of the cases heard at the district level, where trials were held by juries that knew the accused, resulted in convictions, whereas the proportion at the royal county courts was approximately 50 per cent. These percentages, it should be recalled, come remarkably close to those in Scotland, and in both cases the local courts proceeded by jury trial, whereas in the higher courts inquisitorial procedure prevailed.

Some of the conclusions that emerge from this study of witch hunting may not be all that startling. It has long been recognised that local courts pursued witches more aggressively than central courts; that many witchcraft convictions were reversed on appeal; that scepticism appeared first in the central courts. What is not often recognised, however, is the role that state-builders played in this whole process. However much they may have wished for a more homogeneous population, however much they may have desired to discipline the lower classes and help the church wipe out superstition, they also were firm advocates of what has come to be called the rule of law, and that often meant adherence to strict legal procedure. These two goals, of social control and judicial restraint, came in conflict with each other, especially in cases of witchcraft, and the state found itself regulating over-zealous local authorities who exceeded the bounds of royal justice. If we wish to speak about reason of state and absolutism in connection with witch hunting, we should look less at the celebrated introduction of state-sponsored prosecutions and the application of judicial torture, and much more at the central regulation of local justice.

J. T. Swain

The Lancashire Witch Trials of 1612 and 1634 and the Economics of Witchcraft

An important theory was put forward by Alan Macfarlane and Keith Thomas to help explain the incidence of witchcraft accusations at a local level in early modern England. They noted the fact that the witches were often poor old women who were usually accused by more prosperous younger neighbours, following a refusal of charity. Thomas and Macfarlane saw the economic changes of the sixteenth century, with rapid population growth putting pressure on limited resources and with enclosure increasing the number of the landless poor, as factors which accelerated the trend towards a cash economy. The medieval idea of voluntary charity towards the poor as a necessary Christian obligation was rendered obsolete by the advent of the Elizabethan Poor Law which discouraged begging. Thus the move away from a neighbourly, communal ethic to one based more on private property and commercial values led to increasing social tension, as the poor felt the full force of unfavourable market forces and the sanctions of the state. A rejected beggar would often curse his uncharitable neighbour, and, should something then go wrong, the neighbour might attribute his misfortune to witchcraft. Also present is the notion that the victim, aware that he had failed in his social

J. T. Swain, "The Lancashire Witch Trials of 1612 and 1634 and the Economics of Witchcraft," *Northern History* 30. Copyright © 1994. Reprinted with permission.

obligations, sought to exonerate himself by transferring the guilt he felt to the beggar.

Macfarlane admitted that there were problems with this model, and later repudiated his original ideas, claiming instead that the individualistic characteristics of the English were present in medieval times and did not arise specifically in the sixteenth century along with witchcraft accusations. Nevertheless, Macfarlane's original ideas, together with those of Thomas, remain very influential, whilst his later ideas have not been as widely accepted. The purpose of this investigation is to assess the extent to which economic factors played a part in what are, arguably, the most famous witch trials in English history—those of the Lancashire witches.

The Lancashire or Pendle witches are justifiably famous. Two historical novels based on the events of the 1612 trial have contributed most to the legend: Harrison Ainsworth's *The Lancashire Witches* (1849) and Robert Neill's *Mist over Pendle* (1951). Neill's book has the merit of being based more heavily on the chief historical source, *The wonderful discovery of witches in the country of Lancaster*, published in 1613 by Thomas Potts, the judges' clerk at the fateful Assizes of August 1612 where the chief witches were condemned to death. . . .

The immediate events which led to the first trial began on 18 March 1612 when Alizon Device met a Halifax pedlar called John Law near Colne. She wanted some pins, but he refused to sell or give her any. He then suffered a stroke, and accused Alizon of bewitching him. Apparently, she later confessed to the crime of witchcraft both to Law and to his son, Abraham, a Halifax cloth dyer. On 30 March, a local J. P., Roger Nowell, Esq. of Read, questioned her together with her brother James and her mother Elizabeth Device. Nowell interrogated others and mutual recriminations followed; finally, on Saturday 4 April, he sent for trial at the next Lancaster Assizes, Alizon, her eighty-year-old grandmother Elizabeth Southerns alias Old Demdike, and two women from another family thought to be notorious witches, Anne Whittle alias Old Chattox (also aged about eighty) and her married daughter Anne Redfern. Old Demdike had confessed to Nowell that she had given her soul to the Devil twenty years before and let her familiar, called Tibb, suck her blood. Alizon also admitted to a demonic pact sealed two years previously, apparently at her grandmother's instigation. Anne Whittle similarly confessed to making a pact fourteen or fifteen years before with a devil called Fancy.

The following Friday, Good Friday 10 April, relatives and friends met in Pendle Forest at Old Demdike's house called the Malkin Tower. No doubt they were alarmed and confused about the arrests and naturally wondered what to do next. Nowell got to hear of the meeting, assumed because of the day chosen that it was a witches' sabbat (despite the fact that no evidence of the Devil's presence was discovered) and, after further examinations, sent several more prisoners to join the other four in Lancaster Castle. There, they were interrogated again, and details of an incredible plot emerged, notably that they had intended to rescue the four prisoners, kill the Lancaster gaoler and blow up the castle.

This was only seven years after the Gunpowder Plot, and so perhaps naturally the authorities took the case seriously, particularly since accusations of witchcraft were involved. On the other hand, to what extent did the authorities pressurize those who were accused? In theory, torture was not allowed in English trials that did not involve treason, but some of the confessions seem too incredible and far-fetched to be the result of anything other than the product of unscrupulous tactics by the prosecution, whether by the use of force, methods such as prolonged periods of sleep deprivation, threats, suggestions that others had already confessed or promises of leniency if the accused admitted to what the authorities wished to hear. Whatever did happen inside the dungeons at Lancaster, it was too much for Old Demdike, who died before the trial. At his trial in August, the labourer James Device "was so insensible, weak and unable in all things as he could neither speak, hear or stand, but was holden up."

The star witness at the trials which followed in August was nine-year-old Jennet Device, the sister of Alizon and James. She provided evidence about those who had attended the Malkin Tower gathering, including information against her own mother, Elizabeth Device, and her elder brother and sister! The shock of this was too much for Elizabeth, who had refused to make any confession, but finally broke down in court when Jennet, backed up by James and Alizon, accused her of witchcraft. Not all the prisoners pleaded guilty, and one who refused to confess was Alice Nutter of Roughlee, whom Potts describes as standing out because, unlike the others, she was a rich woman. Not only was she charged with attending the Malkin Tower meeting, but, incredibly, she was also accused of consorting with Old Demdike and Elizabeth Device to kill Henry Mitton of Roughlee because Demdike, when on a begging expedition, has been refused a penny by Mitton! This is not the only piece of implausible evidence accepted by the courts and Potts. Some were acquitted, including a further group of alleged witches from Samlesbury.

Nine, however, were condemned to death and, together with a woman from Windle near St Helens, were taken out and hanged the following day. Another woman who had apparently attended the ill-fated Malkin Tower meeting, Jennet Preston of Gisburn in Craven, had been previously tried at the York Assizes in July and had been executed too. . . .

What was the economic background to the Pendle witch trials? The term "Forest of Pendle" is somewhat misleading because the area was not a forest at all in the modern sense of the word. Originally, the area was a forest or chase in the legal sense and was therefore reserved for hunting deer, but, in the latter Middle Ages substantial vaccaries (cattle farms) were established. During the fourteenth century the area was leased, and farmers had the opportunity to develop the resources of the forest on their own account. Pendle Forest, as part of the Duchy of Lancaster's Honour of Clitheroe, became part of the Crown lands when Henry IV usurped the throne in 1399. Leasing continued throughout the fifteenth century until in 1507 the forests of the Honour of Clitheroe were granted to tenants by copy of court roll, according to the custom of the adjacent manors such as Colne and Ightenhill.

This was a decision which benefited the Crown in the short term—rents rose by 39 per cent in Pendle—but in the longer term prospects were more to the advantage of the tenants since they gained security of tenure with copies of their tenancy agreements which could be demonstrated if necessary in court. In addition, the forest copyholders were permitted to inherit their holdings automatically, provided that they paid an entry fine of just one year's rent. The rents themselves were fixed, so, in real terms, the copyholders became increasingly better off during the sixteenth century as prices rose. By contrast, many tenants in other areas faced great hardship, often being evicted if the landlord wished to enclose his lands, or at the very least were subjected to rapidly rising entry fines and rents.

Not surprisingly, the opening up of these forest areas—in Pendle's case, 7,289 acres—on such advantageous terms led to rapid population growth. There had been just twenty-four tenants in Pendle Forest in 1443 but the number had grown to exactly 100 by 1527. In response, a new corn mill was built at New Carr in 1542 and Newchurch itself was officially consecrated in 1544 and separated from St Michael's Clitheroe. Other areas of Pendle Forest were contained in three adjacent chapelries: Barrowford in the north-east was in Colne chapelry; to the south-east, Burnley chapelry contained Reedley Hallows, Filly Close and New

Laund; to the south-west, Higham, West Close and Heyhouses were part of Padiham chapelry. All formed part of the huge parish of Whalley.

Exact population figures are impossible to obtain, but a total of 100 tenants in 1527 suggests a population of at least 400–500, and this must be regarded as an absolute minimum since it takes no account of families existing as subtenants or those officially landless but illegally squatting. Moreover, the population seems to have continued to grow. In Newchurch chapelry there were sixty-four households according to the communicants' returns of 1563, and 150 in 1650. Making allowances for the sections of Pendle Forest in the other three chapelries gives an estimate of 145 households in the whole of Pendle Forest in 1563 and 340 in 1650. This suggests a total population of 580–725 in 1563, and of about 1,620 people living in Pendle Forest in 1650. The communicants' returns may be somewhat unreliable, but the non-communicating and largely Catholic population was not very numerous in this area. It seems reasonably safe to conclude that the population had more than doubled between 1530 and 1650.

The harshness of the climate and the unproductiveness of the land for arable crops meant that the predominant form of agriculture was pastoral, taking the form largely of stock-raising with some dairying. In 1608, four years before the first witch trial, the forest tenants of the Honour of Clitheroe pointed out that there were "great and mountainous commons extremely barren and unprofitable" and since the disafforestation of 1507, the copyholders' had been put to considerable expense:

> not only in the enclosure of the same copyholds and the continual manuring and tilling thereof, being before that time in respect both of the nature of the country and the soil thereabouts extremely barren and unprofitable and as yet capable of no other corn but oats and that but only in dry years and not without the continual charge of every third year's new manuring, but also in the building of their houses and habitations thereon having no timber there nor within many miles thereof, and having from time to time ever since enjoyed the same and therefore paid a rent and fine at the first as much or more and now very near the value thereof, have nearly disposed, employed and placed all the fruit and increase of their ancestors and their own labours and industries and the estates and maintenance of themselves, their families and posterities upon the same copyholds. . . .

The copyholders, needless to say, were exaggerating, for the petition was designed to persuade the Duchy that they were too poor to be able to pay a large sum of money for the confirmation of their copyholds. The picture was certainly not as bleak as they painted it; for example, probate inventories record crops other than oats growing in the Pendle area, such as barley and wheat.

In the early years after the disafforestation of 1507, when land was plentiful, some copyholders chose to treat their sons equally and practise partible inheritance. In 1532 the Duchy noted with alarm the subdivision of holdings, fearful that the small farms created would be incapable of supporting a tenantry sufficiently prosperous to pay their rents. A decree was therefore issued that no tenant in Pendle, Trawden or Rossendale forest was to sell, lease or surrender part of their lands unless the new tenants' lands were worth £1 6s. 8d. above all charges, on penalty of seizure of the holding by the steward. No examples of seizure have been found and, since there were some extremely small holdings, perhaps the decree was ignored. It may have influenced the copyholders to move away from partible inheritance, for the wills available for the late sixteenth and early seventeenth centuries reveal the universal practice of primogeniture, whereby the eldest son acquired the holding and the land was only split if there were daughters but no sons. This was quite logical in an area where land was not particularly productive and where pressure on resources was becoming apparent. Moreover, the heir did not get everything his own way, for if his mother were still alive he was obliged by custom (and it was often stated in the father's will) that she should have a quarter of the holding as her dower; sometimes even more than this was left to the widow. She was also entitled to a third of the personal estate or moveable goods. If the heir had younger brothers and sisters too, he was often obliged to provide them with cash portions when they came of age. All of these burdens might force an heir to sell or mortgage part of the holding, and so the years immediately following his father's death could be extremely difficult for the eldest son.

It is therefore not surprising that all types of household chose to try to earn a living by means other than simply agriculture in order to make ends meet. The inventories reveal a wide range of other activities, including coal-mining, quarrying of slate and limestone, tanning and brewing. It is clothmaking, however, that was particularly widespread, notably production of a coarse woollen cloth called kersey. Some 70 per cent of "supra" inventories (i.e., where the personal estate was valued at £40 or more) listed clothmaking tools. Over half of these Pendle households possessed cards or combs (52 per cent) and spinning wheels (56 per cent), and nearly two-fifths (38 per cent) owned looms.

These inventories reflect the middling wealth levels of society; the very poor did not make wills and hence left no inventory, and few "infra" inventories (less than £40 and proved locally) have survived, but those that are extant reveal a similar picture. We know from the witchcraft evidence that the very poorest and youngest in society might be involved in textile production. For example, Anne Whittle alias Old Chattox was hired by the wife of James Robinson to card wool about six years before the trial of 1612, despite being in her seventies, almost blind and apparently a witch of eight years experience! She carded on a Friday, Saturday and the following Monday, but then apparently soured the ale after drinking from it—what did she do with it/in it? Another example comes from the 1634 evidence. The star witness, Edmund Robinson junior, aged ten or eleven, said that his mother had brought him up to spin wool and fetch home the cattle.

There are, however, no local examples of putting out, the system of production whereby a cloth merchant or capitalist clothier gave out the wool to be made up into cloth in the workers' own homes, paid piece rates and then sold the cloth and took the profit for himself. On the contrary, inventories and lawsuits reveal a picture of independent, small-scale producers, often buying their wool from merchants (or "broggers" as they were called) and selling the finished material themselves.

Is it possible to tie in particular economic crises with the Pendle witch trials of 1612 and 1634? . . . [One] source of crisis was the Duchy's decision to call into question the security of the copyholders' estates. Duchy lawyers found loopholes in the original grants of 1507 and in 1607 started proceedings against the tenants of the Blackburnshire forests for allegedly unlawful entry. This legal chicanery was really designed to produce a large cash sum from the tenants in return for confirmation of their titles. James I, always short of money, was exploiting every expedient he could. A settlement was reached whereby the tenants agreed to pay twelve years' rent in three instalments in 1609. The total amount paid by the Pendle tenants was £1438 2s. 6d., and, large as this payment was, it should be noted that subtenants were often paying far larger sums to the copyholders. Thus the Duchy's demand for twelve years' rent in a single year may not have caused a severe problem and certainly seems to have led to few copyholders being forced to sell or mortgage part of their holding. Nevertheless, the Pendle composition, paid by the end of 1609, may well have contributed somewhat to the social tension which produced the accusations of witchcraft in March 1612. Some of those brought to trial, such as Old Demdike and her grand-daughter Alizon Device, seemed to have lived partly by begging and the accusation of acts of witchcraft sometimes centred on a curse following refusal of charity by a wealthier neighbour, who presumably had less to spare after the composition payment.

The witchcraft accusations in 1612 and 1634 do not tie in neatly with other economic indicators such as periods of crisis mortality, high bread prices or data for sales and mortgages of land. The years 1612 and 1633–34 were not years of crisis mortality in this area. The worst year for this during the period 1600–1640 was 1623, which seems to have been largely famine-induced, and yet witches do not appear to have been blamed for this natural disaster. Crop pieces were certainly far higher than usual in 1612–13, but were not out of the ordinary in 1633–34, so the pattern here is inconsistent. Transfers of land for money payment in Pendle Forest are more difficult to correlate since it was not necessary to register a land transaction which had been made out of court until up to the third halmote (manorial court) following, which might be eighteen months away. Certainly there were more transactions in 1612–14 (nineteen) than in the period 1609–11 (six), but the three-year period 1615–17 produced still more transactions (twenty) rather than a return to "normal." . . .

Clearly, as the population grew, land increasingly became in short supply and therefore more valuable. The rental of 1650, which lists subtenants, records a total of 155 Duchy copyholders and 33 tenants who held land only from copyholders (18 per cent of the total). This is far from a total record of all the subtenants in the Pendle area since only subtenancies for longer than a year and a day had to be registered before the halmote, at which an entry fine was also payable to the Duchy; leases for shorter periods might be agreed without surrender and fine at the halmote. It is undoubtedly true that some of the prominent witches lived as subtenants. For example, Anne Redfern, Old Chattox's daughter, was a tenant of the Nutters of Greenhead in New Laund; one day, about eighteen or nineteen years before the trial of 1612, Robert Nutter junior made unwelcome advances towards her, and, on being rejected, rode off in a rage, saying, "if ever the ground came to him, she should never dwell upon his land." In revenge, Old Chattox allegedly procured Robert's death a few months later with the help of her spirit, rather ironically called Fancy.

There was a sub-society of the landless or virtually landless that had to rely on charity, and many of the leading witches seem to have fallen into this category. An Act of 1589 prohibited the use of a cottage for habitation if it had fewer than four acres attached to it, or taking in more than one family in a cottage as inmates. Landlords could command huge rents for these tiny holdings and were consequently prepared to ignore the Act. Fines were commonly brought by the halmote juries in the fifteen-nineties and sixteen-twenties. In October 1621, for example, thirty-one were presented for this offence; in addition, four were accused of receiving strangers or vagrants, and one of taking a pregnant woman into his house.

Subtenants seem to have been finding it increasingly difficult to pay their rents, particularly in the period 1622–24. From the mid-1610s, the juries began to present individuals for "detinue" of buildings and land; prior to 1615 this was extremely rare, though private suits for detinue were a common feature of court business. Usually, these fines were presented at the Easter rather than the Michaelmas halmote; 78 per cent of the eighty-eight Pendle cases occurred at the Easter court. Rents were usually paid twice a year at Michaelmas and Easter, and subtenants would have found it harder to pay their Easter dues when prices were generally higher and wage labour less available than in the period during and immediately following the harvest. In this connexion, it is perhaps significant that both major Pendle witch outbreaks occurred in the spring, in March 1612 and February 1634, well after the harvest and when people had more time on their hands to allow petty arguments, resentment and jealousies to get out of hand. Perhaps the Devil does find work for idle hands! Macfarlane found from Essex assize records that the greatest number of bewitchings took place from February to June, and the least from August to October, but he noted that the differences were not significant and thus it was not simply a question of hunger which led to witchcraft accusations.

It would be wrong to concentrate exclusively on economic factors in seeking to explain the incidence of witchcraft accusations. Clearly, the social and religious attitudes, both of the political and ecclesiastical leaders in the locality, as well as the beliefs of the mass of the population, must be explored. . . .

. . . [L]ocal people believed strongly in the existence of witches in the Pendle area and in their power to do evil. Although he finally admitted to fabricating the details of the witchcraft accusations in 1634, Edmund Robinson junior did say that he made up the stories against those accused "because he heard the neighbours repute them for witches." As a further example, the son-in-law of Old Demdike, John Device, was so afraid of the spells of the other leading witch, Old Chattox, that he agreed to pay her a measure of meal each year in return for an undertaking that she would not harm him or his goods. It seems that he had insufficient confidence in the magical powers of his mother-in-law to protect him! On his death-bed, he attributed his condition to the non-payment of the meal. There was bad blood between the two families which seems to have originated about eleven years before the trial when the Device house was burgled and goods worth £1 stolen, a crime which they attributed to Old Chattox's family. The rivalry between these two families was important; Potts described Old Chattox as "always opposite to Old Demdike, for whom the one favoured, the other hated deadly, and how they envy and accuse one another in their examinations may appear." Conflict was only natural since the two families were in a very real sense competing for a limited market, as healers, beggars, and probably also as witches, and hence reputation was everything.

There is strong evidence that some of those accused of witchcraft were thought to have the ability to heal the sick. Alizon Device said that although she did not have the power to cure the pedlar John Law, her grandmother, Old Demdike, could have done so if she had lived. Some of the local inhabitants seem to have been prepared to enlist the services of the witches to cure their sick animals: John Nutter of the Bull Hole apparently asked Old Demdike to cure a sick cow, but it died. Some of those who were indicted may have been practitioners of herbal or folk remedies for curing human and animal ills; inevitably sometimes things went wrong, and they got the blame.

It seems likely that some of those accused of witchcraft actively fostered their reputations as witches since it enabled them to make a living by begging and extortion. They exploited and preyed on popular fears of witches and on the omnipresence of sudden and inexplicable illnesses and deaths of both man and beast. No doubt many people, such as John Device with his annual tribute of meal to Old Chattox, paid up a nominal amount rather than risk offending Old Demdike, Old Chattox or their broods. As Potts put it in his description of Old Demdike: "no man escaped her, or her Furies, that ever gave them any occasion of offence, or denied them anything they stood in need of." Nature had not been kind to many of those who were accused—some were old, virtually blind widows such as Old Demdike and Old Chattox, whilst others such as Old Demdike's daughter Elizabeth Device suffered from physical deformity. As Potts says: "This odious witch was branded with a preposterous mark in nature, even from her birth, which was her left eye standing lower than the other, the one looking down, the other looking up." Such people must have felt social outcasts. What better way to achieve social standing, or at least make themselves feared if not respected, and also repay folk for unkindness, than to cultivate a reputation for witchcraft? They exploited popular fears and superstitions about witchcraft and perhaps used, or appeared to use, the paraphernalia of witchcraft, including clay or wax models. They may even have convinced themselves and each other of their supernatural powers.

The trial of 1634 provides clear evidence that accusations of witchcraft might also spring from financial motives. The Bishop of Chester had been told that Edmund Robinson senior had demanded £2 from Frances and John Dicconson in return for dropping the accusations against Frances, but she had advised her husband against paying anything. Edmund Robinson senior later denied that this had happened when questioned in London. As John Webster wrote in 1677, however, Robinson had other charges to face:

> the boy, his father and some others did make a practice to go from church to church that the boy might reveal and discover witches, pretending that there was a great number at the pretended meeting whose faces he could know, and by that means they got a good living, that in a short space the father bought a cow or two, when he had none before.

And what of the Thomas/Macfarlane model, which focuses on the problems created by refusal of charity? Many allegations of injury or death were made in 1612, but in twelve cases the actual cause of the dispute is clearly stated. Only three originated from problems relating to refusal of charity. It seems that the initial incident which triggered off the whole chain of witchcraft accusations in 1612 may be attributed to a refused request for charity, i.e. the pedlar John Law's apparent unwillingness to hand over some pins to Alizon Device when her offer to pay for them was probably not genuine. Secondly, the case of Henry Mitton (previously cited) fits into this pattern, since he was allegedly bewitched to death by an unholy alliance of Old Demdike, Elizabeth Device, and Alice Nutter, for refusing to give Old Demdike a penny. Thirdly, James Device confessed to getting his spirit, Dandy, to kill John Duckworth of the Laund because Duckworth had promised him a shirt but subsequently refused to hand it over.

The other nine cases cover a wide range of allegations, none of which apparently concerns refusal of charity. Three spring from Old Chattox's confessions. The death of Robert Nutter at Old Chattox's hands for making unwanted advances to her daughter, Anne Redfern, and for threatening them with eviction, has already been quoted. Secondly, Old Chattox also claimed to have made her spirit, Fancy, kill a cow belonging to Anthony Nutter because he favoured Old Demdike rather than her. Thirdly, she maintained that she had killed a cow belonging to John Moore, a gentleman of Higham, because Moore's wife had nagged her, even after she had cured his bewitched drink.

Alizon, Device referred to four other cases in her confessions. The death-bed claim by her father, John Device, that he was dying because of the non-payment of the meal to Old Chattox has already been quoted. In addition Old Chattox had apparently bewitched to death Anne Nutter for laughing at her, and Hugh Moore for accusing her of bewitching his castle. Lastly, Alizon Device claimed that Old Chattox had bewitched to death a cow belonging to John Nutter because John's son disliked what she was doing with a can of milk which had been begged from his family.

The two remaining cases refer to confessions made by Alizon's mother Elizabeth and by her brother James. Elizabeth Device claimed that her spirit, Ball, had made her make a clay model of John Robinson alias Swyer of Barley and kill him by drying it so that it crumbled away, all because he had insulted her by saying that she had a bastard child. Her son James confessed that Mistress Anne Towneley of Carr Hall, had been killed by the same method because she had accused James and his mother of stealing her turves and because she had hit James.

Many other witch trials from this period do not provide significant evidence of problems arising because of refusal of charity. Several motives were alleged for witchcraft at Royston (1606), Milton (Bedfordshire, 1612), Northamptonshire (1612) and Belvoir (1619), amongst them being revenge for verbal insults suffered, injuries incurred and unfair dismissal from employment. Failure to provide appropriate charity was mentioned only once out of nine occasions when a motive was clearly stated. J. A. Sharpe's work on seventeenth-century witchcraft in Yorkshire confirms the view that problems relating to refusal of charity did not play a central role in prompting allegations of witchcraft. It therefore does not seem justified, at least for the early seventeenth century, for Thomas to assert that

> the overwhelming majority of fully documented witch cases fall into this simple pattern. The witch is sent away empty-handed, perhaps mumbling a malediction; and in due course something goes wrong with the household, for which she is immediately held responsible.

In conclusion, it appears that the early seventeenth century was a period of considerable economic difficulties for many who lived in the Pendle area, particularly, of course, the poor. There may have been increasing tension between rich and poor, and it is possibly true that the old medieval communal ethic of neighbourliness and charity was breaking down before the forces of capitalism and the agencies of the state, especially the apparatus set up under the Poor Law. It is certainly the case that the Lancashire witch trials do not tie in very closely with periods of obvious economic distress. Strong support for the Thomas/Macfarlane model is difficult to sustain because refusal of charity did not play a part in three-quarters of the detailed allegations of witchcraft in 1612, nor in the main events of the 1634 trial, nor in most of the motives alleged for acts of witchcraft in other contemporary trials. The world of those who were accused of witchcraft seems to have revolved largely around the difficulties of making ends meet. Some seem to have tried to resolve their financial problems by cultivating a reputation for witchcraft, which enabled them to make a living by acting as healers, or by extorting money, food and drink or goods from their neighbours. In these circumstances no one had good reason to feel guilty about refusing charity, only fear at what might befall him at the witch's hands. Many of the Lancashire witches were no doubt completely innocent of the charges brought against them, but to some, witchcraft was a business, a livelihood with enormous risks, for failure meant not bankruptcy, nor the debtors' prison, but the gallows.

Gábor Klaniczay

Witch-hunting in Hungary: Social or Cultural Tensions?

The theme of witchcraft has attracted a great number of scholars in recent decades. I shall single out just one of the many reasons for this: witchcraft is a topic that cuts across the established disciplinary boundaries and provides us with the possibility of fruitful exchanges between various fields of research, including social, cultural and legal history; the folklore

Gábor Klaniczay, "Witch-hunting in Hungary: Social or Cultural Tensions?" *Acta Ethnographica Hungarica* 37 (1991–92). Copyright © 1992. Reprinted with permission.

of magical beliefs, practices and mythologies; and anthropological enquiries into social, moral and cultural meanings, functions or dysfunctions. A combination of these different approaches, together with close scrutiny of archival documents, has led to a number of studies and monographs that in turn link this topic with various other concerns of recent historiography, such as community studies, family history, gender approaches, history of the "reform" of early modern popular culture, historical anthropology, history of *mentalité*. On the other hand, however, the complexity of the problem and the richness of its various forms still defy universal explanations, blur theoretical insights and leave us to hypothesize about why it was that, at given historical moments, large-scale witch persecutions occurred in certain places or regions.

The wide array of theoretical explanatory tools and comparative sets of data stands in puzzling contrast to the ease with which each general proposition can be contradicted. About a decade ago, the anthropologist Rodney Needham characterized these anomalies of current witchcraft research in the following way: "witches are neighbours, or else they are distant; they are relatives, or else they cannot be relatives; they are marginal, or else they are enemies within; they are lowly misfits, or else they are secure and prosperous just because of their witchcraft; they are so categorized that not everybody can be a witch, or else they are such that anyone can be a witch." The more we seem to know about the historical and anthropological details of witchcraft, the more numerous become the intriguing riddles and paradoxes we have to face when researching it. While the individual cases, the local and regional panics seem to obey recurrent patterns, the underlying tensions, the passion-filled testimonies and weird phantasies of the persons involved continue to provide lessons about historical, social, cultural, regional differences.

In the following presentation of the sixteenth- to eighteenth-century witch-hunting period in Hungary, I will try to illustrate the unique nature of the Hungarian cases while taking into account the interpretive possibilities and weaknesses of [a] current set of explanations about the occurrence of witch persecutions that connects it to the social tensions . . . of the period.

Before doing so, however, I shall begin with a brief overall sketch. Apart from a few scattered medieval cases, witch-trials started to multiply in Hungary in the 1560s, and their number rose at a moderate pace throughout the seventeenth century (with two quantitative jumps, in the 1620s and in the 1690s). The real peak of the persecutions came very late in comparison to other countries, between 1710 and 1730 (with more than 200 accused and more than 60 death sentences per decade). Witch-hunting then proceeded fairly actively until stopped from above by the enlightened legislation of Maria Theresa between 1758 and 1766. My calculations are based upon the records of 1,642 persons charged with witchcraft in Hungary between 1520 and 1777, 1,482 of whom were women (89 per cent). The number of known death sentences was 449, and 23 persons died in prison or by lynching, while in 460 cases the accused suffered lesser punishments. Compared with the masses killed, for example, in the South German persecutions, these numbers seem fairly moderate for a country of 3–4 million inhabitants, even if we take into account that in 710 cases the outcome of the trial is unknown, and furthermore that the number of documented trials could be increased by hundreds of additional recorded cases unearthed by recent archival researches and estimations. Witchcraft accusations and trials recurred persistently in Hungarian towns and villages over a lengthy period, but they rarely (in fact only exceptionally) amounted to the type of panic, with mass accusations and group burnings, familiar to some other European countries. . . .

According to a major paradigm of historical and anthropological writing, witchcraft accusations explained individual or collective misfortune by pinpointing the "responsible" human agents within the immediate environment, and gave redress to the damaged parties by purging the community of the "witches" who violated the norms of coexistence. Accusations naturally tended to be embedded in a set of local conflicts; they occurred at "weak points" of social relations; they expressed "deep-felt animosities in acceptable guise"; they served as a social "strain-gauge." Consequently, historians could better understand the occurrence of witchcraft accusations by clarifying their social context. Revealing hidden tensions with apparently no other, more direct, outlets or resolutions, witchcraft conflicts even offer historians and anthropologists a promise of new insights into obscure but important problems within the affected communities.

This approach, which Alan Macfarlane called the "sociology of accusations," provides witchcraft research not only with a new set of explanations, but also with a wide range of previously ignored evidence to be examined, a large number of witnesses' depositions in witchcraft trials, voicing various motives for popular accusations and providing ample evidence of the conflicts that gave rise to witch-trials. On the basis of these sources, Macfarlane and Thomas suggested that the dissolution of traditional communal or neighbourly forms of solidarity in early modern villages, and the rise of a new type of individualistic ethic, could have been among the most typical conflicts leading to witchcraft accusations. This type of investigation has been successfully developed by witchcraft scholars of other regions, who have provided further illustration for this "neighbourhood conflict" thesis. Subsequent studies also support another observation of Macfarlane's—that witchcraft conflicts did not necessarily correlate with a socioeconomic crisis, but correlated rather with periods of transformation favouring certain social strata and disadvantaging others. . . .

At the same time, the simplistic versions of the sociological approach generated widespread criticism. The functionalistic trend that sees in witchcraft accusations a pure expression of "social causes" that lie elsewhere, or a regulating mechanism that serves to resolve those conflicts on the basis of commonly accepted norms—all this has been justifiably rejected. . . .

It does not follow naturally from all this criticism . . . that a sociological account of the history of witch-hunting is impossible or useless. Rather, the criticism provides encouragement to seek the complex patterns of the interwoven social, cultural and magical conflicts with fewer preconceptions and with an open attitude towards integrating an even wider sphere of explanatory factors. The most recent complex regional monograph about witch-hunting, that of Wolfgang Behringer dealing with south-eastern Germany, seems to proceed in this way. Without trying to resolve the debate in general (for each witchcraft panic has to be explained within its immediate context), Behringer advances a set of new observations concerning the correlation of natural calamities and subsistence crises with witch-hunting waves, at the same time showing how contemporary demonological reasoning tried to link natural and social disasters with the problem of witchcraft.

My aim is similar to Behringer's: without setting out to find a sociological key to Hungarian witchcraft prosecutions, I will investigate (within the limited space of this chapter) certain cases that could illustrate their various social contexts. Two of my five examples concern urban witch-trials, one from the onset of the witch-hunts (the Kolozsvár [Cluj] trials of the late sixteenth century), and one from its eighteenth-century peak (the 1728 panic in Szeged). The aristocratic witchcraft accusations in seventeenth-century Transylvania and the shepherd trials of the western counties in the second half of the seventeenth century present two different social extremes. Finally, the witchcraft cases in the borough of Hódmezövásárhely and its neighbouring villages exemplify the mainstream of Hungarian witchcraft conflicts.

The witch-trials of the Transylvanian city of Kolozsvár are of special importance in Hungarian history. They are the first series of trials for which we possess documentation. According to the documents, between 1565 and 1593, nineteen witches were prosecuted here; thirteen were condemned to death by burning (six of these in 1584); the outcome of the rest of the trials is unknown. The fact that Kolozsvár became the first centre of this new type of conflict is instructive in several respects. This city of about 8,000 inhabitants mainly German—originally, but in this period becoming increasingly dominated by a Hungarian majority—was the only Transylvanian city to witness spectacular economic growth and prosperity in the sixteenth century, while the other "Saxon" cities (like Kronstadt [Brasov] or Hermannstadt [Sibiu]) were affected by the general economic decline of Hungarian cities at that time. This rapid expansion was somewhat disturbed by the troubled political climate of Transylvania in the 1580s—which, incidentally, coincided with the 1584 local peak of witchcraft accusations. This correlation, however, cannot be extrapolated too far, since other Hungarian cities with similar or even more alarming economic or political troubles did not experience large-scale witchcraft accusations at that period.

If we try to relate the testimony rendered at these trials to certain more concrete tensions, we find that they do indeed show traces of typical neighbourhood conflicts (stealing the fertility of the neighbour's land or animals), of strained economic relations (accusations against former housekeepers or lodgers, debates about work cooperation). Others can be related to factional struggles: one of the mighty town jurors, Mihály Igyártó, seems to have directed a campaign against his enemies by accusing them of witchcraft—he initiated two witch-trials against women who bore witness against him in another kind of trial. Quantitatively, however, the overwhelming motivation of the accusations seems to lie elsewhere: eight of the nineteen "witches" were healers or midwives, who apparently had no economic or social conflicts with their accusers; three more cases had their origins in jealousy connected to presumed love-magic; in one case a husband accused his wife. In 1565, in the first three trials of the series, legal proceedings seem to have been sparked by mutual accusations of three wise women, each of whom attributed people's illnesses to charms inflicted by the other (with the help of the fairy-like *pulchrae mulieres*). Another of the executed witches (1584) presents traits related to the Hungarian version of shamanism[:] falling into trance, making a soul-journey in the shape of a fly and boasting of other special powers. Still another fell under suspicion because she possessed a "devilish book" which enabled her to detect treasure.

The overall impression is of a generalized fear of magical aggression stirring up traditional folk-beliefs, and the reasons for this scare could be religious and cultural rather than social and economic. Kolozsvár was the centre of Transylvanian religious debates in the period. Lutheranism made its appearance here in the 1540s, represented by Reverend Gáspár Heltai, who founded a famous printing press in 1550 and organized a team that achieved the first complete translation of the Bible into Hungarian. While German inhabitants remained Lutheran, Hungarians tended to become radicalized and to accept the "Helvetian confession," i.e. Calvinism (like Heltai himself), or even to become Unitarians (like Ferenc Dávid, elected twice as the bishop of Protestant Hungarians, then executed in 1579 because of his increasingly radical views). The Jesuits also made their appearance in the 1570s.

Some of the witchcraft conflicts seem indeed to be related to these religious divisions. The Calvinist juror, Igyártó (a militant promulgator of local statutes against adultery and fornication in the same period and one of the main witch-accusers), was in conflict with the presumed witches precisely on account of their participation in Carnival disorders. Another of the notorious accusers, Peter Grúz (who brought the charges of witchcraft against the two first wise women to be burnt), later became the militant leader of the Catholic party, which proposed to Prince István Báthory in 1575 that he should invite Jesuits into the city of Kolozsvár. Each religious party advocated an increasing hostility towards manifestations of early-modern popular culture, the effect of which is shown here by the fact that the accused mostly came under suspicion for having performed traditional fertility rites or healing magic. The criminalization of magical healing (the assertion that it could work only if the "same devil" that is, the healer himself had previously carried out the bewitching) was pronounced in Kolozsvár in 1584—the first occurrence in Hungary.

The aristocratic witchcraft accusations of the seventeenth century present a very different picture, in regard both to underlying social patterns and to their cultural background. As for the former, they conform nicely to the general pattern of conflict-motivated fear of magical vengeance, where the victorious party supposed himself (or his wife) to be bewitched, and accused relatives of defeated rivals of practising witchcraft, thus eliminating them in this additional way. Transylvanian Prince Gábor Bethlen (1613–29), after acceding to power following the murder of Gábor Báthory in 1612, initiated a spectacular witch-trial against the deceased's sister, Anna Báthory, and two high-born widows (Kata Török and Kata Iffju), also intimately related to the deceased. They were banished and their considerable estates confiscated. The accusations ranged from fornication (with Bethlen's ill-fated predecessor, Gábor Báthory) to love-magic and using witchcraft to harm the health of Zsuzsanna Károlyi, the wife of Prince Gábor Bethlen. The long drawnout proceedings, revived several times against Anna Báthory (1614, 1618, 1621) till her final exile and the confiscation of all her properties, were also supported by new legislation concerning the prosecution of witchcraft, enacted by the Transylvanian Diet in 1614.

Similarly, Prince Mihály Apafy (1661–90) staged a major witch-trial between 1679 and 1686, involving twenty-five accused (thirteen noble-women among them), principally Zsuzsanna Vitéz, wife of his defeated rival Pál Béldy. Mrs. Bédly, who was arrested after her political agitation and armed uprising in favour of her exiled husband, was alleged to have bewitched Apafy's wife, Anna Bornemisza, causing not only her recurrent illnesses but also the death of several of her new-born children. Although the charges could not be proved against her, Mrs Béldy died in prison, and investigations of the affair remained a feature of Transylvania's troubled political life for about eight years.

It is no accident that witchcraft accusations permeated the conflictual and intrigue-ridden court life of seventeenth-century Transylvanian princes. The recurrent decline and re-emergence of this charming country—prey to Turkish political machinations, uncertain in its relations with Poland, hesitating whether to side eventually with the Habsburgs against the Turks, menaced occasionally by Romanian *voivods*, and torn also by the intrigues of mighty and ambitious aristocrats aspiring to princely dignity—all this served to enhance the contemporary vision that the fate of this land was being influenced by obscure magical forces. It was not by chance that Transylvania was labelled by contemporaries as

Tündérország (fairy-land) or *Tündérkert* (fairy-garden). Besides, Transylvanians were not the only people to believe in magic operating in the higher spheres of politics; the bewitched fleet of James VI of Scotland is an outstanding example.

From the cultural point of view, two aspects merit attention. One is the stereotype of the aristocratic witch, exclusively female, who did not practise witchcraft herself, but hired professionals (popular wise women, magical specialists) to provide her with effective magical tools to assist her if she wanted to cast spells personally or to harm her enemies in other ways. It is fascinating to see witchcraft notions rearticulated to rely upon this kind of division of labour, appropriate to the new aristocratic lifestyles. The actual bewitchment (the dirty work) was done by a team of popular magicians (magic and superstition having become the label of popular culture); they were used as specialized agents within a whole team of servants hired for evil-doing (spies, killers). Although these servants were declared guilty and punished, the responsibility was shared by the cruel lady-witch who embodied the dimension of moral evil. She plotted the whole enterprise and it allegedly served her pleasures, her perversities, or her personal vengeance.

This witch-stereotype tended to be a crystallization point for moral evil in all its dimensions: Anna Báthory, denounced by Prince Bethlen as "killer devil whore," was accused of incest with her brother and also of killing her own son. Consider also the case of her more famous cousin, Elisabeth Báthory, whose 1609–11 trial (initiated by her two sons-in-law and resulting in life imprisonment and the loss of her estates) depicted her as sort of female Gilles de Rais and precursor of the marquis de Sade, producing testimony that she had tortured and killed several hundred of her maids. According to the depositions of her servants (not surprisingly) she also experimented with witchcraft. In the year 1637, torturing, beating and killing servants, especially maids, was also the central feature of the witch-trial of another aristocratic lady, Anna Rozina Listius, from north-west Hungary.

Finally, and this is the second culturally relevant aspect, the fashions of learned magic in the late sixteenth and early seventeenth centuries also had their impact upon these aristocratic witchcraft cases. Alongside tales of popular magic, we hear about learned astrology, and also about special amulets. The interrelated nature of the emergent hermetic, occult and magical fashions and witch-hunting attitudes in the sixteenth century has been brilliantly analysed for England by Keith Thomas. This same relation still remains to be examined for the Transylvanian and Polish (Cracovian) courts of the Báthory, the Prague court of Emperor Rudolph II, and the smaller German princely courts, which hosted and provided meeting centres for a large number of famous magical experts who came from all over Europe.

My third example takes us to the very different world of shepherds in the western counties under Habsburg rule. They contributed—under the military—economic protection of the mighty and enterprising lords of the region, the counts Zrínyi, Esterházy or Batthyány—to a traditional cattle trade with Venice and with the southern German cities, which, how-ever, tended to decline in the second half of the century. This, together with various other natural calamities of the seventeenth century, and with the burden of the renewed warfare against the Turks, must have produced serious strains in this pastoral society after 1650. A series of mutual accu-sations among shepherds between 1651 and 1687, which led to a dozen witch-trials in Körmend (centre of the Batthyányi estate), Lakompak (centre of the Esterházy estate) and the nearby city of Szombathely, could be viewed as the expression of these tensions. The general complaints were that the accused gave a magical unguent to their own animals "in the name of the devil," diverted plagues from their own animals onto the flocks of neighbouring shepherds, attacked the animals of rivals by setting wolves upon them, or even assumed the shape of a wolf themselves and acted as werewolves. As for the social side, the trials give an interesting picture of the competitive, individualistic shepherd society of the age, and point towards the above-mentioned theories that explain early modern witchcraft accusations by emerging individualistic tendencies.

An examination of the beliefs disclosed in the depositions, however, warns us to be wary of this explanation. Most of the accusations involved belong to the general Hungarian mythology concerning the "cunning shepherds" (*tudós pásztor*), whose positive representatives had been con-sidered types of shamanistic sorcerers right up to modern times. On the other hand, the diabolical elements in these trials (devilish associations, covens of male sorcerers, having their own judges, captains, flags, prac-tising strange rituals, having a familiar devil that can be put in a box) seem very alien to Hungarian witchcraft beliefs. The various werewolf concepts first emerged more than a century earlier (1529, 1531) in two cowherd trials in the city of Sopron, which was inhabited principally by a Germany population. Such beliefs surfaced only sporadically in other Hungarian regions, and then only in the middle of the eighteenth century. They were altogether alien to Hungarian folklore. This might warn us to treat with some caution the foregoing economic and functional explanation and to look for other causes, including foreign influences.

In fact, this campaign was directed not just against shepherds, but also against some other male vagrant sorcerers. All this might be related to the campaign against presumed associations of male sorcerers in neighbouring Styria, such as the *Grindiger Hansel* trial in 1659 or the singular witch scare in the region of Salzburg between 1675 and 1690, known as *Zauberer Jackl* trials, whose several hundred victims were mostly beggars and marginals, and mostly males. These campaigns resulted in a rather unusual stereotype of the target of witch-hunting in these regions, with more male victims than female—and the image of the devilish male sorcerer also recurred persistently in the western border regions of Hungary until the middle of the eighteenth century.

My fourth example is the most significant episode in the history of Hungarian witch-hunting—the scare of the 1720s–1730s in the Szeged region. This involved forty-one accused (and more than 100 denounced persons) between 1728 and 1744—twenty-one of whom were brought to trial in 1728, fourteen were executed and two died in prison[;] the brutality of the Szeged panic seems unparalleled in Hungarian history. The only comparable example is the mass trial of eleven witches in the borough of Somorja (Samorin), near the city of Pozsony (Bratislava), in 1691, which resulted in the mass burning of seven of the accused, the beheading of one and the banishment of three others. Most other panic-type persecutions involved "only" between five and ten persons; the urban scares so common in Germany and other parts of Europe were almost non-existent in Hungary.

Detailed investigations carried out to find an explanation for the Szeged scare have focused upon several underlying causes: natural calamities in the preceding decades (plague in 1709–13, flood in 1712, serious drought in 1728—hence the principal accusation against the witches that they sold the rain to the Turks); a precipitate growth of the city population from 3,000 around 1700, to 7,000 around 1719, and 14,000 around 1728—a result of the arrival of Hungarian, German and Serbian settlers; factional struggles between an "autonomy" party (mainly Hungarians) and a German party. The German faction's candidate for judgeship, György Podhradszky, was one of the initiators of the persecutions, whose most noteworthy victim was Dániel Rósa, a former Hungarian judge of the city (Rósa, a slightly discredited person because of previous local conflicts, was not a member of the local "autonomy" party, but was a useful figure to bring it into disrepute).

The pattern of brutal torture, the enforced adoption of demonological stereotypes, and even the rapid extension of witchcraft accusations from lower social circles (midwives and beggars) to socially more elevated targets (like former judges and other municipal functionaries) conforms very much to western European witch scares. It seems that a kind of witch panic similar to those experienced in Germany a century earlier was starting to gather force in the disrupted and rapidly repopulated southern territories of Hungary. Connections with the mass arrival of settlers and with typical crises of precipitate growth of new urban communities could also make it legitimate to compare these persecutions to the New England cases analyzed by John Demos. The general intellectual and institutional context, however, was different by the 1720s. The notoriety of these later persecutions and the tempering reaction of the Viennese imperial court constrained the Szeged judges to return to "regular," more moderate Hungarian standards of witchcraft prosecution.

The catalyzing effect of the Szeged panic can be observed throughout the whole region (simultaneously affected by similar population growth, similar ethic and social tensions between indigenous and settler populations, and similar natural calamities). Nevertheless, nowhere else did witchcraft accusations give rise to similar panics; they remained rather at the level of heightened manifestations of personal conflicts. Thus— coming to my fifth example—the neighbouring Calvinist borough of Hódmezövásárhely (with 5,000 inhabitants in the 1730s), experienced twenty-four witch-trials between 1729 and 1759, of which six resulted in death sentences. Here the accusations also started with popular healers, easy targets for incrimination. Among the accused there was a considerable percentage of beggars and marginals. One was characterized by her son as follows: "my mother has spent all she had for drinking. As far as I am concerned she could well be burnt." There were also many widows, elderly peasant wives, and relatives of convicted witches (daughter, husband). Altogether the whole picture fits the stereotypes. Neighbourly conflicts, cohabitation and unsuccessful healing have their due share among the accusations. It is noteworthy that some members of the local elite, like the schoolmaster, the chanter, a young *studiosus* and the juror and usurer, István Ceglédi, act also as accusers, adding weight to the mass of depositions from the lower social strata.

Another category of accusers deserves a special mention—that of German soldiers residing in the borough and the neighbouring villages, and being compulsorily maintained by the population. Here, as in many other places, they acted as active witch-finders or accusers, using this imported skill to counteract the hostility of the local population. The most spectacular bewitchment stories are to be read in the accusations of a soldier-servant, who made complaints in 1739 against ten inhabitants of the nearby village of Mindszent, four of whom were eventually brought to court.

The significance of the Hódmezövásárhely trials—besides offering a rich set of data on the local quarrels underlying witchcraft accusations, and a series of popular, highly exotic witches' Sabbath descriptions, told this time not by tortured witches but reworked in the nightmares of the accusers—lies in the remarkable absence of panic reactions to various calamities. There are no traces in the witchcraft documentation of the two contemporary uprisings of the region, the Péró peasant revolt in 1735 and the Töro-Peto *kuruc* revolt in 1752–3; no traces of religious divisions: Hódmezövásárhely was a slightly insecure Calvinist refuge within its Catholic surroundings; and, more importantly, no trace of the terrible cattle plague of 1736 or the plague of 1738 in which half the population (about 2,500) died. Instead of contributing to tensions that would be relieved by witch hunting, these calamities repeatedly brought the rather sporadic witchcraft accusations to a halt. Those who suffered from these calamities apparently found relief in other types of strain-gauges or conflict-solving mechanisms.

To sum up the results of this schematic enquiry into the social causes of witchcraft prosecutions, one could say that this type of enquiry can be of great help in locating witchcraft accusations in their local historical context, but one should not expect from this a definitive explanation of causes. The sociological approach allows us to formulate more specific questions about the occurrence and the significance of various types of witchcraft conflicts, but it does not provide easy answers.

On the other hand, a sociological examination of accusation narratives could provide various other means of enriching our views about how society was reflected in these magical conflicts. Which were the typical social situations that would be likely to support witchcraft accusations (economic or personal jealousy, refusal of alms or neighbourly favours, quarrels about cooperation or payment, rivalry among healers, midwives)? Where could these accusations or threats be communicated (taverns, spinning houses, markets, family gatherings around sick members)? What sites of social life did the witches allegedly select to break into and to rejoice in during their nightly Sabbath gatherings? There is a link between these stereotypes and actual social conditions, but it can only be unveiled if one takes into account the difference between magic and reality.

[The article ends with a discussion of cultural tensions; this section has been omitted.]

Robin Briggs

Witches and Neighbors: The Social and Cultural Context of European Witchcraft

The family has provided the basic structure of all developed human societies. Affective, economic, political and social life have all revolved around it throughout known history. There have been important senses in which the individual could only exist through the family, and this was certainly more true in the early modern period than it is today. With rare exceptions, Europeans lived and died within the milieu of their birth; mobility was strictly limited both geographically and socially. The elites were defined by inherited wealth and position, even at the level of village oligarchies. . . . [T]he affective and social aspects of the family will detain us first, together with their multiple reflections where reality and fantasy meet in witchcraft. The term is itself ambiguous, of course; it applies both to the wider kinship networks and to the household unit. Through most of Europe in the early modern period the latter was typically "nuclear," in the sense that it comprised a married couple and their children, with perhaps a single servant. Large households including grandparents, adult children and grandchildren were relatively uncommon. This was at least partly because the late age of marriage and relatively low life expectancy precluded them in most cases. The most important variation was that found in large parts of Mediterranean Europe, where men typically married much younger girls; in consequence middle-aged widows frequently presided over households of unmarried children. The rich had their own distinctive household patterns, but these only impinged very occasionally on the plebian world where witchcraft beliefs flourished most vigorously.

Marriage was the crucial social transaction in many respects. It was the mechanism whereby families constantly renewed themselves and formed links with others, like cells splitting and recombining. As an exchange in which property was involved as well as persons, with the establishment of a new household, one would be hard pressed to exaggerate its structural significance at every level. No wonder that marriage was surrounded by an elaborate ritual making it out as a "rite of passage," whose repercussions extended far beyond the couple themselves. So many interests came into play that the celebrations carried a necessary subtext of tension and dissatisfaction. Uncomfortable presences at the feast-table might include resentful parents and siblings, rejected suitors with their kin and groups of mutually suspicious new in-laws; other neighbours might be muttering because they had not been invited at all. Eating, drinking and dancing could all too easily become the setting for insults or acts of violence that left a shadow across the future. Jean Grand Didier must have wished he had avoided the marriage feast of Colas Ferry at la Vacherie in about 1586, where he seems to have been in a singularly quarrelsome mood. He got into a knife fight with another guest, who died of his wounds some days later, so that Jean had to flee, then secure a pardon from the duke at a cost of 700 francs. He also quarrelled with the brothers Mengeon and Colas Moullot, nearly provoking another fight; at the end of the evening Jean insisted that Colas have a drink with him as a sign of reconciliation. After several refusals Colas agreed, but instantly felt a great pain in his body when he drank, crying out that he had been given his death-blow. He died after an illness lasting just three days, saying that Jean had given him his death and they should open him after he was dead to find the poison. Fourteen years later his brother testified that they had not done this because they lacked the means, but had always imputed his death to Jean's witchcraft.

The commoner form of animosity dating from the wedding festivities was resentment at not being invited at all, which might appear later as the alleged motive for bewitchment (a theme which passed into folklore in the familiar form of the excluded witch taking her revenge). Marguerite Menginat testified that just three months after her marriage six years earlier, Barbelline Chaperey had come to her house and said to her "that she might well eat and drink, making use of hens and other good food . . . but that her husband's first wife had hardly known any good health while she lived with him, and she would be in the same case, nor would she have children by him or others." Although they had not quarrelled, Marguerite's mother had told her Barbelline was angry because she was not invited to the wedding feast. Since that time the witness had been in poor health in both body and mind, so she suspected the accused of being the cause. Other complications arose in the frequent instances of remarriages, inevitable when so many unions were terminated by a premature death. The complex emotional and financial tangles often associated with such second or third marriages have also left their mark in the trial records. . . .

Witchcraft accusations . . . were very dangerous when they interacted with families. This was a process on multiple levels. Suspicions and charges originating from outside could generate enormous tension and even dissolve the normal bonds between family members. Differences and disputes which began within families not only left their members far more exposed, but often lay at the root of personal reputations. In other cases quarrels between families were expressed through allegations of witchcraft. Many of the elements of fantasy incorporated in witchcraft beliefs had their origin in the crucial early stages of development, so that patterns of infant- and child-care fed through into some of the more outlandish features of confessions. These are among the most obvious of the ways in which one cannot understand how the nexus of beliefs and practices worked without relating them to the familial context. One commonplace observation too often forgotten is that the closest bonds and the most bitter hostilities are linked, as opposite but inseparable polarities; if the ties of blood bind people together, it is often with a special intensity of mutual hatred. Among the most disconcerting features of close relationships is the way they frequently alternate between opposite poles, and encourage patterns of quarrels and reconciliations. Often they also seem to liberate individuals' ability to express violent feelings they would conceal or sublimate in more external situations. The endless dramas played out on this semi-public stage fed into witchcraft, both directly and through the inner psychic worlds they shaped.

Official doctrines of patriarchy made the husband and father the unquestioned head of the family. Although reality was never so simple, at the legal level wives and children had little chance of acting except with his consent, and under his name. This was particularly important when wives were suspected of witchcraft, rumours began to circulate and neighbours insulted them by calling them witch. Failure to respond to such provocations was routinely cited in court as evidence for the suspect's guilt when the trial finally began. In fact it was far from easy for those concerned to know how to react. The best outcome was a formal sentence from a local court awarding damages, but such proceedings could go badly wrong if the other party decided to fight; in such circumstances they could turn into a trial for witchcraft. Action of this kind was likely to be safest if undertaken early on, before suspicions had accumulated to the point where wide support could be mustered for such a counterattack. While there are plenty of judgments awarding small fines, it seems likely that more of these cases were settled by informal arbitration, carried out by local office-holders, clerics, or leading members of the community. That was a prudent low-level response, but many people simply ignored the insults or responded in kind. When answering their judges they resorted to three main strategies to explain their conduct. The first was to claim there had been no witnesses, the second to allege they were too poor to risk losing a case and having to pay themselves, the third to blame their husbands. The latter were said to be too soft or cowardly to help, with the implication that they had chosen to distance themselves from the whole affair. This was understandable, for these men were caught in the problem faced by families more widely; one set of rules enjoined support between kin, another the avoidance of suspected witches.

Neutral attitudes of this kind were evidently common, although they are bound to be over-represented in surviving records, since where husbands took an active part in defending their wives' reputations this is likely to have been quite effective, reducing the chance that these cases would come to court. Given the adhesive quality of suspicions, it was hardly possible to dispel them completely, so damage limitation was a more plausible hope. Husbands could confront potential accusers and ask them to declare their opinions; this might well shame or cow them into silence. Claudon Thonnere believed Mongeatte Johel was responsible for his illness, a suspicion his wife told her and her husband about when they met at the mill. The husband then came to see him, asking if he wished to declare that his wife was a witch; to which he replied that he did not, but if she was such as many suspected he blamed her for his illness." Mutual threats of legal action followed, but Claudon's recovery allowed the matter to be dropped. At other times more direct threats or violence might be employed, or alternatively excuses and pleading, even promises there would be no repetition. Ten years before Catherine Ancel was finally arrested, Demenge Alix had lost many animals, so he and several others from Benifosse resolved to seek out the *prévôt* to ask for her arrest. When her husband heard of this he went to see him, begging him not to proceed, while promising to talk to her and ensure that she gave no more cause of discontent. He touched his hands as he said this, and finally Demenge agreed to withdraw. We may note that in this case, as in a good many others, action was only taken when the husband was dead—and that some of the suspicions came from the wife of Catherine's stepson.

There were occasional allegations that kin had attempted bribery towards gaolers or hangmen, but few substantiated cases. An inherent danger in any kind of intercession was that of being tarred with the same brush as the suspect; there are some cases where married couples or larger groups of relatives were tried. This normally seems to have resulted from widespread pre-existing suspicions rather than the immediate circumstances of the trials, but on occasion confessing witches were put under pressure to incriminate their spouses or children, particularly on the theory that they might have inducted them to the Devil's service and taken them to the sabbat. If the bemused or broken victim complied, horrible and heartrending scenes might follow when they were confronted with those they had virtually condemned to death. Ysabel Seguin declared that her seventeen-year-old daughter Gauthine had been to the sabbat with her, to which the girl replied "that she must be out of her mind and understanding to bring about her death in this way"; the ludicrous response from the mother was that she was in her right mind, but one must tell the truth. It must have taken enormous courage for Gauthine to resist four sessions of torture and win her release. Another line of questioning concerned the deception necessary to attend the sabbat without detection by one's partner. The answers revolved around illusions procured by the Devil, whether the inert body of the witch remained behind (what might, irreverently, be called the doctrine of the witch's two bodies), or some object such as a hayfork took on his or her shape. Some of the witches from Spanish Navarre offered a kind of double insurance policy; the Devil ensured that all other members of the household fell into a deep sleep, but also provided a demon in their likeness to occupy their place in bed. There were households which had a generalized reputation for witchcraft, such that both spouses, or even larger groups, where accused simultaneously. There might be stories of how they had been overheard trading insults, or making other compromising statements. A curious example was that of Ulriot Colas Ulriot, who was (rather implausibly) alleged to have said to his wife eighteen years earlier, "Marie, I have no idea whether you are a witch, nevertheless you have been arrested as such, and brought great dishonour on your family. As for me, I am a witch, yet have not been arrested or dishonoured my family, despite being the master of the witches." Sometimes witnesses put their charges in the form that one or other of a married couple must have caused a bewitchment, perhaps after a provocation offered to the household as a whole. Several witnesses hedged their bets in this way by declaring suspicions against Jean Cachette, his wife Mengette and their daughter Jehenne.

A small minority of husbands revealed themselves as actively hostile to their wives; Bastien Bourguignon actually appeared as a witness against his wife Françoise, to tell how he had become suspicious of her after discovering that she had been accused by a man and a woman on trial at Neufchâteau—he had checked this with a judge at Nancy who had possession of the papers in the case. He had therefore watched her carefully, but could only add that she had sometimes mysteriously got back into the house overnight after he locked her out. Second marriages (like this last example) look as if they were more vulnerable to such breakdowns, with women who remarried in middle life either proving less tractable than their juniors, or bringing dangerous reputations with them. Their husbands may also have been particularly vulnerable to the kind of taunts sometimes recorded from the tavern and similar settings. Sometimes these men appear positively determined to get rid of a detested spouse, on other occasions merely keen to avoid any hint of guilt by association. More ambiguous cases had angry husbands calling their wives witches, with these insults being noted by attentive neighbours and later cited as evidence. Straightforward maltreatment of wives, who were beaten or locked out of the house, could be interpreted in similar ways. Unfortunates subjected to this kind of abuse had to hope for support from neighbours or their own kin, and it was hard to keep such goings-on quiet. In one or two exceptional cases the abuse was so extreme that the husband rather than the wife attracted obloquy and came under suspicion.

The sensational case of Jean Aulbry, who confessed to an impressive list of sexual offences, thefts and blasphemies, came to court after he was so violent to his wife that she fled to take shelter with neighbours, then herself asked the abbot of Étival to take action. The confessions also provide indirect evidence, when women admitted they had been driven to despair by maltreatment, and then succumbed to the blandishments of the Devil. A quarrel with one's spouse competed with poverty as the commonest explanations witches offered for their peculiar vulnerability to the tempter; this is double-edged as evidence for marital relations in general, since the despair might be the result of exceptional rather than typical treatment. Those of either sex who remarried several times were also liable to come under suspicion of having disposed of previous partners, since some of the deaths were likely to have been sudden or unexplained. Jean de Socourt was questioned closely about the deaths of his four wives; at first he offered very sensible natural explanations, but in his final confessions included two of them among his victims, killed because they were disobedient to him.

Women who confessed did sometimes claim, often without evident prompting, that they had killed their husbands. Their responsibilities for providing food and drink made it all too easy to explain how they had slipped in a poisonous diabolical powder. Marguitte Laurent said she had put powder in her husband's soup after he beat her with the fire-irons, giving her a painful blow on the head. After adding that she had killed her nephew she went on to demand her own punishment, saying "it was high time they put her to death, considering how many crimes she had committed over twenty or thirty years." Even more pathetically, Marguitte Digard confessed to following her master's instructions to put black powder in her bedridden husband's soup, because she saw she could not feed him or her children. Admissions of this type were horribly risky, since the judges were liable to treat them as parricide or petty treason, and add gruesome penalties, such as the application of hot irons or burning alive, to the sentence. One can only presume that once the witches started to list the grudges for which they had supposedly avenged themselves, deep-seated feelings of guilt or hostility towards their late husbands surfaced in this pathetic form. A slightly different case was that of the Swiss witch Clauda Brunyé, tried at Neuchâtel in 1568, who had been asked to kill Don Claude Jacquet by his wife Franceysa. Together they prepared poisons, first by using items from a chicken carcass, which had gone green, then part of a donkey's hoof; yet again soup was the chosen mode of administration, and the unfortunate Don Claude "dried up immediately and died in six days." Stepchildren might also bring accusations of this type, as Nicolas le Jalley did against his stepmother Barbelline. He claimed to have left home himself because he was so frightened she might bewitch him, then suggested that his father had fallen ill on drinking some soup which tasted bitter, after which he lost the power to feel or speak. Nicholas asked Barbelline what had been in the soup, adding "that if he did not recover quickly he would go to consult a *devin*, and if he learned she had bewitched him he would have her taken and burned"—as soon as he had said this his father became a little better, although still far from well.

Household responsibilities and conditions are often evident in the sub-stratum of depositions and confessions. Friction naturally arose over money, with women complaining that they were not given enough to feed themselves and their families. Drinking was far the commonest culprit, with gambling and business incompetence occasionally mentioned. Boon companions, blamed for encouraging such conduct, were usually the targets for malice and bewitchment in these cases. Demenge Jean Gerardin told how fifteen years earlier Françatte Camont had spoken to his wife, asking how they could separate their husbands, who got together to drink. Some weeks later he was at her husband's forge with some miners, and they sent for a pot of wine. She drank some from a glass, then handed the rest to the witness, who drank it but was soon afflicted by a chill through his whole body, lost the use of his limbs, then after three months had to take to his bed. A consultation of the *devin* identified Françatte as the cause, leading to his eventual recovery after two separate exchanges with her. When she confessed, she said she had been angry with him because he made her husband go drinking, while there was not enough for their food. Men obviously spent a good deal of time in the tavern, and indeed the uncomfortable physical conditions of most dwellings meant that life was carried on in public spaces as much as weather and convenience allowed. If the tavern was a masculine space, the street and the houses which sheltered the *veillées* were mixed, even predominantly feminine. All this militated against privacy, as did the tendency to share the same roof, especially among the poor. People knew what their neighbours were up to and how they lived; they overheard conversations and spied on one another. Although this nosiness had its virtues—for example it may have protected children against the extremes of neglect and cruelty found in our own society—it was also oppressive and liable to magnify both discords and suspicions once they arose. . . .

If complete breakdowns of family bonds leading to accusations between close kin are rarely apparent, there were other situations which manifested themselves repeatedly. Families were often disrupted by the deaths of adults, and relations between step-parents and stepchildren could never be without problems. Since widows with dependent children did not find it easy to obtain new partners, stepmothers were much commoner than stepfathers; the folkloric commonplace of the wicked stepmother was an exaggeration based on a well-known phenomenon. Women routinely accused one another of failing to feed or care for their stepchildren properly, while as we have seen the adult children by a previous marriage often displayed marked hostility to the replacement wife. Such tensions were exacerbated by latent or open quarrels about inheritance, which could also influence the relationships between half-siblings, with unfairness almost bound to be felt by some if not all parties, whatever efforts were made to avoid it.

These tensions could spill over into the kind of charges made by Didier Hanna against his sister-in-law Thomasse Poirot, whom he believed to have caused the death of two of his daughters, aged eleven and thirteen. Didier had tried to dissuade his brother from marrying her, while there had been various other disputes subsequently, and "a wise-woman had told his wife that another woman who sought to get their property had caused the death of those children." Worst off of all were those children who lost both parents and became orphans; unless they had some property they had to rely on charitable relatives, supposing these could be found, or eke out a precarious existence by minding animals and other similar tasks. Marginal individuals of this kind, who typically wandered from one community to another and lacked any support from kin, sometimes acquired an aura of malevolence which turned into a dangerous reputation. In one spectacular late episode, the Zaubererjackl trials in the archbishopric of Salzburg, such people were to become the specific target of persecution. The rarity of such cases, however, suggests that such an evolution was unusual; orphans were numerous, yet few show up in the records of trials. Most of them probably learned to be subservient towards the more fortunate, and simply could not afford the self-assertion commonly associated with witchcraft. Guardians or tutors would be forthcoming where there was property involved, but these arrangements were often unsatisfactory, giving rise to claims of dishonesty or embezzlement. Conflicts of these types might seethe just beneath the surface of witchcraft accusations, only partially visible to the historian's eye; often they are easier to intuit than to demonstrate.

Parental attachment to children, and valuation of them, is also a widespread theme with complex ramifications. The most persistent note sounded by many of the accused, in respect of their own situation, was not anxiety about their personal fate, but concern for their children. This was true of men as well as women, giving rise to some heart-rending appeals to the authorities. After Jean Pelisson confessed he was a witch he begged the local chapter to have pity on his poor wife, who had no property of her own, and their four small children under seven, otherwise they would have to go begging; he would die more easily if he knew something would be done for them. Across most of Europe, as in this case, the situation was made worse because the property of a convicted witch was confiscated by the authorities, leaving the survivors impoverished. Although evidence for this aspect is limited, it appears to have been common for the family to repurchase land and other goods at less than their official value, perhaps with the connivance of either the officials or the community. Such arrangements could only mitigate the disaster, of course, and had no effect on the other consequence of a conviction, the creation or confirmation of a family reputation which might haunt the descendants through several generations. This was a dangerous reinforcement of the labelling process, with the trials helping to build up family, as opposed to individual, reputations. In most areas persecution did not last for long enough for the full implications to become evident, but there are some signs that a growing proportion of the accused may have been identified on this basis. In other cases there are later reports that the children of convicted witches had later left the neighbourhood, perhaps a sensible move, but one which may well have reduced them to the level of the vagrant poor. Nor was there any guarantee that moving would wipe the slate clean, since incomers were closely scrutinized and reports travelled quite readily over considerable distances.

There are signs that women with dependent children put up a stiffer fight than most; those who made remarks such as "who will feed my children?" sometimes resisted intensive torture to assert their innocence. Those who had no children surviving, or had lost contact with them, on the other hand, plainly felt themselves to be isolated and disadvantaged; one or two felt so unwanted that by their own admission they hoped to secure their own deaths. Nicole Nigal, whose two surviving children had absented themselves long since, tried to drown herself in a well, saying she would rather be drowned than burned, and when on trial continued to say she wished she were dead, since there was no-one to defend her. Claudon Wannier also insisted there was no-one to take her part, crying as she told of the death of her daughter and saying, "a terrible death for me." As a matter of self-interest, all other considerations apart, adult children had good reason to defend their parents as far as they could; the simple awareness that they would bear a grudge against accusers must have been a restraining factor in many cases. In addition to lacking this protection, the childless often seem to have been feared, suspected of envy and malice towards more fortunate neighbours, an impression they were liable to intensify by taking a pathetic interest in other people's children. Admiring a baby or giving a child some titbits could be as risky as muttering a curse if illness followed. Chesnon la Triffatte, a childless widow in her seventies, was alleged to have approached a baby's cot during wedding festivities, remarking, "Jesus, what a beautiful child"; the wet-nurse became alarmed when the child failed to wake, and found its face to be black and swollen. Another servant said in the street that some witches must be burned, at which la Triffatte rose from the bench on which she was sitting, and the infant recovered. It is perhaps significant that during her subsequent confessions the old woman told how her master had instructed her to kill some children in the fields, but when she approached two who were collecting pears she spared them, because they were friendly, one even sharing his bread and cheese with her—a poignant memory of one small act of kindness. Later she added that the Devil feared children, so when she wanted to avoid him she often kept company with them, for which he would beat her.

Children also played a considerable part in creating or worsening disputes between neighbours. Heavy-handed intervention to break up fights and punish another child could easily cause bad feeling, or again activate witchcraft suspicions when illness or injury could be linked to it. Allison Claude testified against her near neighbour Mathieu Margeron, whom she blamed for the death of her son aged seven a decade earlier. The boy had gone out and she had not paid attention to where he was going, as one would not normally bother with children of his age. He had the better of a fight with Mathieu's son, was told off by the accused, then developed a pain under his arm and died in two or three days; the accused was reported to have said he would not recover, while his wife, who saw the quarrel, told the boy "she would have his sauce made for him by the said Margeron." These clashes often involved the familiar projection mechanism, when the aggressor feared punishment and might display symptoms as a form of self-protection. This is evident in the famous case of Mary Glover and Elizabeth Jackson, when the girl had behaved badly to Jackson's daughter and was faced with the prospect of parental discipline. Mary Glover's subsequent "possession" has all the marks, in its early stages, of a hysterical reaction to a persecuting figure readily assimilated with her own parents (as it developed her behaviour was shaped to meet the expectations of those around her). Contemporary physicians seem to have realized that there was something odd about these episodes, rightly feeling that they went beyond simple fraud, without being able to penetrate the powerful psychic mechanisms at work. In other cases mysterious symptoms disappeared abruptly when the suspected witch offered some kind of conciliatory gesture and the threat of punishment was lifted. Jean Mulot testified that a few years earlier his son Jean, aged six, was playing with other children when he called Jacquot Petit Jacquot's daughter "black beast." When Jacquot heard of this he said the boy would repent, then next day he fell ill in an extraordinary fashion, with his stomach very swollen. Jean was considering going to the *devin* to see who had given the illness, but a woman suggested "that she had heard a rumour that he might be cured." Therefore he decided to call some friends to supper, and ask Jacquot and his wife; as they left they visited the sick boy, who had had a blessed candle in his hand all day, and was expected to die. During the night he called out for some bread, ate it readily and next day was recovered, running around the street with the others. We should note the way in which children could transmit or enhance reputations through the familiar practice of name-calling, for one of the favourite insults was to call another child the son or daughter of a witch. This bred quarrels between parents, who may all have been embarrassed by behaviour they could not really control, when as so often children subverted the restraints set by adult society. The process may also have typecast the children of suspects, encouraging them to construct the compromising stories which simultaneously won them a certain respect, if only through fear, and threatened disaster to their whole family.

Title page illustration of a brief witchcraft pamphlet published in Germany in 1555, showing three witches being burned, and another being beheaded. Such pamphlets, with lurid pictures and titles (this one was titled "A shocking history of three witches at Derneburg in the Duchy of Reinstein"), spread demonological ideas and contributed to widespread panics. *(Broadside newsletter, Derneburg (Harz), October 1555. Print courtesy www.geocities.com/pagantheology/woodcuts.html)*

Accusations, Trials, and Panics

Learned demonology, much of it written in specialized academic Latin, had an international audience, and the political and economic developments that provided the context for the witch craze were quite similar in many parts of Europe. When we turn to actual trials, however, what first emerges is a strong sense of the *local*: conflicts, hatreds, and jealousies, but also friendships and loyalties that began and strengthened in the intimate world of the family, household, street, and village.

Cases generally began with an accusation of *maleficia* in a village or town. Very often the incident that led to the charge was not the first, but for some reason the accuser decided no longer to tolerate the suspect's behavior. Once a first charge was made, the accuser often thought back over the years and augmented the current charge with a list of things the suspect had done in the past. The judges then began to question other neighbors and acquaintances, building up a list of suspicious incidents that might stretch for decades. Historians have pointed out that one of the reasons those accused of witchcraft were often older was that it took years to build up a reputation as a witch. Fear or a desire for the witch's services might lead neighbors to tolerate such actions for a long time, and it is diffi-cult to tell what might finally drive them to make a formal accusation.

Once an accusation had been made, the suspect was often called in for questioning, which might involve torture to extract a confession and the names of accomplices. She or he might be stripped and shaved in a search for a "witch's mark" or "pricked" to find a spot insensitive to pain. In central Europe, where authorities were especially concerned with a witch's sexual contacts with the devil, her body might be searched for signs of such orgiastic sexual relations, such as a mole that might actually be an extra nipple for the animal familiar to suckle. These investigations were generally carried out by a group of male officials—judges, notaries who recorded the witch's answers, the executioner who did the actual pricking or other types of torture—with the witch at least partially naked, so that it is difficult not to view them as at least partly moti-vated by sexual sadism. Gradually the circle of suspects widened, and small hunts sometimes grew into large-scale prosecutions.

The geographic and cultural heartland of the witchhunts, where both single accusations and mass panics were most common, was west-central Europe: the Holy Roman Empire, Switzerland, and east-ern parts of France. There are a number of possible explanations for this: much of this area consisted of very small governmental units, which were jealous of each other and after the Reformation divided by religion. The rulers of these small territories often felt more threat-ened than did the monarchs of western Europe, and were largely unhindered in their legal or judicial moves by any higher authority. The parts of France that were under tighter control of the French monarchy and the appeals court of the Parlement of Paris saw far fewer large witch hunts than the areas that bordered Switzerland or the Empire.

Many of the deadliest hunts were in the prince-bishoprics in the Empire, such as Trier, Mainz, Würzburg, Ellwangen, Bamberg, or Cologne, where bishops were both the secular and religious powers in their territories. They saw persecuting witches as a way to demonstrate their piety and concern for order, and were often founding hospitals and universities, building spectacular baroque churches, and modernizing their administrative bureaucracies at the same time that they were hunting witches. These modernized bureaucracies were quite efficient; in one hunt in Ellwangen, for example, over 400 people were executed for witchcraft between 1611 and 1618, and nine prince-bishops were responsible for over 6,000 deaths. One of the bishops of Bamberg later acquired the nickname the "burning bishop of Bamberg."

The first selection in this section comes from just such an area of intense persecution, the many different political units of southeastern Germany in what is now the province of Bavaria. In his huge study, *Witchcraft Persecutions in Bavaria: Popular Magic, Religious Zealotry and Reason of State in Early Modern Europe,* the German historian Wolfgang Behringer examines all known prosecutions for witchcraft in the period 1300–1800. He analyzes them in terms of contexts we have already discussed—learned discourse and social crises—and also carefully describes many, many trials. Behringer finds that witch hunting occurred in waves, often spreading from one town to another as people became concerned they were not taking the threat of witches as seriously as were their neighbors. In the section included here, he looks at the first major wave of persecution, which began in the 1586 and had more or less played itself out by 1592. He describes in detail several initial accusations, looking at the status of the accuser and the events that led to the charge, including illness, accidents, threats, and suspect behavior on the part of the accused. He then turns to mechanisms of persecution, highlighting the role played by executioners who carried out the torture of suspects. Finally, he discusses the way individual accusations grew into a mass hunt, and the pattern through which the panic subsided and persecutions grew less frequent.

The second selection in this section, Robert S. Walinski-Kiehl's "The Devil's Children: Child Witch-trials in Early Modern Germany," picks up in the middle of mass trials in central Germany, and investigates examples of accusations against child-witches. Some of these, such as those in the bishop's city of Würzburg, led to the execution of forty children over the course of two years; others, such as that in the neighboring city of Bamberg, involved only one or two children. Walinski-Kiehl sets the issue of child-witchcraft within the context of a growing emphasis on children's capacity for sins and on the need for all members of society to exhibit proper moral behavior. He also speculates about the motivations of the children themselves, both those who accused others of witchcraft and those who confessed to such activities, sometimes without torture.

Behringer and Walinski-Kiehl focus primarily on Catholic states and cities, and the third article in this section, Julian Goodare's "The Scottish Witchcraft Panic of 1597," looks at a Protestant area. The official Scottish state church, called the "kirk," had been Calvinist in its theology and organization since 1560, with decisions made through representative bodies called presbyteries rather than through a hierarchy of bishops. During the 1590s, King James VI (who would also become James I of England at the death of Queen Elizabeth in 1603) and some of the presbyteries were in conflict over his handling of Catholics that remained in Scotland. In 1596 there was a riot against the king's officials in Edinburgh. The 1590s were also a period of famine, and 1597 saw an outbreak of the plague in Scotland. Goodare's article explores the expanding witch hunt in this year of crisis, and traces the ways in which several local proceedings turned into large-scale prosecutions. The king himself was involved in several of these, and later in the year published *Daemonologie,* a treatise arguing that witchcraft was a serious problem and needed to be investigated thoroughly and punished severely. Several women who were initially accused of witchcraft, but then claimed to be able to detect witches, also played a key role. These "witch-finders" were taken from town to town, and Goodare traces the effects that they had on levels of accusation; he also explores what happened when the most spectacular witch-finder admitted to being a fraud.

Some areas of Europe saw individual trials but not mass panics, and the fourth article explores one of these, Telemark province in southeastern Norway. Norway was at that point part of the kingdom of Denmark/Norway, ruled from far-away Copenhagen; there were witch-trials in Norway beginning in about 1550, but these remained relatively isolated incidents involving one or a small group of accused. In "The Making of a Witch: The Guilty Triangle—as Illustrated in the Case Against Elline Klokkers of Gjerpen," Thor Hall analyzes the case of one woman, Elline Klokkers, accused by a man who became ill and later died of having caused his illness through witchcraft. Hall takes us through the various stages of the investigation and trial, which took several years, and explores the ways in which older traditions of understanding and handling witchcraft blended with newer ideas.

Wolfgang Behringer

Witchcraft Persecutions in Bavaria: Popular Magic, Religious Zealotry and Reason of State in Early Modern Europe

In all the territories [of Bavaria] the persecutions [of 1590] began without reflection; nowhere was there a concerted plan for the systematic expansion of individual trials. Nor was there any special agreement between the territories to collaborate in hunting down witches, or a special body of legislation on witchcraft or even the theoretical foundations for such a law. The basis for the trial of witches in all the towns and territories was the paragraph (article 109) on harmful sorcery in the *Constitutio Criminalis Carolina* [the code of criminal law for the Holy Roman Empire]. The "outbreak" of the wave of persecution in the years around 1590 found the region unprepared. People did not begin to reflect on the events until after their extraordinary character had become apparent. . . .

In the whole region, without any distinction between Lutherans and Catholics or territories and Free Cities, the idea had taken root by 1590 that the Devil's power was on the increase, and that his followers, the witches, with God's permission, were bringing misfortune on the country. . . .

In 1590 almost all the authorities argued for a ruthless persecution of witches. Their eradication appeared to offer a quick means of escape from the "plagues" from which people in the largely agrarian society of the time were suffering. Persecution had not been tried in the region before 1590. The hope it seemed to offer generated a high degree of consensus in all confessions and social groups. . . .

The great persecutions were planned more and more thoroughly and their conduct became a matter of routine. If accusations of witchcraft were made anywhere, the machinery of persecution was set in motion: enquires were made into the life of the accused, reports of "unnatural" harm were collected and checked for their possible connection with the accused. If such a connection was found, the prison was put into repair or a new prison was built, contracts were signed with suitable executioners and reliable court officers and priests were chosen to carry out the persecution. . . .

The greatest persecution in Bavaria began in 1589 in the judicial district of Schongau. Nominally this was under the rule of Ferdinand, the younger brother of the reigning Duke Wilhelm V, but in practice, as in all other trials for witchcraft, the proceedings were directed from Munich by the Court Council. The models for the persecution at Schongau, as one can see from the sources, were the trials at Dillingen in 1587 and in the Margravate of Baden in 1586; in 1591 depositions made by witches executed at Kaufbeuren were entered in the court files. Witches were also executed in the more easterly districts of Weilheim and Tölz in 1590 and 1591, but these trials remained smaller in scale. Several years after the end of the persecutions, it was proposed that a memorial be erected to the greatest witch trial in Bavaria:

> since 63 of the women who had committed the horrid crime of sorcery were brought to justice in about two years . . . and for such a work of solemn justice . . . it could be ordered that an eternal memorial column be built and erected in a place here in the street, not only in memory of the trial itself, and to celebrate the fame of the authorities, but also to serve as a reminder, warning and sign to passing strangers and the multitude. . . .

The persecution at Schongau was directly related to the preceding harvest failures, which had been caused by thunderstorms. Whole villages around Schongau sent deputations to the judge, demanding relief by the burning of the witches, whom they held responsible for the disaster. They may have been stimulated by the example of the trials in the Bishopric of Augsburg, or those in the district court of Rettenberg in 1586–7 and at Schwabmünchen, which had begun a few months before the persecution at Schongau. In particular the catastrophic hailstorm of 26 June 1588, which destroyed the grain harvest in several places, so that even seed corn had to be brought in, was blamed on witches. There had also been a thunderstorm on 20 May 1589, "a frightful thunderstorm, so bad that it was feared everything would be ruined." The villagers even offered to have the executioner of Biberach brought in at their expense, if that would speed up the persecution. One of the first witches to confess admitted that she had caused the storm which had destroyed the crops. But the villagers were not satisfied with one witch, they wished to tackle the evil at the root and burn them all. The method of finding the other witches was the normal one: to demand the names of the witch's accomplices at the witches' sabbaths, under torture. The tortures were applied by Master Jörg Abriel of Schongau. . . .

Important though they always were, it was not chiefly the denunciations that caused the wave of persecution to spread; in most cases local causes were decisive in beginning the persecution, while denunciations helped it to expand within a town or territory. The wave of persecution could only expand if the authorities accepted the persecution paradigm and kept witch trials under close supervision whenever they heard of them. It was impossible for a persecution to develop unless the authorities were involved, but the lower courts could avoid trials if they resolved complaints at their level. The example of persecution in adjoining territories influenced both subjects and their rulers. Villagers demanded that their superiors should follow the example of their neighbours and burn witches, governments followed the procedure adopted by their neighbouring territories, and often called in their executioners to conduct their trials. In many cases this allows the wave-like expansion of the persecution to be reconstructed in detail.

Often the beginning of the persecutions revealed a pent-up demand for persecution, which shows that no steps had been taken in the previous decades against those who had long been under suspicion as witches or sorcerers. In many cases earlier witch trials were raked up again. . . .

Though witchcraft was the most secret of all crimes, often the cause and effect seemed to be so closely linked that the act of sorcery or witchcraft resembled a "public and undoubted misdeed" (Article 16 of the *Carolina*) and attracted an immediate public suspicion of witchcraft.

The witchcraft trials in the court of Zusmarshausen (Bishopric of Augsburg) began with an apparently overt case of sorcery, which occurred at the meat market in Augsburg. A mother had put her eight-year-old daughter down for a moment while buying meat, and an old woman from Oberhausen, near Augsburg, gave the child a piece of bread. Soon afterwards the child went pale, began to gasp and breathe heavily, and her face swelled up before the eyes of the horrified crowd. The mob accused the old woman of witchcraft, the Bishop's administrator in Augsburg had her arrested and transferred to the district court of Zusmarshausen, to which she was subject. The incident took place on 6 June 1590. The very next day the Court Council in Dillingen ordered an inquisition for witchcraft against the woman, and ten days after her arrest the executioner Christoph of Biberach, who was still carrying on a persecution at Schwabmünchen, was ordered to travel to Zusmarshausen to torture the old woman. On 12 September she was condemned to be burned, but by then she had denounced numerous other women of Oberhausen. Three months later the first of the women she had denounced was burned, and the persecution at Zusmarshausen continued into 1591. Some of the denunciations spread to nearby Burgau, Göggingen and Augsburg.

The persecution at Nördlingen also began with events that seemed to eye-witnesses to be obvious cases of witchcraft. A children's nurse, under whose care all three children of a family had died, was suspected of witchcraft. Her refusal to approach the deathbed of one of the children had already aroused suspicion. When she was finally compelled to approach the bier, the "sign" occurred: the body of the child began to bleed again, an event which had been taken as proof of the presence of the murderer as long ago as the *Nibelungenlied*. This "bier test" transformed the popular suspicion into a certainty, and the nursemaid was accused as a witch.

One may regard such events as chance coincidences, but there is undoubtedly a certain statistical probability that they were repeated. Amazingly, even in 1590, trials that began with such events did not necessarily end in executions. In the Free City of Augsburg a butcher's wife visited a bath-house with her child in 1589. The child urinated unintentionally on a woman employed in the bath-house, who asked the name of the child. Soon afterwards the child's chest began to swell, and the butcher's wife publicly accused the bath-house attendant, a widow, of witchcraft "not only in the public bath, but in the neighbourhood, at the butcher's and elsewhere," and this caused grave difficulties for the attendant and for the master of the bath-house. The council of Augsburg, unlike the Bishop's administrator, critically examined the credibility of the accuser and concluded that she behaved "as if she were not right in the head." The bath-house attendant, who had been the subject of such serious charges, was released without being threatened with torture, and her accuser was forbidden to make further accusations against her, on pain of punishment.

A similar case in Dillingen might have had a more dangerous outcome. A student accused a woman of "doing something to him in the bath," after which he had developed a "strong gripe." The doctor diagnosed an "unnatural" sickness, and the woman probably only escaped with her life because the student withdrew his charge and convinced the court that the gripe was the fault of his unreasonable diet. The woman was again denounced as a witch during the persecution of 1591.

Children and Fools Tell the Truth (Proverb)

As a rule it was dangerous to utter suspicions of witchcraft, for every unprovable accusations rebounded on the accuser. Unless it was a case of an overt act, therefore, victims were reluctant to bring charges before the authorities, but tried instead to counter the sorcery by using traditional means. Two groups could not exercise this self-control, and it was no coincidence that they often provoked trials and persecutions, either by incriminating themselves or by accusing others, mostly old women. The statements of children and "fools" give an undistorted reflection of contemporary points of view on witchcraft, by which they felt threatened or even bewitched. . . .

In general three groups of "fools" tended to provoke witchcraft trials: those who thought they were witches, those who believed they had supernatural gifts that enabled them to recognise witches, and the "possessed." The third group was dangerous because of the widespread view that possession was caused by witches, who induced a demon to enter the body of their enemy. In the Catholic rite of exorcism the victim of possession was explicitly asked if the demon had entered his or her body on the instructions of a witch. As exorcists commonly also asked the name of the witch, exorcism repeatedly led to trials for witchcraft.

The persecution at Nördlingen in 1589 was triggered by a woman who thought that she was possessed, and on the other hand also had traits of a witch herself. The affair of Ursula Haiderin of Nördlingen is almost a test case for the tolerance of the Free City towards social and mental deviants. Like most of the "possessed," Haiderin was a relatively young woman. She was one of the poorest of the poor in the city, and had neither property nor relatives; she also suffered from physical and mental fits and seizures. Her mother and her father, who had been a local carrier, were long dead. For years the woman had had the impression of a "tumbling and rumbling" in her head. At times she was unable to speak or hear. Ursula Haiderin thought she was possessed, but suffered from struggles with the Devil that went beyond the normal bounds of diabolical possession; in her imagination the Devil often visited her at night in the form of a peasant lad called "Papperlin." She had sexual relations with him in this shape.

Ursula Haiderin had already told other women of her lover before the witch trials began, but they had only laughed at her. They made fun of her by asking about her lover, and it was generally agreed that the woman was mad; she was called "Papperlin's fool," but no more significance was attached to her foolish words. Not until after the events connected with the "bier test," mentioned above, did Ursula Haiderin's confessions gain plausibility. She had an attack of possession at the home of a relation of one of the dead children, and admitted in the presence of witnesses that she had killed the children by "smearing on" a salve—the usual method chosen by witches. Only then was she reported to the authorities as a witch.

After the hearings of witnesses had confirmed the statements of the plaintiff, Ursula Haiderin's trial began. In her mental confusion, she now withdrew her previous confessions but at the same time told the court of her flights through the air and her relations with the Devil. The council decided to put her to torture. Under torture she was repeatedly asked about her "accomplices" at the witches' sabbaths. All the women she named were arrested in the following months and burned as witches. Ursula Haiderin herself was burned to death on 15 May 1590, the first victim at Nördlingen, six months after the trial had begun, with two of the women she had first denounced.

Women accused themselves of witchcraft in other persecutions elsewhere in the region. In 1590 a woman confessed voluntarily at Schongau, without being asked. Her village had not been previously affected by denunciations, so far as one can judge from the trial records. Under the impression of the persecutions in the neighbouring court of Schwabmünchen, a young woman subject of the chapter of Augsburg, an unemployed servant girl, accused herself of witchcraft. Her trial in the capitular court at Dinkelscherben brought further denunciations in its wake. At Grossaitingen, another of the chapter's courts, a woman was burned as a witch as a result. The further course of this case cannot be reconstructed. . . .

Threats were important in the persecutions of 1590. As so often, the threats actually uttered in practice were distinguished from those that the theory of the persecutioners seems to expect. For direct threats of sorcery were rare, in most cases they remained vague or simply warnings that God's justice would not suffer a wrong to go unpunished. Occasionally a simple prediction was interpreted as a threat. During the persecutions in the Bishopric of Freising, where weather spells were important, the remarks of an old woman after a violent thunderstorm led to the expansion of the inquisition into witchcraft. The city judge reported to the Bishop's Governor:

> On the next Sunday evening there was a very violent shower, and all kinds of talk, and some people let themselves be heard saying that we could expect a greater and more violent storm this week . . . and so there was some suspicion of these women, so that it is suspected that they caused this weather . . .

The summer of 1590 was unusually hot. The chronicles record that the corn harvest began on 10 July. The thunderstorm at Freising on 4 June was soon followed by another, so that the "threats" of the old woman appeared to be fulfilled. She was arrested and handed over to the executioner, who was to torture her and look for the *stigma diaboli.*

A woman's predictions about storms and the prospects for the harvest also helped to start the persecutions at Schongau, at least, here too there were predictions that there would no more good weather that year. The villagers concluded that she could influence the weather, and in the course of the persecution the woman, the wife of the judge of Schwabsoien, was considered to be one of the chief culprits behind the damage to crops caused by the thunderstorms of the past year.

Actual or alleged threats were often made to the health of man or beast. In a village near Hindelang (in the district of the court of Sonthofen-Rettenberg), a woman was suspected of witchcraft following a quarrel between neighbours. A seven-year-old child stole pears from a neighbour's garden, and the owner of the pear tree threatened that she would soon "salve the pears so that he must not steal many more of them." Not long afterwards the child was struck suddenly lame, and was confined to his bed for ten years. The desperate parents increasingly suspected witchcraft on the part of their neighbour, and tried to force her to withdraw the spell.

The great persecution at Ellingen began with a vague threat of witchcraft.

> This execution or rooting out began in such a way. A poor serving maid who was not willing to stay any longer in the service of her mistress at

Ellingen, offered to serve another, and had agreed with her for the coming term. When she came home again, and told her of this, her mistress was rather unwilling, and a neighbour who happened to be present scolded the woman, saying: you should not have done it, and you will not have any more good luck. The next night the same neighbour came to the maid in bed, gave her a pinch in the arm, from which she soon began to suffer inhumanly great pain in the arm, and because she says that this woman said such words, and that she came to her by night and gave her a pinch, she could only think that she had caused her such pain. When this became known, the said Lord [Walbrecht von Schwalbach of the Teutonic Order's Commandery of Ellingen: WB] had her taken into custody, and she not only admitted the devilish sorcery herself, but also revealed others in the same place . . .

Remarkably, the threats cannot be classified in a particular social context, as some anthropologically oriented historians have appeared to accept. Even if we are unwilling to dismiss as implausible Stone's suspicion that "witchcraft was the weapon of the weak against the strong," we must conclude from the sources we have investigated, that a difference in social level between the person uttering the threat and its intended victim was by no means a precondition.

At least in 1590 all threats which appeared to have been fulfilled, without a direct cause and effect being demonstrable, seem to have been regarded as potential grounds for an accusation of witchcraft. . . .

It was therefore not so far fetched for the Bavarian instruction on procedure in witchcraft trials of 1590 to require the homes of the sorcerers to be searched for suspect objects, such as "poison, hosts, toads, human limbs, wax images stuck with pins and needles," for these objects and many more were repeatedly found when houses were searched. Hosts were found in the homes of the witches of Werdenfels, and one of the witches of Schongau was found to have no fewer than forty-eight suspect objects, dozens of amulets, magic bags, salves, roots, oddly shaped stones, hosts, a small wooden horse whose legs were bound with twine, wax dolls, cryptic characters on slips of paper, papers of powders, bundles of herbs, magical plants, feathers, human skin, animal bones, coal, pitch, old iron, axle grease, roots knotted in leather, rotten wood sewn into bags, pots, pans and buckets full of objects whose purpose was not recognisable, and which therefore could only be of magical significance. Such mysterious objects repeatedly aroused the fear and suspicion of neighbours who had suffered any kind of apparently "unnatural" ill luck.

Suspect behaviour could also arouse mistrust in a climate of tension, especially if its repetition seemed to suggest a magical rite. A woman of Freising was observed to walk around a church several times for no apparent reason. The city judge reported to the Governor that

> item we have found that the witch early yesterday morning, Monday, walked four times around the church of St George, and behaved as if she had lost something and were looking for it. Why it happened is not yet known at this time. . . .

The same woman was also under suspicion because she had left the city several times on the same day and visited a certain cornfield. Particular suspicion fell on those who were seen in the open field during a violent thunderstorm, as sources from Freising, Nördlingen and Schongau illustrate. A woman of Schongau who was seen in the vicinity of a witches dancing place (the Peissenberg) during a severe hail shower aggravated the suspicion by apologising for it without being asked; her excuse later proved to be false. . . .

. . . Oversimplifying, we could say that while complaints are always to be understood in their individual context, the triggering events often followed an accumulation of circumstantial evidence, which in the end made an accusation of witchcraft acceptable.

For example, . . . In Schongau complaints of 1587 we find a conflict between neighbours, the work of soothsayers, personal "faults" of the accused (quarrelsomeness, threats), and the raking up of old accusations. . . . It may be that such an accumulation of factors was typical of the beginning of large persecutions, as it can be recognised wherever the sources allow a more detailed reconstruction of the events. Yet to assume a typical process behind the beginning of the trials, on the basis of this hypothesis, takes us little further, for the accumulation of specific factors still means that the events were no less individual. It seems that there were in fact certain typical constellations of events that made trials for witchcraft more likely, but that no constellation led automatically or necessarily to a persecution. All the individual main factors are found in trials which did not lead to executions, and even when several of them were present, they did not necessarily lead to persecutions. . . .

In most places where trials for witchcraft were held in the years around 1590 it was the executioner who determined the way in which suspects were tortured and for how long. Not every executioner was competent to conduct a witch trial. Although the extraordinary brutalisation of criminal justice at the end of the sixteenth century meant that many smaller places had their own executioners, in essence five men determined the course of the proceedings in the region: the executioners of Biberach (all of Swabia, the Bishopric of Freising and minor territories in southern Middle Franconia), of Schongau (all of Bavaria and the Bishopric of Freising), of Lauingen (Pfalz-Neuburg, all parts of the district), Oettingen (County of Oettingen and Margravate of Ansbach) and Eichstätt (northern Bavaria, parts of the Upper Palatinate and the whole of Middle Franconia). They were reputed to be exceptionally experienced in dealing with witches, and were called in to conduct trials in distant places, where they set an example to the local executioners. Only a few authorities made no use of their services during the persecution of 1590. As a rule the Free Cities relied on their own executioners, while Bavaria and Pfalz-Neuburg as well as Oettingen and Eichstätt depended almost exclusively on the executioners named, so far as the sources allow us to judge, except when there were too many simultaneous trials for them to cope with. Skill in "recognising" witches and in performing the proper rites and procedures to extract a confession from them was regarded as a kind of arcane knowledge, in which they excelled over the other executioners and the officers of the courts. The notorious executioners purported to be able to tell a witch by her appearance, her figure, her gestures, her eyes and from the witches' mark (*stigma diaboli*) that was tested by the needle test. Often the woman's fate was decided at her first meeting with the executioner; if he found no stigma and saw no other grounds to suspect her, she was released. During the persecution at Werdenfels the executioner Hans Volmair of Biberach inspected twenty-seven women during a tour of the lower courts at Garmisch, Partenkirchen and Mittenwald, and found ten of them to be "sorceresses." The other suspects were released. Even after the suspects had been removed to prison the executioner still determined the course of the proceedings in 1590. The executioner's "art" began long before the actual torture. On his instructions special meals were prepared for the prisoners, who were given holy water and baptismal water as well as consecrated salt. The mate of the executioner of Eichstätt said:

> For when a witch comes into the prison, she must strip naked, and then his master puts consecrated salt in her mouth, as much as he can hold between two fingers, and a drink of holy water and a drink of baptismal water. After this he inspects her for the sign, which is a little mark, as if

it was scratched, and when he has found this he sticks a needle in it, and if she is a witch it does not bleed, and she does not flinch.

The so-called "needle test" was regarded even by the executioners themselves as such a delicate matter that the executioner of Schwabmünchen asked the government in Dillingen to bring in the Master of Biberach to perform it, a whole year after the persecution had begun. The witches' mark was considered to be important circumstantial evidence for the application of torture by the persecution courts during the wave of persecution in 1590.

The torture itself had to be ordered by the government, but in the territorial district courts the way in which it was carried out was decided, as we can see from the trial records, by the executioners. Examples of torture have been described time and again in the literature; here we shall merely cite the procedure of the Master of Biberach in the first persecution of the wave of 1590:

> When we reminded him of this point only, and he did not wish to admit it, as always, he was handed over to the Master for hard torture, orders having been given, and at 2 in the afternoon he was racked and until 4 he was strewn with fire, pitch and brandy, mixed with gunpowder. And also harshly tormented with two red hot irons which were placed under his arms, so that his skin was burned from the genitals to the head, but he would not confess or say the least thing. . . .

After several such tortures the Oberstdorf herdsman Stöckhlin had confessed everything that the trial judge wanted to know, following the questions sent down from Dillingen. The brutality of the tortures led to many deaths in prison. During the persecution in Rettenberg-Sonthofen, six of twenty-three named prisoners died before they could be brought to trial, or more than a quarter of all the accused. Naturally many women whose "guilt" had been "proven" by the finding of the witches' mark, confessed during the "amicable" hearings that preceded the "territion" (the showing of the implements of torture) and the torture itself. Women also committed suicide because of suspicions of witchcraft or tried to escape trial by flight. . . .

Once the first witches had been interrogated . . . a wave of arrests began in those places where persecutions were held. In most cases the arrests were guided by the plausibility of the denunciations. The first batch of suspects arrested was tortured with unbelievable frequency and cruelty.

Of two women of Nördlingen one was interrogated fourteen times and tortured four times, the other sixteen and six times. The confessions of the second wave of victims confirmed the statements of the "first witches" and added to their credibility. This programmed an expansion of the persecution in advance: the court believed the confessions and used every means to obtain more. Yet, to begin with, the expansion of the persecutions was not precipitate. The reason for this was very simple: the capacity of the prisons was too small. The dungeons of the castle of Werdenfels held twelve prisoners, the witches' prison at Schwabmünchen only six. The persecutions therefore went ahead in stages, for only when the previous prisoners had been executed or released could new suspects be imprisoned. Often the scanty prison accommodation had to be repaired or new cells provided.

At first the persecution expanded geographically. As the arrests were made on the basis of plausibility, the judges selecting the most suspect from the larger number of those denounced, the persecutions expanded within the local vicinity. The persecution at Schwabmünchen of 1589–91 was at first confined to the village of Bobingen, spread first to nearby Wehringen, and then to the neighbouring villages of Oberottmarshausen and Kleinaitingen, before jumping to the more distant towns of Schwabmünchen and Augsburg after the denunciation of persons who can be shown to have had close personal ties or relationships with prisoners who had been interrogated. The geographical expansion, therefore, was not systematic but casual. It originated in the circle of the "first witches" and depended on the plausibility of their statements. No persecution in southeast Germany was conducted by the courts using abstract or systematic criteria.

The "social expansion" of the persecution began at the latest in the third stage of arrests, that is after two collective executions. As the credibility of denunciations increased, the social standing of those arrested changed. Persecutions were no longer confined to outsiders and those at the bottom of the social scale, but affected the urban and rural middle classes. The plausibility of accusations was borne in mind during this "social expansion" as well. Otherwise it would be hard to explain why denunciations hit particularly hard at those trades and professions which had dealings with magical practices because of their occupation (e.g. midwives, cowherds, apothecaries) or were in contact with foodstuffs (tavern keepers, butchers, bakers). The latter were seen as particularly capable of causing "unnatural" sicknesses by poisoning or bewitchment. As the persecutions progressed, the witches became freer in the choice of their alleged accomplices. Consequently, suspects facing death tended not to name friends and relations any longer, but to chose their enemies and members of the local elites, persons of wealth or standing, or both. In Schwabmünchen, for example, several wealthy farmers' wives and tavern keepers were burned, in Oberstdorf several women bore the names of families with coats of arms, and in Garmisch too the gentry families were hit. In the Free Cities the persecutions spread to the patrician families during this stage. In Nördlingen a tavern keeper and the widow of a councillor had been executed as early as the second burning of witches, and in the fourth the keeper of the town hall, the city paymistress and the widow of a burgomaster were executed. Among the thirty-three women burned in the city between 1590 and 1594 there were two former burgomasters' wives, two wives of town councillors, two close relations (mother and daughter) of councillors and the wife of a high official who was eligible to sit on the council. Besides seven women from families with the right to serve on the council, several wealthy tavern keepers and a sister-in-law of Count Friedrich of Oettingen were burned. The wife of the former town clerk, the daughter of a high Württemberg official, had to flee to Stuttgart. Because of the duration of the persecution, the higher ranks of the citizenry were disproportionately overrepresented. When the persecutions were broken off, the wives and daughters of several councillors in office and local noblemen were on the list of the denounced. It was the same wherever persecutions were held. . . .

The Breakdown of Consensus

The statement that persecutions were ultimately led into absurdity by their inner expansionist mechanism is not quite correct, to the extent that it is an abstraction from the deeds and thoughts of those who took part, which anticipates and simplifies the results of a very laborious learning process—a learning process characterised by many reverses and which by no means described a straight line.

Though influences from the past and from outside should not be denied, it is nevertheless clear that the persecutions of 1590 in the region created a constellation of conflicts of a new type, which formed the starting point of discussions of witchcraft in the following decades—when the "witch craze" in Germany and other parts of western Europe reached its peak. From 1590–1 a "party" existed in most towns and territories which spoke up for further persecutions on the model of 1590. Likewise, from this time there was an opposition party in most towns and territories, which was not willing to become involved in such excesses again. . . .

In fact a more or less open breaking off of the persecutions can be demonstrated in several territories. In general one could say that until the summer of 1590, the crest of the wave of persecution, a relatively unbroken mood of persecution is recognisable among the governments. In the autumn of 1590 the persecutions in several territories in Swabia and Bavaria came to a halt, though in almost all the places where persecutions had been held there were still prisoners suspected of witchcraft. They had been denounced by the witches already executed, and the governments could not make up their mind to release them. New arrests were already being carried out, in general, with more caution, as was the use of torture. Attempts were also made to prevent the persecutions spreading. The government at Dillingen ordered that parish priests should "forbid the outcry against witches from the pulpit" and thus calm the mood of the people. In the Bishopric of Freising no new arrests were undertaken in 1591, nor were there any in Schongau or Munich. In the second half of the year a few women under particular suspicion, on whose release it had not yet been possible to decide, were executed in Freising and Ingolstadt, and then the persecution lapsed. The Bavarian Governor in Ingolstadt received an order from the Duke forbidding him to arrest any more witches. . . .

The breaking off of the persecutions by no means meant that the new idea of witchcraft had been abandoned, or that persecution was no longer acknowledged to be necessary. On the contrary. The persecutions had been discontinued because people had become convinced that innocent victims had suffered; this was seen as a particularly treacherous device of the Devil, who not only brought harm on humanity through the witches, but also compromised the authorities, who were incapable of distinguishing the innocent from the guilty. The belief in the existence of witches had, however, been cemented by the numerous confessions and executions. With the breaking off of the persecutions in the years after 1590, the last word had not been spoken.

Robert S. Walinski-Kiehl

The Devil's Children: Child Witch-Trials in Early Modern Germany

During the fourteenth and fifteenth centuries when witchcraft theories were being developed and the number of persecutions was gradually accelerating, the main concern was with adult witches. Children's involvement in witch-trials was mostly confined to that as recipients of the witches' harmful sorcery. The infamous demonological text, the *Malleus maleficarum* (1486), made scant reference to children and, when it did mention them, it focused mainly on their role as victims. The *Malleus* stressed that children were offered as sacrifices to the devil or were killed and dismembered by witches, so that their limbs could be used for magic potions. However, the *Malleus* also suggested *en route* that children could play a more active part in the demonic process, since it argued that a proclivity to witchcraft was hereditary, particularly in the female line:

> Finally, we know from experience that the daughters of witches are always suspected of similar practices, as imitators of their mothers' crimes; and that indeed the whole of a witch's progeny is infected. And the reason for this and for all that has been said before is, that according to their pact with the devil, they always have to leave behind them and carefully instruct a survivor, so that they may fulfill their vow to do all they can to increase the number of witches. For how else could it happen, as it has very often been found, that tender girls of eight or ten years have raised up tempests and hailstorms, unless they had been dedicated to the devil under such a pact by their mothers.

The possibility of children being witches was confirmed further by the numerous confessions from imprisoned adults that they had been seduced into witchcraft during their childhoods. Although it was recognized that

Robert S. Walinski-Kiehl, "The Devil's Children: Child Witch-Trials in Early Modern Germany," *Continuity and Change* 11: 2. Copyright © 1996 by Cambridge University Press. Reprinted with the permission of Cambridge University Press.

children could be witches, the prosecutions throughout much of the sixteenth century concentrated primarily on adult females. The situation only began to change during the mass trials of the 1580s that affected the German territory of Trier. In the course of this witch-hunt, children were discovered who claimed to be witches, and they denounced others whom they had supposedly seen at the witches' secret, nocturnal meetings—the sabbats. This marked the start of children's active involvement in the witch-hunts, and by the early seventeenth century they began to figure prominently in some of Europe's major persecutions. They played a central role in the trials that affected the Basque country between 1610 and 1614. Here about 1,384 children were implicated and many provided lurid accounts of having attended witches' meetings. Children also featured noticeably in the mass trials that affected southwestern Germany during the 1620s. The leading expert on these prosecutions has noted that "From 1627 on, every large witch hunt began with children." Europe's final outburst of witch-hunting in the late seventeenth century was similarly dominated by children. The Swedish Mora panic of the 1670s, the German prosecutions in Calw during the 1680s and the contemporaneous Austrian "Jackl the Sorcerer" trials all involved children as central participants.

The distinguishing feature of these prosecutions was that children were mostly suspected of indulging in witchcraft practices themselves rather than simply being victims of adult witches' harmful magic. Historians are generally more familiar with children's participation in witch-trials when the emphasis was on them as the subjects of bewitchment. The most famous example of such an occurrence was in 1692, when accusations from bewitched, "demonically possessed" girls gave rise to the Salem witch-hunt in North America.

As soon as children began to be suspected of actually practising witchcraft, the judicial authorities were compelled to clarify the legal position of minors in such cases. Prior to the 1580s jurists had paid little attention to this and even the eminent demonologist Jean Bodin added nothing new to the topic. He simply reiterated the *Malleus maleficarum's* observation that children of witches were almost certainly suspect because their parents usually initiated them. Peter Binsfeld, the suffragan bishop who had actively encouraged the 1580s Trier witch-hunt, provided one of the first discussions on how to proceed with child witches in his 1589 demonological study. Drawing upon his experience of the Trier panic, Binsfeld deviated from the views of traditional jurists when he approved the torture of minors, that is, of children under 14 years of age. He also stepped outside conventional judicial practice by allowing the testimony of children to be used against adults. This was a disturbing legal precedent as it gave children the opportunity to play a decisive role in judicial proceedings. Binsfeld justified such legal innovations by arguing that witchcraft was an exceptional crime and, therefore, extraordinary methods of detection were valid.

Jurists from other parts of Europe, such as Henri Boguet, Franche-Comté's demonologist, followed Binsfeld's lead and began to consider the legal problems posed by minors in witch-trials. While traditional legal thinkers advised that, under normal circumstances, culprits under 14 years of age should not suffer the death penalty, Boguet vehemently approved the execution of child witches. He justified such a harsh view by stressing the gravity of the offence "which is the most abominable of all crimes that can be imagined." Boguet also recommended executing such children because he viewed them as extremely dangerous offenders, invariably incapable of reform, and observed: "we have seen that he who has once been caught in Satan's net can never, except with the greatest difficulty, escape from it." However, Boguet's harsh views were not universally accepted and no judicial orthodoxy was established on the appropriate means of dealing with children; a range of conflicting attitudes existed instead. Some magistrates displayed caution and were reluctant to accept children's testimonies. The Genevan judges fell into this category: they regarded the confessions of juveniles as unreliable, and consequently no children were prosecuted for witchcraft in the Republic. For those who believed that children were capable of such acts as making satanic pacts or attending witches' meetings, problems could still arise over the child's culpability. In Sweden during the Mora panic children were thought to have attended witches' dances (*Blåkulla*), but were legally regarded as minors who had been seduced by adults and who were not, therefore, punished for witchcraft. This had dangerous legal implications because it allowed children to denounce adults as sabbat accomplices without fear of punishment. Alternatively, some authorities adhered to the views of the north German cleric Henrich Dreckmeier, who stressed children's guilt and the need for firm action to be taken against them. He argued that children possessed a sound religious knowledge and knew perfectly well what they were doing when they repudiated Christianity and made a satanic pact; such children had not simply sinned through youthful ignorance but were aware of the gravity of their actions. Dreckmeier adhered to Boguet's harsh view that children found guilty of witchcraft deserved death.

The existence of these disparate views helps to explain why the judicial response to child witches was far from uniform. Some parts of early modern Europe such as Germany experienced prosecutions fairly frequently and it is, therefore, appropriate to focus more closely on its child witch-trials. Unfortunately to date no quantitative survey of Germany's prosecutions involving children has been undertaken, because the abundant archival materials on witchcraft from many regions have still not been examined systematically. Although we have to await a comprehensive study, some of the salient features of Germany's child witch-prosecutions can be discerned by concentrating on a number of case studies.

Prosecutions in Würzburg

It is useful to commence with a consideration of the trials in the Franconian territory of Würzburg, since this region gained notoriety for its extensive persecution of children during the reign of the prince-bishop, Philipp Adolf von Ehrenburg (1623–1631). Würzburg's child witch-trials did not occur in isolation but were part of a major hunt which engulfed the principality in the 1620s. When such mass trials occurred, the search for sabbath accomplices became so intense that the stereotype of the witch as an old woman frequently lost credibility, and hitherto atypical suspects such as adult males and children became increasingly implicated. Clearly this is what happened in Würzburg, and at the height of the witch-hunt, between 1627 and 1629, at least 160 persons were executed in the city, 41 of them children. Würzburg's intensive child witch-persecutions were centered around the city hospital, the Julius-Spital. This was used as a temporary prison to house the growing number of persons denounced as witches, and children from the school and orphanage attached to it soon began to be suspected of witchcraft. In January 1628 ten schoolchildren, ranging in age from 8 to 13, were examined. They claimed that their parents had seduced them into witchcraft practices, that is, renunciation of God, rebaptism in the devil's name and attendance at witches' dances. Two schoolgirls, who had especially bad reputations and had confessed to having sexual intercourse with the devil on numerous occasions, were executed, while the rest were handed over to the *Hausvater* for supervision and reform. On 4 May 1628, a judicial commission headed by two of the prince-bishop's leading experts in witch-trials, Drs Faltermair and Fabricius, arrived at the Julius-Spital to examine children suspected of witchcraft. These two over-zealous witch-hunters were mainly responsible for Würzburg's high rate of child prose-cutions and executions. The trial of 13-year-old Hans Philipp Schuh provides a useful example of Dr Fabricius' skills at extracting confessions from children. Schuh, the son of a choirmaster, initially denied the charge when he was examined in October 1628. He still maintained his inno-cence after he was subjected to judicial torture in the form of 46 stripes from the lash. However, after receiving a further 77 stripes he made a full confession. He admitted to having been introduced into witchcraft by a classmate who persuaded him to renounce his Lord God. The youth then provided his interrogator with a standard demonic witchcraft con-fession. Schuh, in common with other child witches, seemed eager to offer his examiners details about his sexual experiences, and told of in-dulging in intercourse with a young girl whose private parts were soft and warm. He also admitted to introducing other classmates to witchcraft and thereby helped to provoke further arrests. On 9 November 1628, he was executed for his supposed crimes.

The total number of child witch-trials will never be known, since many of Würzburg's primary sources on witchcraft have been lost. How-ever, the comments in a letter from Würzburg's chancellor in August 1629 suggest that they were extensive. The chancellor ruefully observed:

> In conclusion of this lamentable matter, there are some 300 children of three or four years who have had intercourse with demons. I have seen children of seven executed, brave scholars of ten, twelve, fourteen and fifteen years. I can write no more about this misery.

Even allowing for the fact that the horrified chancellor may have exag-gerated the situation, the surviving material is ample testimony to the brutality and extensive nature of child witchcraft prosecutions in Würzburg. These particular trials fell into a distinct category of prose-cutions, that is to say, those types of panics which occur in institutional settings. Group dynamics were clearly important in sustaining the trials, for accused schoolchildren such as Hans Philipp Schuh invariably claimed that they had initiated classmates and consequently the number of suspects escalated.

Although he was concerned with modern organizations, the insights of the sociologist Erving Goffman into institutional behaviour seem relevant here. Goffman emphasized the power of psychiatric institutions to rob people of their identity and to mould behaviour so that it complies with official definitions of mental illness. He has demonstrated that patients incarcerated in asylums gradually learn to behave in ways that conform to the institution's definition of psychological disturbance. The staff apply appropriate sanctions to those inmates who refuse to act the role of mental patient. In the Julius-Spital the pressure of interrogations and the time spent enclosed in the institution also ensured that the Würzburg children relinquished their individuality and conformed to their new ascribed demonic role. . . .

Prosecutions in Bamberg

Child witch-trials have been considered so far in their collective form as panics. However, prosecutions also took place which involved only one or two suspects. The prosecution of an unnamed nine-year-old boy in the Catholic bishopric of Bamberg in 1629 provides a relevant example of such a trial. Although the case occurred at the height of Bamberg's large-scale persecutions (in contrast to the situation in the neighbouring territory of Würzburg), few children were suspected of witchcraft. The surviving records indicate that in Bamberg between 1626 and 1630 only seven persons aged 14 and under were prosecuted.

This trial offers valuable insights into childhood witchcraft, because it was based on quite substantial documentation. The source material consists of 24 manuscript pages which record the boy's various judicial examinations made between 3 April and 17 May 1629. Throughout his trial, the boy was very compliant and readily provided a confession without being subjected to torture. He admitted that he had been introduced to witchcraft about two years previously by his friend Georg, who had promised to teach him spells to make fleas. This suggests rather prosaic magical ambitions, but is consistent with the views of a child, for in folk belief the creation of small animals or insects, such as mice or fleas, was regarded as the lowest grade of sorcery. The boy went on to describe his demonic rebaptism, his renunciation of God and his oath of loyalty to the devil, which he wrote with his own blood in a book. He subsequently admitted to flying on a pitchfork to three sabbats. His comments about the witches' meeting were limited and mainly confined to a brief description of a meal and a circular dance that occurred before and after the repast. In this respect the boy's statements conformed to the general pattern of German children's confessions, which concentrated on the festive rather than the demonic aspects of the sabbath. While children's descriptions were usually less grotesque, adult suspects were able to offer graphic accounts of the sabbath's perverse practices (such as crude back-to-back dancing, kissing the devil's posterior, indulging in homosexual or incestuous orgies) that mirrored those found in the demonological literature. However, it is unlikely that children were completely unfamiliar with demonic witchcraft notions, particularly in areas that experienced mass panics. They would have overheard adult conversations discussing the trials, and they had the opportunity to obtain information by attending the public executions where the witches' demonic confessions were read out aloud. But children's perceptions and preoccupations were not identical to those of adults, and they would have had difficulty in assimilating this macabre information and accommodating it effectively into their immature world-view. Children's appropriation of demonological concepts was selective, and in the process of comprehending this perplexing, disturbing material, they tended to distort and transform it. They drew upon familiar experiences and amalgamated them into their demonic confessions. When recounting details of the sabbats, they focused attention on their festive qualities, because they were familiar with such activities. Feasts and festivals constituted important components of early modern popular culture and children could, therefore, easily integrate them into their accounts of the collective assemblies.

Although the Bamberg boy's description of the sabbath corresponded with those made by other children, his confession also contained original, distinctive features. Most children provided details about illicit sexual activities. For example, five-year-old Andreas Förster from Bamberg, who was also examined in 1629, admitted that he had engaged in sexual acts with a young girl who had entered his bedroom. However, there are no similar sexual references in the unnamed Bamberg boy's confession. While the boy displayed a lack of interest in sexual matters, throughout his confession blasphemy was constantly stressed. The boy's blasphemous acts were excessive and went well beyond the more cursory, monosyllabic repudiations of Christianity that most suspect children had until then admitted. At the conclusion of a lengthy examination, held on 4 April 1629, the youth cried out resolutely:

> I do not want to belong any longer to God; and in the devil's name I spat three times in His face. My soul ["my star"] should burn in hellfire and I want to belong to the devil for ever and always. I have renounced God in Heaven, the blessed Virgin Mary and the four angels St. Andrew, St. Michael, St. George and St. Jacob.

Besides making these sacrilegious utterances, he also confessed to desecrating a crucifix by either spitting on it or playing with it in various impious, childish games. None of the other numerous Bamberg witch-suspects' confessions contained such excessive blasphemous elements, and its unique qualities were probably a product of the boy's personality and capacity for fantasy and exaggeration. His readiness to name accomplices and his evident glee at recounting acts of *maleficia*, such as blinding an ox, or poisoning people's food and drink with a powder made from the ashes of a child's corpse, are indicative of a fairly malicious nature. His malevolence was further revealed by his comment to the magistrates: "If I was an inquisitor, and had to deal with witches who did not want to confess, I would stretch them for so long until the sun could shine through them." This confession was not only spiteful and blasphemous but it was also extremely elaborate and clearly exceeded the expectations of the examiners, who usually had to content themselves with more perfunctory statements from suspects. Hans Sebald, a sociologist who has studied this prosecution, suggests that the confession's excesses may have been partly the result of the boy's "mythomanic" personality. The term "mythomania" derives from the work of Emile Dupré, an early-twentieth-century practitioner of forensic medicine, and refers to individuals who have a chronic compulsion for lying, exaggerating and myth-making. Dupré believed that mythomania was usually found in children who were particularly vain, malicious or sexually precocious. The Bamberg boy's behaviour certainly seems to correspond with one element from this psychological profile, for he displayed characteristic malice during his judicial examination. Mythomania may also help to explain confessions in other childhood witchcraft prosecutions, especially in cases involving children who were not denounced by others but confessed voluntarily, such as seven-year-old Margaretha Gebelin from Ellwangen; in 1611 she provoked fear in the community by bragging about riding to various sabbats. It is certainly possible that children who were inclined to make vivid and detailed confessions without much judicial prompting may have possessed mythomanic tendencies.

In some instances where children confessed the psychological process known as "brainwashing" may have occurred. The essence of "brainwashing" is that, as a result of intense psychological pressure and persuasion, an isolated prisoner's personality is gradually transformed and a new identity assumed. In the case of witch-trials this would lead suspects to identify themselves as witches and accept completely the false confessions of witchcraft that they had been persuaded to make. The Bamberg youth may have been subjected to this process, for he experienced some of the pressures associated with this form of psychological interrogation: he was kept in solitary confinement for long periods, so that he was disoriented, and had to endure frequent interviews designed to convince him completely of this new identity as a servant of Satan. However, it is difficult to establish whether the boy was actually persuaded of his guilt because of experiencing "brainwashing" or whether this was the result of a mythomanic personality convinced of its own lies. Sebald is probably correct in his assumption that the youth's elaborate confession was a product of the convergence of both factors: the "brainwashing" techniques of the magistrates, combined with the boy's mythomanic inclinations.

Parents, Children and Moral Reform

We have seen that Germany experienced a variety of child witchcraft prosecutions and they did not all conform to the Bamberg model. Obviously, methods of interrogation varied and child suspects were not confined to individuals who displayed signs of psychological disturbance. Although the prosecutions were not uniform, certain features were mostly present. Child witch-trials were usually brought about by a combination of adult pressure (whether from judges or parents) and the testimony of children whose vivid imaginations often led them to blur the distinction between fantasy and reality; occasionally children confessed voluntarily and without any adult prompting. It is difficult to determine what motivated children in specific instances to denounce friends and relatives as witches. Did children sincerely believe in the guilt of those they denounced? Or was it simply the result of the kind of thoughtless malice described by the historian Rossell Hope Robbins as "the wanton mischief of undisciplined youngsters." Unfortunately these questions cannot be answered conclusively, for the source materials are too fragmentary and no historical methodology is available to determine the veracity of such early modern statements. We can, of course, speculate on the possible motives that prompted children to make denunciations. By denouncing adults, particularly parents, children gained power over them and could revenge themselves if they had been subjected to parental ill-treatment. Such confessions could have been cathartic and emotionally beneficial to children, because they allowed them to dramatize familial tensions symbolically. Similarly, denunciations provided an ideal opportunity for deprived children to draw attention to themselves and become for a brief moment the centre of adult interest. However, children's testimony could also be manipulated by adults, so that they denounced individuals of whom their elders disapproved. We should not over-estimate the ability of children to exploit witch-trials for their own ends.

It is necessary in order to gain a more complete understanding of early modern childhood witchcraft not only to focus on the trials themselves but also to consider wider issues, such as religious and cultural factors, which could have promoted the prosecutions. Children may have become more susceptible to witchcraft accusations because, from the Reformation era onwards, greater adult emphasis was placed on youth's capacity for sin. Lutheran moralists, in particular, were keen to stress children's natural inclination to iniquity, and used this to justify a policy of repressive upbringing as the best way to create good, pious Christians. Catholics were similarly concerned about the sins of children. A *New treatise on the seduced child witches* (1629) from Catholic Mainz argued that one of the main reasons for the increase in such crimes was children's sinful behaviour, particularly their swearing, blasphemy, covetousness, lewd talk and immoral games. However, the growth of juvenile witchcraft was not blamed entirely on children's vices. The 1629 *Treatise* tried to demonstrate that much of the responsibility lay in the bad examples set by parents to children. The author asked how it was possible for children to be brought up correctly when fathers led unchristian, dissolute, drunken lives? He solemnly advised that "Children are our greatest and costliest treasure, let us protect them with the greatest of care. . . ." The *Treatise's* essential message was that childhood witchcraft was a symptom of both parental neglect and the sins of their offspring, and could only be avoided if the whole family led a more pious, virtuous life.

Adult concern with child witches was, therefore, linked to the issue of family discipline while such preoccupations with the family were themselves related to a more general process of moral policing. Although historians are undecided whether it was a novel movement or merely an extension of an earlier process, it is now generally recognized that many early modern states attempted to impose moral discipline on subjects. It was, of course, easier to promulgate morality ordinances than to put them successfully into practice and we should, therefore, guard against overestimating the extent to which actual behaviour was transformed. For evidence that campaigns of moral reform were under way in German states we have only to look at the growing severity in sentences for such sex-linked crimes as infanticide, sodomy and adultery. The suppression of urban prostitution and the imposition of female dress codes that stressed modesty and decorum are further indications of the move towards a more rigid, family-based ethic.

Punishing child witches could also be used to enforce Christian morality and define the parameters of conformity, particularly among the young. Witchcraft was generally regarded by the educated élite as a complete antithesis to the existing moral order, and consequently suspect children were perceived as disturbing embodiments of depravity and evil. The activities to which child witches confessed certainly represented an extreme inversion of the pious behaviour that children were increasingly expected to cultivate. Parents were probably shocked by the accused children's uninhibited accounts of their sexual exploits at the sabbaths. These descriptions were usually devoid of the sexual perversions outlined in the learned demonologies, but they could still disturb adults as they undermined notions of childhood sexual innocence. Two trials from the Catholic city of Cologne during the seventeenth century offer useful examples of such accounts. Seven-year-old Maria Cecilia told her examiners that she and her companions had danced with the devil and "afterwards they undressed themselves and one lay on top of the other." Similarly, ten-year-old Entgen Lenart, who admitted to attending 30 witches' dances, claimed that she had intercourse with the devil "just like husband and wife did together."

While such confessions were mostly based on childhood fantasy, children with specific reputations for sexual delinquency were especially vulnerable to witchcraft accusations. This can be illustrated by the prosecution in 1660 of 13-year-old Hans Ulrich Fasnacht, a butcher's son from the Protestant city of Reutlingen. At his trial a witness revealed that three years previously Hans Ulrich had indecently assaulted his daughter. The youth laid much of the responsibility for this act on his already imprisoned father, who had encouraged him to seek out whores and lie with young girls behind hedges. Hans Ulrich's father was an extremely reprobate character and, when questioned, readily admitted to engaging in bestiality with a calf and also confessed to homosexual acts. Given such a negative adult role model, it is hardly surprising that the youth was a juvenile sex offender and suspected witch.

Children and adolescents who were involved in disreputable activities such as begging were also potential witch-suspects, particularly from the late seventeenth century onwards, when poverty and the dislocation brought about by warfare caused a vast increase in the vagrant population. Gangs of vagrants, often comprising many adolescents and young men separated from their families, roamed the countryside. The precarious nature of their existence compelled these marginal groups to live by their wits and to indulge in a range of dubious practices such as begging, trickery, fraud and theft. Some individuals also experimented with various forms of sorcery because of the potential power over nature that magic might give them. When these persons came before a court, often initially on theft or vagrancy charges, they also admitted to performing witch-craft practices. The most notorious case involving vagabond youths, the "Jackl the Sorcerer" affair, erupted in Salzburg between 1675 and 1690. Salzburg's reigning prince-bishop, Max Gandolf von Khuenburg, used the trials to mount a general crusade against vagrancy; at least 56 boys ranging in age from nine to 16 years were executed. Under interrogation which usually included the lash, boys confessed that they had been cor-rupted and seduced into witchcraft by the legendary sorcerer, Jackl, and admitted to renouncing Christianity. They also confessed to membership in a demonic sect, engaging in sodomy and committing a variety of sacri-legious crimes. This intensive panic rapidly spread beyond the confines of Salzburg and it was not long before the nearby territory of Bavaria wit-nessed similar trials. The prosecution of these young beggars as witches is indicative of attempts made by ruling élites to impose a new ethic on populations. In this case it involved stigmatizing as deviant those mobile social groups whose life-style ran completely counter to the pious, family-based morality that the élite advocated.

It was, therefore, not simply fortuitous that child witch-trials were prevalent during an era when many states were making great efforts to enforce social and moral discipline. They can be interpreted in a simi-lar manner to the adult witch-prosecutions; that is to say as one of the consequences of the general movement of reform and repression. In those territories where they occurred, child witch-trials certainly had the potential for instilling obedience into young people. The evil actions of juvenile witches could be held up as warnings and dramatic examples of behaviour that should be emphatically avoided by all good, Christian children. Furthermore, the harsh judicial treatment that many child witches experienced would have acted as a powerful deterrent and made young people aware of the fate that awaited those who strayed too far from the righteous path.

Although the authorities may have been concerned with moral reform, the accused children's preoccupations were obviously different. It is, of course, difficult to reconstruct the mental world of the child witches because of the limited nature of the historical sources. However, the surviving confessions often provide us with brief expressions of their thoughts and feelings. Through the medium of the confession—that curious amalgam of fantasy, wish-fulfillment and real experience—children were provided with an opportunity to express hidden desires and conflicts. It is, therefore, hardly surprising that the confessions tended to dwell on issues, such as sexuality, that the authorities were most keen to repress. Occasionally children gave dramatic expression to their conflicts and inner turmoil, as the case of the anonymous boy from Bamberg demonstrates. His extreme blasphemous utterances possibly reflected an intense aversion to the type of pious, Christian society that the territory's Catholic ruling élite were attempting to establish. While the confessions provided an outlet for such deep-rooted aggression, the comment of the historian Lyndal Roper that "interrogations were not conducted as analytic discussions" is appropriate here. The judicial interviews may have provided children with the chance to express anger or rebellion but the examinations were hardly designed as therapeutic sessions. Ultimately, children had little scope to influence the proceedings and the trials affirm their lack of power when they became entangled in the legal web of witch-hunting.

"Moral Crusades" Against Witchcraft

This study has demonstrated that children first became significantly involved in the witch-hunts from the 1580s onwards when the combination of the judges' credulity and the vivid imagination of the young had fateful consequences. We have seen that child witch-trials tended to occur at a time when régimes were making concentrated efforts to reform manners and morals. The sociological term "moral crusade" seems an apt description of these attempts to transform moral values, for it has been noted that "In moral crusades, there is always social pressure to publicly dramatize the evil and to make symbolic examples of particular cases." To early modern moral crusaders the child witch could act as a particularly potent symbol of the evil and malevolence that threatened to negate the pious magistrates' vision of a devout, Christian society. However, moral crusades concerned with children suspected of satanic contamination were not simply confined to intolerant, religion-obsessed pre-industrial societies. The recent moral crusade in Europe and America that has focused on the issue of children and their alleged involvement in "satanic-ritual abuse" demonstrates that these campaigns can reappear, albeit not in an identical form. In the modern variant, children are primarily perceived by those who believe in the reality of contemporary satanist abuse as victims rather than as culprits. While distinctions need to be made between the early modern moral crusade involving children and the devil and its appearance in the late twentieth century, the fact remains that such events are deeply disturbing and socially disruptive whenever they occur.

Julian Goodare

The Scottish Witchcraft Panic of 1597

By far the most detailed information about the panic of 1597 comes from Aberdeenshire, where a remarkable dossier of trial records survives. Concern about witchcraft arose in three separate Aberdeenshire localities in January and February. The initial investigations were by three different local authorities and the witches concerned were not linked to each other. However, it is quite possible that news of one prosecution was picked up by neighbouring authorities, encouraging them to act.

The earliest actual trials were in Slains, 15 miles north of Aberdeen. The local magnate, the earl of Errol (one of the Catholic earls), obtained a commission of justiciary that enabled his officials to execute several witches. In Dyce and Fintray, 5 miles to the north of the city, two kirk sessions began investigations that would eventually lead to the execution of a prominent local charmer, Isobel Strachan alias Scudder. And in the city itself, the magistrates obtained their own commission of justiciary to prosecute Janet Wishart, a burgess's wife with an evil reputation, and six of her relatives and associates. Wishart, like Strachan, attracted public interest because her neighbours swarmed to accuse her of maleficent acts, and she was executed on 19 February. But neither Wishart nor Strachan were

Julian Goodare, from *The Scottish Witch-Hunt in Context*, 2002, Manchester University Press, Manchester, UK. Reprinted with permission.

themselves interrogated, and prosecutions based on their reputation could extend no further than the associates credited to them by public opinion. Strachan's daughter was prosecuted but acquitted.

It was a few days after Wishart's execution that the snowball was set rolling. Her son Thomas Leys was interrogated, confessed to having made the demonic pact and attended a witches' sabbath, and named a number of women as having been present. Hauled in themselves and (like Leys) probably tortured, several of these women also confessed and named further names. The Aberdeen magistrates now panicked in earnest, and rushed back to Edinburgh to seek a further commission of justiciary—not to try named individuals this time, but to try all cases of witchcraft. A five-year general commission was granted on 4 March to the magistrates and sheriff depute of Aberdeen.

The newly-empowered commissioners spent the rest of the month interrogating and burning their way through the suspects generated by Leys. They then turned to the Lumphanan and Cromar area, 25 miles to the west, remembering that the previous national panic in 1590–1 had produced two prominent witches from that area. Margaret Bain, the sister of one of them, was a sitting target, a midwife with a magical reputation; interrogated, she too named further suspects. This was not enough for the commissioners, who summoned the local lairds and kirk sessions of half a dozen parishes in the area to provide yet more names. Some were distinctly reluctant, either providing no names or warning that their local charmers had nothing maleficent known against them. Nevertheless, this systematic trawl netted a number of witches in March and April. The commissioners also raked over the embers of the earlier prosecutions in Slains to obtain more names from that locality. A few further witches, either isolated individuals or small groups, were identified elsewhere in the sheriffdom by local elites who heard of the prosecutions, and the Aberdeen tolbooth saw a constant succession of trials.

By the end of May, the Aberdeenshire panic had burned itself out. Records are incomplete but at least twenty-seven people had been executed, and there had been one suicide and one death in prison. Eight people had been convicted of non-capital magical offences, and five had been acquitted. Thirty-four people had been named formally as witches and their fates are unknown; some had at least initial proceedings taken against them and some may even have been executed. A revival of interest in the autumn and winter would lead to four more prosecutions—three acquittals and one execution. This makes a total of at least eighty people caught up in the panic, thirty of whom died as a result of it.

The Aberdeenshire panic can open a window into events elsewhere that are otherwise obscure. In other parts of the country, we have *indications* that similar events were taking place, but little or no detailed information. When sources speak merely of "many witches burned" this should be regarded as evidence that trials similar to those in Aberdeenshire were taking place, even if the detailed evidence on the trials has disappeared. Two features of the Aberdeenshire panic might help to identify the scale of prosecutions in other localities. Firstly, the earliest trials were under individual commissions of justiciary, for the trial of specific, named witchcraft suspects. Once the trials started to snowball and further suspects were uncovered, a general commission was obtained. A general commission is thus a strong sign of large-scale prosecutions. Secondly, witches who were interrogated were likely to generate further names of suspects, while those prosecuted on the basis of neighbours' information alone were likely to remain isolated cases. Evidence of interrogations may also be evidence of large-scale prosecutions. . . .

Witch-hunting began in Fife in January, when the kirk session of Anstruther Wester began proceedings against Janet Fogow that led to her execution. That session heard five witchcraft cases in 1597, though in other years the number never exceeded two. Witch-hunting was organised in the Pittenweem area by the courtier Colonel William Stewart, commendator of Pittenweem, in consultation with the presbytery of St Andrews. In June he had draft dittays against four witches, including Janet Fogow; they and perhaps others had been burned by 7 July. One intense episode was reported by the English ambassador Robert Bowes. King James spent several days in St Andrews, to purge the university's presbyterians "and for the trial and punishment of witches":

> The number of witches exceed; many are condemned and executed chiefly for their revolt from God and dedicating themselves and services to the Devil, by especial sacrament (as they term it) in receiving the Devil's mark set in their flesh and in secret part as it has been confessed by and seen in many and wherein many of several sorts are accused. They profess sundry fantastical feats to have been executed by them, all which shall (I think) be published, as I forbear to trouble you therewith.

Another set of Fife witch-hunters, the bailies of Burntisland, panicked so badly that they wholly lost sight of justice. On 26 July, Janet Finlayson complained to the privy council that the bailies had tried her for witchcraft under a commission of justiciary, and the assize had acquitted her. Despite this, the bailies had ordered the burgh clerk not to "delyver the process of hir tryall and clengeing" and were planning a fresh trial. The bailies, who offered no defence, were ordered to desist. Witch-hunting in Fife was not seriously checked, since on 4 August, six members of the presbytery of St Andrews were commissioned "to examine the weimen of the paroche of Largo suspected of witchcraft." On 11, 14 and 17 August the magistrates of Kirkcaldy took cautions for the entry to trial of twenty-two women and three men—a large-scale operation which, as we shall see, also spread to nearby Inverkeithing.

Perthshire seems to have experienced large-scale witch-hunting. The prominent witch of late 1596, Christian Stewart, had been from Perth. The Chronicle of Perth noted: "Ane great number of witshes brint, through all the partis of this realme in June 1597." In July 1597, the bailies of Perth were ordered to "retene ane wiche unburnt" until the king could come. If James meant to pardon the witch, the order would probably have said so. Presumably he wanted to interrogate her or him in person, as he had done with Christian Steward and would do with others.

The chronicler Patrick Anderson wrote a brief but important account of the panic. Although he focused (as we shall see) on a witch from Fife, his paragraph on the subject was headed "Sorcerie in Atholl." His statement that "speciallie in Atholl both of men and women ther was in May att one convention upon a hill in Atholl to the number of 2300 and the Devill amongst them" may be unique in the annals of Scottish witch-belief. Atholl seems to have had a reputation for witchcraft. However, it was more than simply a remote and uncanny Highland locale for Lowland stories, since a complaint to the privy council in March 1598 catches the echoes of a witch-hunt that the earl of Atholl had apparently been conducting for some time, using two imprisoned witches to identify others.

The single most important witch of 1597 was Margaret Aitken, the so-called great witch of Balwearie. Balwearie in Fife had long associations with the supernatural. James V in 1539 had had a terrifying nightmare about Thomas Scott, son of its laird, who on his deathbed visited the king "with a company of devils." Sir Michael Scott of Balwearie, a thirteenth-century physician, had passed into folklore as a wizard. Anderson's account of the panic of 1597 began as follows:

> Much about this tyme there was a great number of witches tryed to be in Scotland, as the lyke was never heart tell of in this realme; speciallie in Atholl both of men and women ther was an May att one convention upon a hill in Atholl to the number of 2300 and the Devill amongst them; a great witch of Balwearie told all this and said she knew them all weill eneugh And what marks the Devill hade given severallie to everie one of them.

Most of what we know about the great witch of Balwearie comes from Archbishop John Spottiswoode, who wrote an ecclesiastical history in the 1620s. In 1597 he was a parish minister in Midlothian, but already involved in national affairs.

> This summer there was a great business for the trial of witches. Amongst others one Margaret Atkin, being apprehended upon suspicion, and threatened with torture, did confess herself guilty. Being examined touching her associates in that trade, she named a few, and perceiving her delations find credit, made offer to detect all of that sort, and to purge the country of them, so she might have her life granted. For the reason of her knowledge, she said, "That they had a secret mark all of that sort, in their eyes, whereby she could surely tell, how soon she looked upon any, whether they were witches or not" and in this she was so readily believed, that for the space of three or four months she was carried from town to town to make discoveries in that kind. Many were brought in question by her delations, especially at Glasgow, where divers innocent women, through the credulity of the minister, Mr John Cowper, were condemned and put to death. In end she was found to be a mere deceiver (for the same persons that the one day she had declared guilty, the next day being presented in another habit she cleansed), and sent back to Fife, where first she was apprehended. At her trial she affirmed all to be false that she had confessed, either of herself or others, and persisted in this to her death; which made many forthink their too great forwardness that way, and moved the king to recall the commissions given out against such persons, discharging al proceedings against them, except in case of voluntary confession, till a solid order should be taken by the Estates touching the form that should be kept in their trial.

The "discharge of all proceedings," although not quite as Spottiswoode represented it, probably refers to a proclamation of 12 August (to be discussed shortly). The chronology thus suggests that Aitken was exposed about 1 August. When "for the space of three or four months she was carried from town to town," this must have begun some time in April.

Aitken's success inspired imitators in her own locality. Several of those caught up in the large-scale Kirkcaldy witch-hunt were denounced by Agnes Ewing, "trayare of witchcraft and sorcerie." The magistrates of Kirkcaldy at one point loaned Ewing to their colleagues in Inverkeithing, making special arrangements to ensure her return. Ewing was still active on 17 August, despite the proclamation of the 12th.

The Aitken affair was notable for subjecting witchcraft suspects to the water ordeal. No reference to the swimming of Scottish witches has yet been found for any other period, but the evidence for 1597 is clear. Anderson concluded his account: "Ther was many of them tryed by sweiming in the water by binding of ther two thumbs and ther great toaes together for being thus casten in the water they fleeted ay above." This is corroborated by James's *Daemonologie*, when he mentioned "two good helps" to the detection of witches. One was the search for the Devil's mark, which was to become a standard procedure in the Scottish witch-hunt. The other was

> their fleeting on the water: for . . . it appears that God hath appoynted (for a super-natural signe of the monstrous impietie of the Witches) that the water shal refuse to receive them in her bosom, that have shaken off them the sacred Water of Baptisme, and wilfullie refused the benefite thereof.

These distinctive proceedings suggest that a special commission, using special procedures, was established to carry Aitken around the country. James's passage on the water ordeal indicates that he took an interest in the commission and approved of its activities. He may even have pressed later for its special procedures to be adopted by statute, as we shall see. But, as Spottiswoode's account makes clear, the trials ended abruptly when Aitken was exposed as a fraud.

The Aitken fiasco led to the proclamation . . . [by the king's privy council revoking all existing commissions] on 12 August. . . .
    . . . To some councillors, the Aitken fiasco probably marked the beginning of a new, more cautious approach. Preventing future injustice meant treating future requests for commissions differently. Rather than handing out commissions indiscriminately, these councillors wanted to ask

questions, and refuse commissions where the answers were unsatisfactory. They were also perhaps going to make more effort to ensure that requests for commissions came before them, instead of being presented to the king via informal court channels that did not necessarily allow for expert scrutiny of the evidence presented. Spottiswoode remembered the order as "discharging all proceedings" . . . except in case of voluntary confession"; although wholly inaccurate as to the letter of the order, this may reflect something of the cautious spirit in which some councillors intended it.

However, to others the order could be a mere public-relations exercise. Those who were still panicking no doubt regretted the execution of innocent people in the Aitken affair, but they were not going to let that prevent them from pursuing the genuine witches who, they were convinced, were still at large. Some public response had to be made to the Aitken affair because the public had witnessed miscarriages of justice. Hence the recall of the existing commissions. But witch-hunting councillors must have noted that the effect of the order need be no more than to call in commissions issued to one or two people, replacing them with commissions issued to three people.

One of those who wanted to continue the prosecutions was the king. . . .

On 5 September, one of Bowes's Edinburgh informants put the king's anti-witch concern at the head of a long list of news items:

> The king has his mind only bent on the examination and trial of sorcerers, men and women. Such a great number are delated that it is a wonder, and those not only of the meanest sort but also of the best. Hereat all estates are grieved and specially the church, affirming that the form of proceeding is neither conform to the law of God nor man.

These reports contradict the impression given by Spottiswoode—that pressure for witch-hunting came from over-zealous ministers. Instead they show the king leading, and "the church," or at least a vocal part of it, sceptical. . . .

So a new series of trials was launched in late August and September, by which the king attempted to rehabilitate witch-hunting. Although his views are clear, there is no need to pin all the responsibility on him: no doubt others supported him. Few details of these trials are known, and even their locations are doubtful, not being given by Bowes on 15 August or 8 September or his informant on 5 September. James himself flitted about to avoid the plague, being mentioned in Edinburgh, Falkland, Hamilton, Linlithgow, Perth and Stirling.

Stirlingshire was one area where there was undoubtedly a local panic at this time. On 7 September, Stirling presbytery commissioned certain ministers "to try and examin thais women alreddie apprehendit and to be apprehendit heiraftir for witchcraft, and qwhat thay find, to report the samin to the presbyterie that thay may judge thairon befoir any of thame thoill ane assyss [i.e. undergo criminal trial]." The investigation was large-scale enough to require bureaucracy: Elizabeth Hamilton was "accusit of witchcraft and abusing of the pepill, as at lenth is sait doun in the Register thairof." On 5 October the commissioners reported that Katherine Kello and Janet Crawford "ar apprehendit for witchcraft with quhome thay have enterit in tryell as thair confessionis bearis in thame selfis in the Register thairof." As in Aberdeenshire, the use of confession evidence may well indicate that names of accomplices were being obtained. The "Register" appears to have been a dossier of evidence for use in a criminal court; possibly it was used to solicit a commission of justiciary, but it seems more likely that a commission had already been obtained and that the execution of Hamilton, Kello, Crawford and others was a foregone conclusion.

The king still wanted to interrogate witches personally, and took an active interest in the Stirlingshire panic. On 16 September he ordered the magistrates of Stirling to send an unnamed "prickat wiche" to him at Linlithgow, "that scho may be reddy thair that nycht at evin attending our cuming for hir tryell in that deposition scho hes maid aganis Capitane Herring and his wyffe." So the Stirling authorities were using witch-pricking as well as extracting confessions—another indication of a large-scale panic. Patrick Heron and his wife Christian Reid had a bitter property dispute with Sir William Menteith of Kerse and his son, and the Menteiths were surely the people who had arrested the "prickat wiche" and shaped her deposition to promote their interests. On 19 October, Heron (who had prudently fled) was being prosecuted for witchcraft by the Menteiths and the lord advocate in a special session of the justiciary court. The case was continued to the next Stirlingshire justice ayre in response to a letter from the king, and disappears from the record. The Menteiths worked together with the Bruces of Airth; William Bruce younger was their cautioner in the Heron dispute. The witchcraft commission to Sir Alexander Bruce, mentioned above, probably dates from this period. The Stirlingshire panic seems to have been widespread. . . .

Interest in witchcraft at a national level continued into November. On 28 November, Lord Ochiltree's commission as lieutenant and warden of the west march included witchcraft among the list of crimes he was empowered to prosecute—the first Border commission to do so. But after so many executions, the supply of actual witches was probably dwindling. In Aberdeenshire, an attempted revival of witch-hunting in November led to one execution, that of Andrew Man; he named numerous further suspects, but a potential snowball of trials was halted abruptly when the first three to be prosecuted were all acquitted. St Andrews kirk session in late October punished for slander a woman who had accused a neighbour of witchcraft. . . .

Let us attempt an overall assessment of the panic. The first issue is the scale of the events involved. The most intense episodes of known witch-hunting were in Aberdeenshire (mainly March to May), Fife (May to August), Perthshire (June and July), the numerous places visited by the Aitken commission including Glasgow (April to July), and Stirlingshire (August to October). Of these five, there are incomplete figures for Aberdeenshire only: 80 known cases including 27 known executions. There were numerous further cases outside these areas, and much evidence is missing. The best guess that can be made at an overall figure is probably to multiply the Aberdeenshire figures by five and say cautiously that there may have been about 400 cases overall during 1597, mostly between March and September. Something under half of these are likely to have have resulted in execution. Although nothing can match the 660 cases of 1661–2, these figures make the panic of 1597 one of Scotland's largest.

Witch-hunting was normally a consensual process on which the authorities agreed. That consensus broke down in 1597. The Aitken affair led to obvious governmental disagreement; the order of 12 August, which was probably intended by some councillors to curtail the prosecutions, was followed by a much-criticised push to rehabilitate witch-hunting in September. Who among the Scottish elite gained from the burnings, and who lost?

Spottiswoode implied that James was the hero of the Aitken affair, but James was the hero of his whole book. At the time, the king did not come well out of the business; if he had, he would have been the first to say so. Whatever people thought of his promotion of the Aitken commission while it was riding high, they were shocked by its collapse in August, and there was explicit criticism of James's role in September. When *Daemonologie* appeared in print, public praise for the learned royal author was conspicuous by its absence.

The dissident presbyterian ministers failed to grasp the opportunity that this presented to them. Some of them, notably in the radical-dominated presbytery of St Andrews, were among the ministers who criticised the king in September, but they were unable to capitalise on the royal discomfiture—presumably because many were known to have been zealous supporters of witch-hunting up to the moment when Aitken was exposed. . . .

. . . Witch-hunting had backfired, and nobody wanted to take responsibility.

So the great witch-hunt of 1597 ended, with little or no credit by anyone involved. Even the Catholic earls, entrenched opponents of the presbyterians, had blood on their hands. The only possible gainers, and then only in the long term, were the councillors who had hoped to use the order of 12 August (which Archbishop Spottiswoode praised, even if he misrepresented its nature and authorship) to curtail witch-hunting. One of these councillors may well have been Alexander Seton, . . . who later became earl of Dunfermline and chancellor of Scotland. He also became Spottiswoode's greatest rival, so it is not surprising that the archbishop gave him no credit. Spottiswoode was no positive enthusiast for witch-hunting, but Seton definitely disapproved of it. In 1614 he marshalled his colleagues on the council to exclude women's testimony from witchcraft trials—a move that would have reversed a personal initiative of the king in 1591, and would greatly have impeded future witch-hunting. Seton's move did not set the precedent he hoped; intense witch-hunting recurred in the late 1620s, and it would be a further half-century before witchcraft panics were finally curtailed in Scotland. But when he sought to inject procedural caution into witchcraft trials he surely had the panic of 1597 in mind. One significant legacy of the panic may have been that it took so long—three decades—before there was another one.

Thor Hall with Herbert W. L. Burhenn

The Making of a Witch: The Guilty Triangle— as Illustrated in the Case Against Elline Klokkers of Gjerpen

The time is 1619.

The place is Gjerpen—or, more specifically, Bratsberg *len*, a subdivision of Telemark province presided over by the old provincial capital of Skien (or, then, "Scheen").

Telemark, even then, was rich farming country, with many prosperous old farms—properties that had been passed on through true and tested bloodlines for centuries—and with a number of large estates, which had been bought and built and were now owned by a powerful Danish nobility that had migrated North since the unification of Denmark-Norway in the late fourteenth century. Bratsberg itself was originally such an estate. Gjerpen, in addition, had had much land that belonged to the church and the crown. Much of that land had been lost at the time of the Reformation, but much had been reclaimed in the years since. The district was well established, well administered; church and state were closely integrated. . . .

In Denmark-Norway, witchcraft had long been condemned by law and punished. But in the old land-laws it had been considered a capital offense only in the form of malevolence to persons, which was considered a crime against society. In the form of medical witchcraft or other such benevolent activities, it was considered a lesser, "religious" offense and given a milder punishment. . . .

Thor Hall with Herbert W. L. Burhenn, "The Making of a Witch: The Guilty Triangle— as Illustrated in the Case Against Elline Klokkers of Gjerpen," *Scandinavian Studies* 60 (1998). Used by permission of Scandinavian Studies.

Toward the end of the sixteenth century, however, the Lutheran state church, then moving aggressively toward orthodoxy, put renewed pressure on the authorities to take stronger action against sorcery and witchcraft in all forms. . . . When Christian IV, fancying himself as strong a defender of the faith as was James I in England, in 1617 issued his law "On troll-people and all their coconspirators," making the death penalty mandatory for all forms of witchcraft except milder forms of medical beneficence, the campaign against witchcraft seems to have intensified all over Denmark-Norway. The case against Elline, the wife of Andres Klokker, sexton of the Gjerpen parish, tragically became an early reflection of these developments. . . .

Elline was not on the surface a likely candidate for witchcraft charges, though those who knew her well had knowledge also of some unfortunate things in her past. . . .

The young woman's name, when she married Andres Klokker, was Elline Ingenmandsdatter ("Nomansdaughter")—the church records thus recorded that she was born an illegitimate child. Rumors had it that her father was a nephew of the king, a Danish prince who had once visited the Bratsberg estate. Elline's mother, Sissel of Almedal, a daughter of the rich and powerful Borge clan, had been a young lady-in-training at the estate at the time—she was engaged to be married, but that had not prevented the Danish prince from violating her. A week after Elline's birth, her mother, out of shame, had taken her own life by drowning. . . .

. . . The Borge clan had become an exceedingly rich and powerful family, the owners of no less than seven large estates up and down the valleys of Telemark. They were greatly admired—and greatly envied. Theirs was old wealth.

Elline's husband, Andres, as he preferred to be called (not Anders, as the local people would say), was also related to the Borge clan. He was apparently well reputed, though people had things to say about him as well. He had come to Gjerpen from Seljord, where he was raised on one of the Borge family's outlying farms; he was apparently a distant cousin of Elline . . . When Andres was given the position of sexton in Gjerpen, it was probably because of his good connections within the hierarchy, possibly also because of his family connections to the Borge clan. But then he had married this "nomansdaughter," Elline. That was not something a sexton would ordinarily do.

As sexton, Andres was in some sense part of the ecclesiastical establishment—though not on the level of officialdom. Sextons were good and pious men of the people, often trusted more than the clergy, who as state officials were generally considered to be compromised and corrupted by their closeness to the seats of power. How Andres was perceived by the common folk is difficult to say. It is possible that the people of Gjerpen held some resentment against him, . . . because of his family connections with the powerful Borge clan. But if he was criticized, it was perhaps primarily because of his marriage to the "nomansdaughter," who, by marrying her distant cousin, had obtained respectability far beyond what she had been born to.

What then was the case against Elline? . . .

It all started in the summer of 1619, when one Hans Grytestøper was cutting timber for Andres Klokker in Gjerpen. One day, while at work, Hans suddenly took ill: . . . "With blood streaming from nose, mouth, and ears, "he lay there screaming, not able to talk'." Shortly thereafter, he died.

That is probably how it all would have ended had not Hans Grytestøper, before he died, blamed the [sexton's] wife, Elline, for having caused his illness. Such deathbed charges, according to the law, were to be taken very seriously—they were often, in fact, considered positive proof in trials for murder. The consensus was that no person in the grip of death would dare lie.

With the accusation the process against Elline got its start. Hans Grytestøper's widow went to court.

On June 14, 1619, three witnesses were examined before a grand jury at the Rising courthouse in Bratsberg. The hearing revealed that there had been bad blood between Hans and Elline for some time. Hans was obviously a big fellow who never backed down from a fight. What the cause was of the most recent trouble is not clear, but Hans had apparently come after Elline, and she had barely escaped into the house, finding safety behind locked doors. Hans had threatened her from the outside—Elline, from the inside, threatening him in return. She declared that she was going to file a complaint against him with the sheriff, that he would come to shame, and that he would never cut timber again. Apparently, when Hans took ill, he immediately set this in connection with Elline's threats. He had told a neighbor's wife that Elline had threatened his life—by promising him that he would never cut another tree—and that he believed he would not be able to do so. Elline on her side had allegedly said that Hans's illness was nothing more than he deserved.

With Hans's dying testimony and the explicit testimony of witnesses to previous threats, there was proof sufficient to charge Elline with murder—murder by *forgjøring* (literally "doing in"), i.e., by sorcery or witchcraft. Both in Christian IV's Norwegian law of 1604 and in the old laws from the time of Magnus Lawmaker, it was determined that in cases of murder the testimony of the victim should be given decisive value: . . . "If he who is wounded can speak when he is found, then the person he first gives case [names], if he otherwise has his wits about him when he makes the charges, is the killer."

At another session of the grand jury, later in the fall, additional testimony was taken. A woman in the neighborhood had heard Elline call Hans Grytestøpher a thieving rascal who was constantly on the war-path against her and her husband. She had allegedly added that he deserved a "devil's trip." This was all that happened in the case in 1619.

Eighteen months later, in March of 1621, the grand jury met at Gjerpen to reconsider the earlier testimony.

Why it should have taken that long to get back to the case is difficult to say. Hans's widow may not have thought it wise to press charges; there may have been some doubt about the justification for the case; there may have been some hesitancy about starting a "hex-process" against the sexton's wife. But then [the] *lensherr*—the chief legal officer in Bratsberg *len*, the Crown's representative—began to take the initiative. He was himself in the chair at the meeting.

The grand jury was still, apparently, hesitant. The case was judged too complicated to be adjudicated immediately and was delayed for another month.

The following month, the grand jury was asked—again by [the] *lensherr*, who presided—either to absolve Elline or to commit her to the trial prescribed by law, but once again the members hesitated. The proofs were too weak to warrant charges of murder, yet too strong for Elline to be found innocent. [The] *lensherr* therefore determined that Elline should *gå sin døl* ("go her dole")—she could free herself of the charges by the so-called *Nektingsed* ("oath of denial"). Such an oath was common practice in Norwegian law at the time. Elline, in order to clear herself of all suspicion and further charges, would have ten weeks in which to swear to her innocence together with eleven just and nonpartial women from the district—seven of whom were to be chosen from a roster of twelve selected by the grand jury, and four of whom were to be of her own choosing. If the eleven women confirmed her plea of innocence, Elline would go free; if any one of them objected, Elline's guilt would be established according to law. The members of the grand jury were clearly hesitant about this turn of events—eleven of the twelve jurors refused to sign the protocol of the meeting and were later fined for it. Moreover, Elline herself was apparently not aware of the need—or did not consider herself obligated—to go her dole. She did nothing. Another eighteen months passed.

On October 18, 1622, Elline was called before the grand jury in Skien, once more by [the] *lensherr*. It had come to his attention that the oath of denial had not been sworn; he wrote Elline that [he] was therefore of the opinion that she had caused Hans Grytestøper's death. At this meeting of the grand jury, six witnesses were also called on behalf of Andres Klokker, Elline's husband. Andres's intention was clearly to counterbalance earlier testimony in the case and to clear Elline's name. Although we do not know what transpired at the October 18 meeting, Andres was evidently not successful. By then, he was having troubles of his own. Since the charges against Elline had surfaced, he had apparently stayed away from Holy Communion—probably out of reverence for the sacrament and respect for his own position as sexton. The church, however, did not consider itself well served by a sexton who did not "gå til alters" (literally, "go to the altar," "take communion") and had complained to the bishop. Andres had in fact received a threat of excommunication from the new bishop of Oslo and Hamar diocese, the mighty Nicolaus Simonis Glostrupius. Thus, both the ecclesiastical and the legal establishments were stirring against the sexton and his wife.

Two months later, on December 16, 1622, the *bygdeting* ("district court") in Gjerpen was called to hear further "proofs" presented by the district [judge] and the local *lensmann* (sheriff). Five new witnesses stood forth to give additional testimony against Elline. In her youth, she had been in training on a farm in Gjerpen owned by Nils and Anne Gulset—and Anne, who was widely reputed for her sorcery, had finally drowned herself. Others in service at Gulset at the time could now remember various suspicious events: a farm hand, frightened by a fierce black dog, had heard Elline say that it would not hurt him; she had picked the dog up and carried it into the house. Another farm hand had heard steps and noises from the attic on one or two occasions; obviously, Elline had been there engaged in some unholy business. A maid had also heard strange noises in Gulset — as though someone with huge shoes had walked through the house and out into the yard, to the henhouse — but without anything visibly occurring.

With these developments we are at the point when the legal and ecclesiastical establishments enters into an open pact with the local rumor mill — with popular fantasy, superstition, and insinuation. Attention is no longer on the facts of the case; general circumstances and certain personal impressions associated with the person charged are taking center stage. Elline, by association and innuendo, is thought to stand in relation to some supernatural evil force. The charges assume an increasingly abstract character. What we are seeing makes clear the anatomy of the classical hex-process.

Andres Klokker, with explicit charges of witchcraft now presented against his wife, decided at the December 1622 meeting of the district court to move to defend Elline's innocence in the strongest possible manner. He made the claim that the district *fogd* would never be able to find any person who would go to his or her death swearing that Elline was a witch. The move did not work — though it did buy Elline a little time. Three months later, however, the district *fogd* had his witnesses.

On March 21, 1623, Elline's fate was sealed. At *lagtinget* ("the provincial court") in Skien, she and another woman, Marte Langøen from Bamble, stood charged with witchcraft before a grand jury of twelve citizens. [The] *lensherr* himself was present.

Why the case was not adjudicated in the district court but went directly before the provincial court in the city (normally an appeals court), is not altogether clear. Perhaps the legal establishment had had enough of the procrastinations of Andres and Elline's neighbors out in the district. At any rate, the [*lensherr*] was now ready to play the prosecutions' trumpcard: confessions of three persons from the Telemark interior who shortly before had been executed for witchcraft and who during interrogations — most likely by way of torture — had implicated a number of others as having been part of their activities. They had sworn on their grave under oath that Elline Klokkers and Marte Langøen had been with them at a witches' sabbath at Skrehelle (the Norwegian counterpart to Bloksberg) and that they had otherwise associated and cooperated with them in sorcery.

The public prosecutor, obviously arguing on the basis of Christian IV's law of 1617 and setting aside the legal reservations of 1547 and 1558 against such testimony from convicted folk, presented these proofs as sufficient to warrant the death penalty for the two women. Yet he indicated that he was still willing to give them an opportunity to go their dole, so that no one would have reason to complain. He announced that the court-appointed women had already been called and were present in court.

As the case then stood—resting on incriminating rumors and insinuations and with the confessions of executed "troll-folk" on record—the outcome was of course given. Under such circumstances, Elline would never be able to find anyone who would swear to her innocence. The prosecution knew this—the conspiracy between the legal establishment, the religious authorities, and the unenlightened and superstitious populace was then complete. One by one, as the potential character witnesses were called, they answered, as the protocol puts it, that they personally knew of nothing for which the two women could be condemned but had heard of the confessions of those executed earlier or of Elline's possibly being involved in Hans Grytestoper's strange and unnatural demise, or of her having been raised by Anne Gulset, whose reputation for artistry in witchcraft was widely known.

It was an open and shut case. The two women, having failed to obtain the oath of innocence, were condemned to death by fire. The provincial court in Skien made them the fourth and fifth victims of the series of hex-trials that was going on in the Bratsberg district of the province of Telemark during 1623.

In all, there were seven women and two men executed in Bratsberg for sorcery or witchcraft that year. . . . They were put to the stake on a small island in Hjellevatnet called "Galgeøya" ("Gallows Island," obviously a place used for several different types of execution). We do not know what methods were used—whether the victims were tied to a pole on top of a woodpile, which was then lit, or were tied to a ladder, which was subsequently pushed over a flaming fire. The latter method would be considered the more humane—but then the hex-processes themselves do not give evidence that the authorities or the populace in general had much sensitivity for such concerns. We know only that the execution was carried out by burning. . . .

It is clear, in Elline's case, that the judicial system under which she was tried was a combination of old Norwegian practices and the new royal regulations and laws concerning "troll-folk." It was not on the surface unthinkable that even under this system she could have received a fair trial. The apparent procrastinations of the district grand jury seem to indicate that there was some gnawing uncertainty about the new procedures, and the willingness of the prosecutor to let Elline go her dole is also an indication of an intention to follow old established rules of the court. As the case wore on, however, the new ways of proceeding against witches seemed to gain status. Andres challenged the prosecutor, obviously on the basis of traditional standards of testimony, to find witnesses who would swear that Elline was a witch. To him, such testimony was unthinkable. The prosecutor succeeded, however, in obtaining sworn testimony from other condemned witches, most likely by way of torture, and clearly on the basis of the exceptional processes then allowed in witch trials. Those were procedures that the local court had to accept.

We thus find ourselves left with the guilty triangle . . . a conspiracy between three primary interacting forces in sixteenth- and seventeenth-century European society: the presence of popular folk traditional and superstitions, the development of official church doctrine on demonology and witchcraft, and the hardening of the systems of law and justice under the domination of religious and churchly interests. . . .

Elline's case clearly illustrates the transition from the image of the witch as an individual worker of harm to the notion of the witch as part of a large-scale demonic conspiracy. Elline was originally accused simply of *maleficium*—causing Hans Grytestøper's death. Given the scantiness of the evidence and the structure of the traditional legal system, she might well have escaped the charge, had she not subsequently been caught up in a witch scare of wider scope and accused under the new rules of evidence of having participated in that archetypal conspiratorial pastime, the witches' sabbath. It is only in the context of the more widespread, church-fed witch scare that the persistence of the legal establishment's pursuit of Elline's case even begins to make sense—if it makes sense at all.

An old witch embracing her young demon lover, from Ulrich Molitor's *De lamiis et phythonicis mulieribus (The witches and divining women)*, first published in 1489. In this early demonological treatise, Molitor limits witchcraft to women, though he also questions whether confessions obtained through torture were valid. *(From MOLITOR (Ulrich), De lamiis et phitonicis mulieribus (Cologne, Cornelius de Zierikzee, about 1500), quarto (An—y.13). Print provided by Glasgow University, Department of Special Collections.)*

PART

IV Gender and Witchcraft

In central and western Europe, learned authors and unlettered villagers, male and female, generally agreed that most witches were women, and the gender balance among those accused, tried, and executed reflects this belief. Women were widely recognized as having less physical, economic, or political power than men, so that they were more likely to need magical assistance to gain what they wanted. Whereas a man could fight or take someone to court, a woman could only scold, curse, or cast spells. Thus in popular notions of witchcraft, women's physical and legal weakness was a contributing factor, with unmarried women and widows recognized as even more vulnerable because they did not have a husband to protect them.

Women also had close connections with many areas of life in which magic or malevolence might seem the only explanation for events. They watched over animals that could die mysteriously, prepared food that could become spoiled unexplainably, nursed the ill of all ages who could die without warning, and cared for children who were even more subject to disease and death than adults in this era of poor hygiene and unknown and uncontrollable childhood diseases. Because women often married at a younger age than men and female life expectancy may have been increasing, women frequently spent periods of their life as widows. If they re-married, it was often to a widower with children, so that they became stepmothers; resentments about preferential treatment were very common in families with stepsiblings, and the evil stepmother became a stock figure in folk tales. If a woman's second husband died, she might have to spend her last years in the house of a stepson or stepdaughter who resented her demands but was bound by a legal contract to provide for her; old age became a standard feature of the popular stereotype of the witch.

For learned authors, the link between women and witchcraft was supported by classical and Christian authorities. Aristotle regarded women as defective males, as more passive and weaker not just physically but also morally and intellectually, which to learned demonologists explained why they were more likely to give in to the devil's offers. Christian authors such as Jerome, Augustine, and Tertullian were often deeply suspicious of women, viewing them as seductive temptresses who lacked rational capacity. As Stuart Clark and others have stressed, these attitudes were shaped by one of the primary underlying concepts in both Greek and Christian thought, a dichotomy between order and disorder, which was linked to other polarities, including culture/nature, reason/emotion, and mind/body. In all of these, men were linked to the more positive first term and women to the more negative second. Witches were women who let these qualities—links with nature, their emotions, and their bodily drives—come to dominate them completely; they were both dis-orderly and actively bent on destroying order. Witches disturbed the natural order of the four elements and the four humors in the body by causing storms and sickness. They disrupted patriarchal order by making men impotent through spells or tying knots in a thread, and subjecting their minds to their passions in a double emasculation. The disorder they caused was linked to the first episode of disorder in the Judeo-Christian tradition, the rebellion and fall of Satan.

Witchcraft also represented an inversion of the normal order, with witches often portrayed riding backwards on animals or their pitchforks to sabbats where they did everything with their left hand, ate nauseating food, and desecrated rather than honored Christian symbols; witches also often passed on their powers from mother to daughter, an inversion of the way property normally passed from father to son. Women accused of witchcraft were often argumentative, willful, independent, and aggressive, the inversion of a "good woman," who was expected to be chaste, pious, silent, obedient, and married. As the indictment of Margaret Lister in Scotland in 1662 put it, she was "a witch, a charmer, and a libber."[1] The last term carried the same connotation and negative assessment of "liberated woman" that it does today.

The first selection in this section, Hans Peter Broedel's *The Malleus Maleficarum and the Construction of Witchcraft: Theology and Popular Belief,* analyzes the classic expression of these ideas. The *Malleus Maleficarum (The Hammer of [Female] Witches)* was published in 1486 and traditionally attributed to two German Dominican monks, Heinrich Krämer (c. 1430–1505—also known by his Latinized name Institoris) and Jacob Sprenger (c. 1436–1495). In 1484, Pope Innocent VIII (pontificate 1484–1492) authorized Krämer and Sprenger to hunt witches in several areas of southern Germany. Krämer oversaw the trial and execution of several groups—all of them women—but local authorities objected to his use of torture and his extreme views on the power of witches, and banished him. While in exile, he wrote a justification of his ideas and methods, the *Malleus Maleficarum;* the treatise also gave Sprenger as an author, but recent research has determined that his name was simply added because he was more prominent and respected than Krämer, and that Krämer was its sole author. A long, rambling, and difficult work, the *Malleus* draws on the writings of many earlier authors as it lays out Krämer's theories about the nature and danger of witchcraft, and provides advice about how to identify and prosecute witches.

In the chapter excerpted here, Broedel examines the roots of Institoris' and Sprenger's assertion that women were much more likely to be witches than men. He finds many medieval authors who believed that women were more superstitious and mentally weak than men, and more likely to use magical means to get what they wanted. What was new in the *Malleus,* Broedel argues, was the authors' obsession with the sexual connection between witches and the devil. To them, the essence of witchcraft was an abjuration of faith by women, and an abjuration directly connected to sex with demons; women's unbridled lust led them to seek sexual intercourse

[1]Quoted in Christina Larner, *Witchcraft and Religion: The Politics of Popular Belief* (London, Basil Blackwell, 1984), p. 85.

with the devil, through which they gained power over men, particularly over men's power of procreation.

As Broedel—and others—note, the *Malleus* is arguably the most misogynist of witchcraft treatises, and it became quite well known. It was written in Latin, and there were a number of Latin editions in the sixteenth and seventeenth centuries, printed in Germany and France. In these areas, the *Malleus* shaped ideas about witchcraft held by learned scholars and officials, and the actual conduct of trials under their direction. Recent historians have warned against overemphasizing its importance, however. In England, Scandinavia, eastern Europe, and southern Europe, the *Malleus* was much less influential, and the works of learned demonologists from these areas share some of Krämer's concerns, but not all. Other than a Polish partial translation from 1614, the first translation of the *Malleus* into any vernacular language was an incomplete English translation made in 1928, so that only those who could read Latin (or Polish) could actually read it in the early modern period. Thus it indirectly shaped popular notions of witchcraft in Germany and France through trial proceedings, but shorter, vernacular works, such as that of the Protestant pastor Frisius analyzed by Charles Zika in Part One of this book, both shaped and reflected popular ideas more closely.

Sexual relations with the devil rarely (and in some parts of Europe, especially Scandinavia, never) formed part of popular ideas about witchcraft, and other aspects of the learned stereotype of the witch also never became part of the popular stereotype. The *Malleus* is convinced that witchcraft is particularly rampant among midwives, "who surpass all others in wickedness . . . No one does more harm to the Catholic Faith than midwives." [2] This is not reflected in popular denunciations for witchcraft, and considering that most midwives were part of the population group from which the majority of witches were drawn—older women—their numbers are probably not over-represented among the accused. The second selection in this section explores a group of women involved with childbirth who *were* more often charged with witchcraft, the lying-in maids who

---

[2]Translated and quoted in Alan C. Kors and Edward Peters, eds., *Witchcraft in Europe 1100–1700: A Documentary History* (Philadelphia: University of Pennsylvania Press, 1972), pp. 114, 129.

took care of the mother and infant immediately after birth. In "Witchcraft and Fantasy in Early Modern Germany," Lyndal Roper investigates several trials of lying-in maids, noting the ways they were portrayed as inversions of good mothers, charged with actions that destroyed, rather than sustained, infants and children, such as drying up a woman's milk or menstrual flow, or poisoning children with food. Lying-in maids were often accused by the mothers whose infants had suffered or died under their care, and Roper explores the psychic world of both the accuser and accused in these intense situations. Using trial records, she attempts to understand what she has elsewhere described as "the emotional dynamic of envy, dependence and terror, which for over two hundred years issued in acts of appalling ferocity against apparently harmless old women."[3]

Roper uses the word "fantasy" to describe the story that people told to themselves to express and relieve that powerful emotional dynamic, exactly what Stuart Clark describes as "thinking with demons." In the third selection in this section, "Women's Stories of Witchcraft in Early Modern England: The House, the Body, the Child," Diane Purkiss analyzes the way that women involved in witch trials "thought with demons," the fantasies they created to negotiate their own fears. She also finds that anxieties surrounding childbirth and motherhood emerge very frequently, as do those about women's role in providing food for her family and otherwise caring for the household. Both Purkiss and Roper emphasize that the gendered nature of witch-beliefs is much more complex than simply a story of patriarchal suppression of women, or even of male fears—or projections—about female sexuality.

The fourth essay in this section encourages us to think about the connection between women and witchcraft in yet another way. We might assume that women would do everything they could to avoid getting a reputation as a witch, but in actuality such a reputation could protect a woman for many years. Neighbors would be less likely to refuse assistance, and the wood, grain, or milk which she needed to survive would be given to her or paid as fees for her magical services such as finding lost objects, attracting desirable

---

[3]Lyndal Roper, *Witchcraze: Terror and Fantasy in Baroque Germany* (New Haven: Yale University Press, 2004), p. xi.

suitors, or harming enemies. In "Marriage or a Career? Witchcraft as an Alternative in Seventeenth-Century Venice," Sally Scully looks at two women who clearly viewed witchcraft, or at least the practice of magic, as an employment option more lucrative than most open to them. The women, who were half-sisters, were both tried several times before the papal Inquisition in Venice; as was common in Italian witchcraft trials, neither lost her life, and one died a wealthy woman in her own bed. In southern Europe, the fate of most women accused of witchcraft was quite different than that of accused lying-in maids and bad housewives of northern Europe. Like Roper and Purkiss, Scully views these women as active agents, but active in the economy of Venice, not in the development of ideas about witchcraft. If we are to understand those accused of witchcraft as they saw themselves, she asserts, we should perhaps stop using the label "witch," for doing so lets their accusers have the last word.

Hans Peter Broedel

The *Malleus Maleficarum* and the Construction of Witchcraft: Theology and Popular Belief

That "a greater multitude of witches is found among the weaker sex of women than among men" was so obviously a fact to the authors of the *Malleus* that, despite scholastic custom, it was completely unnecessary to deduce arguments to the contrary. Witches, in their view, were entirely more likely to be women than men. The experience of the next two hundred years appeared to vindicate this judgment. Throughout most of central and western Europe, where witchcraft persecution was most intense, between 70 and 80 percent of convicted witches were women.

Hans Peter Broedel, from *The* Malleus Maleficarum *and the Construction of Witchcraft*, 2004, Manchester University Press, Manchester, UK. Reprinted with permission.

Institoris and Sprenger's learned successors in the sixteenth and seventeenth centuries—demonologists and their skeptical opponents alike—concurred with their evaluation: to the well informed, witches were almost always women.

It is possible, however, that Institoris and Sprenger's own construction of witchcraft prejudiced the issue: were women singled out for persecution by later witch-hunters precisely because Institoris and Sprenger had already arbitrarily defined witches as women? Was, in Christina Larner's apt phrase, witch-hunting actually woman-hunting? Or are Institoris and Sprenger basically right—that without any learned coaching, people more often accused women of witchcraft than men? In other words, is the gender bias of texts like the *Malleus* descriptive or prescriptive in nature?

Many modern scholars incline toward the latter view, and look to medieval clerical misogyny, masculine anxieties about the changing social, economic, or familial roles of women, women's control over proscribed medicinal or magical activities, or changing notions of gender to explain why witches were women. Institoris and Sprenger, however, are adamant that their characterization of witches as predominately female is no more than an accurate description of reality: their own first-hand experience and the reliable testimony of trustworthy witnesses show this to be true. Though this claim of objectivity has often been dismissed by scholars, who point out that prior to the *Malleus* men were at least as often identified as witches in learned treatises as were women, it may have substantial validity. Notions of gender intersected the various constituent categories of witchcraft in different ways, and because different authors had quite different notions about what witchcraft was, their opinion of the probable gender of witches varied accordingly. . . .

Clerical authors had for centuries been unanimous in their opinion that women were more prone to superstitious beliefs and observances of all types than were men. In the penitentials of the early Middle Ages, women were consistently singled out as the most likely practitioners of condemned magic and superstition. . . .

The authorities of the late-medieval Church agreed that, by their very nature, women were more superstitious than men. John of Frankfurt, writing in 1412, remarked that

> women are less vigorous in reason and understanding than men, and this is why they are more readily held in the snare of superstitions and are less easily dissuaded from them.

Jean Gerson argued that similar mental weaknesses made "old women, girls and boys, and the slow-witted more prone to observing and believing such superstitions. [Johan] Nider in his *Praeceptorium* elaborated upon this theme, and gave what would become the three canonical reasons for women's inclination to superstitious practices. First, women were simply more credulous than men, and since false and erroneous faith was a principal aim of the devil, he mercilessly exploited this weakness. Second, women were especially vulnerable to diabolic assaults because their impressionable natures made them more apt than men to the influences and revelations of spiritual beings. Finally, because they had "slippery tongues," women were unable to conceal from their sisters what they had learned by their magic arts, and, since they were not strong, they were easily inclined to seek revenge though *maleficium*.

Nider's concluding remark is especially relevant, because it links superstitious belief directly with the practice of black magic. Of course, as has already been pointed out, the practice of *maleficium* was a species of superstition, and insofar as women were more prone to superstition, it made sense to assume that they were also especially prone to witchcraft. Gerson was making just this point when he wrote that because of their propensity for superstitious practices, old women had earned their French epithet "old sorceresses." Nider, however, suggests that women who practice witchcraft are guilty of a specifically moral error rather than an intellectual one. Associating women with superstition, Nider combines ideas drawn from a somewhat different tradition in which women, specifically, were suspected of being *maleficae*.

Other sources, too, attributed harmful sorcery especially to women. As Nider observed, because women were thought less able than men to gratify their thirst for revenge through overt violence, they were widely believed to employ occult means. In his penitential, Burchard warned that some women, "filled with the discipline of Satan," would remove turf from the footprints of unsuspecting victims "and hope thereby to take away their health or life." In a canon devoted to the sins of women, the Anglo-Saxon penitential of Egbert also remarked upon the female propensity for magical harm, charging that

> If a woman works witchcraft and enchantment and [uses] magical philters, she shall fast for twelve months . . . If she kills anyone by her philters she shall fast for seven years.

In the late twelfth century, Peter of Blois accused women of making wax and clay figurines either for the purposes of love magic or for straight-forward revenge. Aragonese laws of the same century condemned to death women guilty of harming men or beasts through ligatures, herbs, or *facticiosa*. Late thirteenth-century Swedish law similarly stated that a woman who killed a man through *maleficium* should be burned. In short, although the sources are not unanimous, and although men were certainly thought able to work magic if so inclined, it seems, as Nider in effect argued, that the common association of women with supersti-tious practices in general, and their inability to exact revenge through other means, combined to make them especially liable to charges of practicing *maleficium*. . . .

Maleficium was not, however, a clearly defined, homogeneous cate-gory, but an amalgamation of harmful conditions that could in some way be linked with particular superstitious practices (from the perspec-tive of the learned observer), particularly meaningful events, or particu-larly motivated individuals (from the perspective of the victim). Some effects, motivations, and practices were more closely associated with the domain of women than were others. To take the most obvious example, love magic of various sorts was invariably recognized as the specific provenance of female magicians. Magic of this type acted principally to increase or diminish sexual passion and marital affection, or to cause sexual dysfunction, sterility or abortion. There were many practices associated with these kinds of *maleficium*, but ligatures, weaving, and binding magic were most common. For this reason, clerical authorities thought that magical operations of this sort were among the most com-mon, and, because they seemed so obviously superstitious and diaboli-cal, they provided clerics with a basic paradigm for "popular" magic. The constant insistence on the part of theologians that such magic was, indeed, diabolical cast women's magic in an increasingly sinister light from the thirteenth century onwards.

Moreover, because problems of impotence, loss of marital affection, and infertility remained widespread, reports and accusations of this type of magic intruded regularly into the pastoral experiences of the clergy. By the fifteenth century, among both witch-theorists like Institoris and Sprenger and clerics less intimately involved in the witch debates, love magic came to be seen not so much as a species of superstition, but as evidence of an overt and explicit pact with the devil. Gabriel Biel (d. 1496) was one of many clerics whose interest in *maleficium* was restricted principally to its practical effects upon marriage, but who nonetheless agreed with the witch-theorists that women did not work their spells through any power of their own, but only "through the help of demons whose pacts and sacraments they employ." . . .

Institoris and Sprenger's innovation was not their insistence that women were naturally prone to practice *maleficium*—in this they were simply following long-standing clerical traditions. Rather, it was their claim that harmful magic belonged *exclusively* to women that was new. If this assertion was granted, then the presence of *maleficium* indicated decisively the presence of a female witch. In the *Malleus*, the field of masculine magic is dramatically limited and male magicians are pointedly marginalized; magic is no longer seen as a range of practices, some of which might be more characteristic of men, some of women, and some equally prevalent among both sexes. Instead, it was the effects of magic that mattered most, and harmful magic, the magic most characteristic of witches, belonged to women. Men might be learned magicians, anomalous archer wizards, or witch-doctors and *superstitiosi*, but very seldom did they work the broad range of *maleficium* typical of witches. . . .

Institoris and Sprenger's misogynist arguments ought not to be taken for granted. Although such views were, no doubt, common in the late Middle Ages, nowhere else are they so forcefully linked to notions of witchcraft. No other fifteenth-century demonologist . . . went much beyond Nider's brief enumeration of women's relevant weaknesses. Institoris and Sprenger, however, conceived of witchcraft as essentially rooted in and defined by women's sins, and as all but inconceivable without it.

Nonetheless, although their misogynist views are violent and striking, they occupy a relatively small part of Institoris and Sprenger's text, being for the most part confined to the single *questio* devoted to women and their natures. This chapter is also more straightforwardly a collection of classical and scriptural passages than is any other in the *Malleus*; on the subject of women, the authors' personal experience, so evident elsewhere, is notably absent. Neither is their pervasively misogynist argument entirely self-consistent, since, if all or most women were indeed so thoroughly evil, then all or most women should be prospective witches, and this is clearly not the case—only certain identifiable women are likely to be witches.

Although the *Malleus* represents women with a variety of shared, inherent weaknesses, and although these weaknesses created a propensity for a variety of sins, one weakness and one sin—carnality and lust, respectively—were especially characteristic of witches. Women, Institoris and Sprenger observed, are more carnal than men, "as their many carnal depravities make clear. By this defect, woman are more enslaved to their desires and the lusts of the flesh, and are correspondingly less rational, spiritual, and intelligent than men. So closely are women and the sin of lust identified in the minds of the authors that they use the very word "woman" as a kind of metaphorical shorthand for lust. Institoris and Sprenger advise that whenever one reads censures of women, these "can be interpreted to mean bodily concupiscence, such that 'woman' is always understood to refer to the lusts of the flesh."

From women's unsatisfied sexual desires sprang their unequaled malice: the most malicious of women were the most lustful; and the most lustful of women were witches, whose sexual appetite was insatiable, and who, "for the sake of quenching their lusts, excite themselves with devils." A witch's perverse sexuality was echoed in her magic: the sexual dysfunction caused by her spells, impeding procreation and legitimate sexual relations, revealed "that witchcraft arises more often from adulteresses, fornicatresses, etc." Other vices characterizing witches, notably infidelity and ambition, paled beside the witch's sexual demands. For this reason, the authors add, "those among ambitious women who burn more to satisfy their depraved lusts—as do adulteresses, fornicatresses, and the concubines of the great—are more infected." This was of enormous concern to Institoris and Sprenger, who worried that, through their magic, witches were gradually insinuating themselves into the highest ranks of European society. A witch in such a position had the power to poison her lover's mind, infecting him with a mad love that no shame or reason could gainsay,

> which threatens both the extermination of the faith and intolerable daily danger, because witches know how to change their minds so that they will permit no harm to be done to them, either by their lovers themselves or by others. And so their numbers daily increase.

In this way, in a few sentences, the authors transform the lust of women into witchcraft, and then into an apocalyptic vision of a world overrun with witches and sexual deviance. . . .

In the *Malleus* witchcraft, femininity, and sexual sin form a tight constellation of interrelated ideas: unbridled feminine sexuality led to witchcraft, which expressed itself most typically in sexual, reproductive, or marital dysfunction; the defining act of the witch was sexual intercourse with the devil; men who committed adultery, whose lusts were unrestrained like a woman's, became liable to the spells of witches; and this feminine vice led directly to a second inversion of the natural order, because such men then allowed themselves to be dominated by women. To Institoris and Sprenger, witchcraft, adultery, and feminine domination lead logically to a coherent, closely interconnected conception of a wide-ranging occult conspiracy against society.

In an interesting passage, the authors ask rhetorically: what is the use of finding remedies for witchcraft when men are so sunk in depravity, and when

> the landed magnates, prelates, and other rich men are most often involved with this wretchedness; indeed this is the time of women . . . , since now the world is full of adultery, especially among the nobles— why should those who hate the remedies write about them?

Institoris and Sprenger believe themselves to be living in an age of adultery, an age of witchcraft—an age of women. The "wretchedness" referred to, which emasculates the great men of the world and makes them subject to their mistresses, may be either witchcraft or adultery, but it matters little, since in Institoris and Sprenger's minds sexual and diabolical sins are so closely identified. Thus, the relationship between sexual deviance and witchcraft was reciprocal: disordered sexual relationships engendered witches, and witchcraft, in turn, disordered sexual relationships.

To Institoris and Sprenger, notions of "witches" and "witchcraft" served to reify, in the form of a wholly corrupt female body, the threats and the anxieties posed by human sexuality. Categorizing witches as embodiments of sinful female sexuality provided the authors with a useful means to control the unbridled sexuality of women that led to misfortune and disaster. As Guido Ruggiero puts it, witches were "sexual outsiders," whose activities, from the perspective of the dominant culture, threatened the natural order of society with the wrath of God. Faced with the possibility of another Sodom, Institoris and Sprenger defined witchcraft so as to localize the responsibility for sexual sin in the bodies of particular women, bodies which could be discovered, punished, and burned. Further, by the very act of categorization order *was* imposed: through the creation of an ordered semantic and intellectual system, Institoris and Sprenger provided the necessary terms for a satisfactory symbolic discussion of human sexuality, order, and power. In this new conceptual field, disordered sexuality is identified with the devil, inverted gender roles and sexual dysfunction with witchcraft, and defective social and political hierarchies with women and women's sins. None of this, however, is possible without the use of witches and witchcraft as an ordering term; witchcraft, as it were, provides the conceptual grid which binds this cognitive map together.

In theoretical terms, such a model makes considerable sense. If one accepts the fiction that women were controlled within an imposed sexual hierarchy, and that feminine power and influence within society were subsumed within a discourse of gender and sexuality, then any disordering manifestation of women's power, influence, or behavior must be understood in terms of sexual perversity. In other words, because men in late-medieval and early-modern Europe tended to view women as sexual beings, existing within a rigidly defined sexual hierarchy, any perception of feminine deviance could logically be interpreted as a manifestation of sexual deviance. As soon as *maleficium* began to be seen as a particularly feminine crime, it became correspondingly necessary to view witchcraft within the rubric provided by sexual perversity. Such a construction seems even more probable if the village discourse of magic conceals a hidden discourse of women's power and of negotiated female social roles. . . .

Taken as a kind of symbolic discourse, the construction of witchcraft and the constellation of related ideas that revolve around it in the *Malleus* are thus neither unique nor unreasonable. It is in this context, perhaps, that we should understand Institoris and Sprenger's otherwise risible fascination with the penis-stealing exploits of witches. It is doubtless true, as Mary O'Neil has suggested, that much of the evidence for this practice was found in a tradition of bawdy, rustic joking which the inquisitors lamentably misunderstood. But, while it may seem absurd to suggest that anyone could seriously believe that a witch could steal a man's penis and keep it alive and well in a bird's nest on a diet of oats, and that, when the owner finally came to retrieve his missing property, the witch would admonish him to put back the largest of those he found because it belonged to a secular priest, it is not absurd to suggest that, by so doing, the witch is only doing in a singularly literal way what she and her sisters were accustomed to do more figuratively: make a man into a woman.

A similar conceptual move may explain why one of the most common forms of *maleficium* was to cause impotence. The fact that men were peculiarly susceptible to such magic suggests that masculine sexuality was itself fragile and easily disturbed: physically, witches could prevent erections and inhibit the flow of semen; psychologically, witches could cool the desire necessary for satisfactory sexual performance. When enchantments permitted a man to perform sexually only with a witch, he acquired a passive, "feminine" social role, a role that mirrored the witch's own sexual servitude to the devil. . . .

Throughout the *Malleus*, Institoris and Sprenger try to establish a reciprocally defining relationship between their construction of witchcraft and the persons of real individuals who might plausibly be suspected of such a crime. For this endeavor they created a very detailed image of the archetypal witch. She was a woman, certainly, but she was not just any woman—so inclusive an ascription would have made nonsense of the category the authors worked so hard to make sensible. Rather the witch of the *Malleus* was determined first by the parameters of the category which Institoris and Sprenger had constructed: more than anything else, a witch to them was a person with a reputation for possessing and using harmful occult powers. Yet Institoris and Sprenger were not satisfied to model their witch so straightforwardly upon popular perceptions of unwelcome sorcerers. The unmodified village magician provided them with no easy points of contact with the larger conceptual field of witchcraft as they understood it. True, any use of magic could be diabolized through the theory of the demonic pact, but there was a considerable difference in their minds between magic, even of the most diabolic stripe, and witchcraft. Much of this difficulty evaporated, however, as soon as the authors chose to emphasize the essentially feminine nature of witchcraft. With witches defined exclusively as women, a fortuitous homology was formed between them, night-flying *strigae*, and the women of the *bonae res*, traditions which formed the core of numerous alternative visions of witchcraft.

Yet the witch in the *Malleus* was also not simply a female sorcerer; she was also the personification of deviant or "bad" female sexuality. For all their misogyny, Institoris and Sprenger never accuse chaste virgins of witchcraft. Indeed, one of the most remarkably virtuous characters to be found in their text is a woman, a "poor little virgin and most devout," who was able to cure bewitched persons by merely reciting the Lord's Prayer with complete faith. Witches instead were adulteresses, murderous midwives, and evil mothers, women defined by the authors as personifications of feminine sexuality. The witch's relationship with the devil was not defined in terms of conventional notions of heretical cults, but through sexual relations: the witch did not worship the devil, she slept with him. The link thus established between female sexuality and physical harm of all sorts gave Institoris and Sprenger's conception of witchcraft an explanatory power that rival conceptions lacked. Witchcraft provided a coherent system through which a whole constellation of socially disordering forces could be understood; it created a conceptual field in which anxieties about social order and material well-being could be arranged, understood, and at least potentially resolved.

Lyndal Roper

Witchcraft and Fantasy in Early Modern Germany

In January 1669, Anna Ebeler found herself accused of murdering the woman for whom she had worked as a lying-in-maid. The means were a bowl of soup. Instead of restoring the young mother's strength, the soup, made of malmsey and brandy in place of rhine wine, had increased her fever. The mother became delirious but, as the watchers at her deathbed claimed, she was of sound mind when she blamed the lying-in-maid for her death. As word spread, other women came forward stating that Ebeler had poisoned their young children too. The child of one had lost its baby flesh and its whole little body had become pitifully thin and dried out. Another's child had been unable to suckle from its mother, even though it was greedy for milk and able to suck vigorously from other women: shortly after, it died in agony. In a third house, an infant had died after its body had suddenly become covered in hot, poisonous pustules and blisters which broke open. The baby's seven-year old brother suffered from aches and pains caused by sorcery and saw strange visions, his mother suffered from headaches, and the whole household started to notice strange growths on their bodies. And a fourth woman found her infant covered with red splotches and blisters, her baby's skin drying out

Lyndal Roper, "Witchcraft and Fantasy in Early Modern Germany," *History Workshop Journal* 32 (1991), by permission of Oxford University Press.

until it could be peeled off like a shirt. The child died most piteously, and its mother's menstruation ceased. All had employed Ebeler as their lying-in-maid. Anna Ebeler was interrogated six times and confessed at

> the end of the second interrogation, when torture was threatened. She was executed and her body burnt on March 23, 1669—a "merciful" punishment practiced in place of burning in the humane city of Augsburg. She was aged 67. Just two months had elapsed since she was first accused.

Anna Ebeler was one of eighteen witches executed in Augsburg. As many more were interrogated by the authorities but cleared of witchcraft; others faced religious courts and yet further cases never reached the courts. Augsburg saw no witch craze. Unlike its south German neighbors, it executed no witch before 1625 and its cases tended to come singly, one or two every few years after 1650. Witchcraft of an everyday, unremarkable kind, the themes of the cases can tell us a great deal about early modern psyches. For Ebeler's crimes were not unusual. It was typical, too, that of her accusers all except one should have been women, and that her victims were young infants aged up to about six weeks and women who had just given birth.

One dominant theme in witch trials in Augsburg is motherhood. Relations between mothers, those occupying maternal roles, and children, formed the stuff of most, though not all, witchcraft accusations in the town. To this extent, early feminist works which focused on birth and midwives in their explanations of witchcraft were making an important observation. But though the trials were concerned with the question of motherhood they were not, if seems to me, male attempts to destroy a female science of birth nor were they concerned with wrestling control of reproduction from women. What is striking is that they were typically accusations brought by mothers, soon after giving birth, against women intimately concerned with the care of the child, most often the lying-in-maid and not the midwife.

Many investigations of witchcraft proceed by trying to explain why women should be scape-goated as witches or what other conflicts may have been at the root of the case—conflicts involving issues with which we are more comfortable, such as struggles over charity, property or political power. However, I want to argue that the cases need to be understood in their own terms by means of the themes they develop. As historians, I think we may best interpret them as psychic documents which recount particular predicaments. Witchcraft cases seem to epitomise the bizarre and irrational, exemplifying the distance which separates us from the past. What interests me, however, is the extent to which early modern subjectivities are different or similar to ours. I shall argue that unless we attend to the imaginative themes of the interrogations themselves, we shall not understand witchcraft. This project has to investigate two sides of the story, the fears of those who accused, and the self-understanding of people who in the end, as I shall argue, came to see themselves as witches.

Our perplexity in dealing with witchcraft confessions derives in part from their epistemological status. As a profession used to assessing documents for their reliability, it is hard to know how to interpret documents which we do not believe to be factual. But witchcraft confessions and accusations are not products of realism, and they cannot be analyzed with the methods of historical realism. This is not to say that they are meaningless: on the contrary, they are vivid, organized products of the mind. Our problem is not that early modern people had a different ontology to our own, believing in a world populated by ghosts who walked at night, devils who might appear in the form of young journeymen, severed arms carrying needles, or wandering souls inhabiting household dust. Rather, all phenomena in the early modern world, natural and fantastic, had a kind of hyper-reality which resided in their significance. Circumstantial details were ransacked for their meaning for the individual, and for what they might reveal about causation and destiny. Causation, which could involve divine or diabolic intervention in human affairs, was understood in terms both moral and religious. Consequently, we need to understand confessions and accusations as mental productions with an organization that is in itself significant. This means analyzing the themes of witchcraft not to tell us about the genealogy of magical beliefs . . . but to tell us about the conflicts of the actors.

In the cases I have explored, witchcraft accusations centrally involved deep antagonisms between women, enmities so intense that neighbours could testify against a woman they had known for years in full knowledge that they were sending her "to a blood bath" as one accused woman cried to her neighbours as they left the house for the chancellery. Their main motifs concern suckling, giving birth, food and feeding; the capacities of parturient women's bodies and the vulnerability of infants. This was surprising, at least to me: I had expected to find in witchcraft a culmination of the sexual antagonism which I have discerned in sixteenth and seventeenth century German culture. The idea of flight astride a broom or pitchfork, the notions of a pact with the Devil sealed by intercourse, the sexual abandonment of the dance at the witches' Sabbath, all seemed to suggest that witchcraft had to do with sexual guilt and attraction between men and women; and that its explanation might lie in the moralism of the Reformation and Counter-Reformation years, when Catholics and Protestants sought to root out prostitution and adultery, shame women who became pregnant before marriage and impose a rigorous sexual code which cast the woman as Eve, the temptress who was to blame for mankind's fall.

Some of the cases I found certainly dealt with these themes; but the primary issue in what we might term a stereotypical case of witchcraft was maternity. The conflicts were not concerned with the social construction of gender but were related much more closely to the physical changes a woman's body undergoes when she bears children. While these clearly have a social meaning and thus a history, the issues were so closely tied to the physical reality of the female sex and to sexual identity at the deepest level that they seemed to elude off-the-peg explanations in terms of female roles and gender conflict. . . .

Witchcraft accusations followed a pattern with a psychic logic: the accusations were made by women who experienced childbirth and their most common type of target was a post-menopausal, infertile woman who was caring for the infant. Often, as in the case we have just explored, she was the lying-in-maid. . . .

What was the substance of the witches' crime? The grief and terror of the witnesses concentrated on the bodies of those who were the victims of witchcraft. Their bodies bore the signs of their martyrdom. As one mother put it, her dead child was covered in sores so that he looked like a devotional image of a martyr. Strange signs were seen: nipples appeared all over the body of one infant, erupting into pussy sores. The legs of another were misshapen and bent. Repeatedly, witnesses stress the physical character of the victim's agony, incomprehensible suffering which cannot be alleviated by the onlookers or by the mother, and which excite hatred, revenge and guilt feelings in part because of the sufferer's innocence. In emotionally laden language, the witnesses describe the "piteous" way a child died, and their own failure to get the child to thrive. It is in this collective world of gossip and advice that the rumors of witchcraft first began, in the grief and guilt of the mother at the loss of the tiny baby, and as the women around them sought to identify the cause of this inexplicable, unbearable suffering. Such gossip could be deadly. It was her employer's tongue, her "wicked gob" as Barbara Fischer put it, using the term applied to animals' mouths, which caused one lying-in-maid to retaliate against her maligner by poisoning her.

The themes of the injury are not only pitiful but frightening. These terrors circle around nourishment and oral satisfaction, evoking powerful pre-Oedipal feelings. The breast, milk and nourishment were its key images. The food the witch gave the mother was sprinkled with white or black diabolic powders or the soups she was fed were poisonous; and these of course influenced the milk the infant received in a very immediate way. Attacks on the mother's food were thus attacks on her infant as well. When the witch killed, she often used poison, perverting the female capacity to nourish and heal. So one grandmother was interrogated three times and tortured because her young grandson suspected witchcraft when he felt queasy after drinking an aniseed water tonic she had given him. The witch could be a kind of evil mother who harmed instead of nourishing her charge. The flow of nourishment could be disrupted so that the child dried out and died. In one case, the witch was accused of literally reversing the flow of the maternal fluids, herself sucking the infant dry and feeding on it. Its mother described how

> its little breasts had been sucked out so that milk had been pressed out from the child's little teats contrary to nature, . . . and from this time on the child had lost weight so that it look as if hardly a pound of flesh remained on it.

Another baby was found to be covered with a myriad of tiny teats as if it had become a mere drinking vessel for the thirsty witch; yet another baby's teats produced "a little drop of white watery liquid." The signs that sorcery was afoot were clearly written on the infant's body. Its skin dried out for lack of fluid, or else erupted in sores as if evil fluids within its body were forcing their way out. Its entire little body might become "red and blue, all mixed up, and rigid and hard, like a plank of wood." The infant might be unable to drink from its own mother, yet when given to another woman, he was "so hearty in sucking that it made her weep." . . . In all these cases, the infant's feeding had been disrupted so that no satisfactory nourishing could take place and the relation between mother and child was destroyed. Feeding had been reversed and the infant's young rosy flesh was wasting away while the old witch thrived.

These beliefs rested on a whole economy of bodily fluids. A post menopausal woman, the old witch was in a sense a dry woman who, instead of feeding others well, diverted nourishment to her own selfish ends. Older widows were believed to have the power to ruin young men sexually, and youths were warned against such women because they were sexually ravenous, and would suck out their seed, weakening them with their insatiable hunger for seminal fluid and contaminating them with their own impurities. The old witch's fluids did not flow outwards. Often her magic was directed against fertility, making women barren. As was well known, witches could not weep, and old widows could neither menstruate or suckle children. Instead, so the science of demonology explained, she was nourishing the Devil. The warts for which the executioner searched her naked body were the diabolic teats on which the Devil sucked. . . .

Witches were women who did not feed others except to harm them. Failed exchanges of food typified a witch's interactions with her neighbours. So one woman, suspected of being a witch, offered two sisters who lived in her house a dish of Bavarian carrots. Yet this was a two-edged peace offering. The woman insisted the sisters eat the food, and sat with them until it was all consumed. One of the two was pregnant, and the dish made her ill. The witch said the food would strengthen the child within her, yet this wish for the child's health actually meant its opposite. Like the fairies of fairytale who are not invited to the baptism, the old woman's evil "wishes" for the infant's future blighted its life. And this could happen in a trice, even without the witch's intention: Maria Gogel explained how "if a person ate plain milk, peas, meat or cheese, and chanced upon a child and merely said 'Oh, what a beautiful child' immediately it is bewitched."

Witches' other means of harming was by "trucken," pressing down on the infant or its mother. The verb may also refer to the effort of pushing down in labour. In witchcraft it is used in at least three different contexts: to describe the way the Devil forces one woman to do evil, the smothering of an infant, and a mysterious kind of oppression felt by the woman who has just given birth. Georg Schmetzer's wife complained of feeling that something was coming to her at night, lying on her and pressing her so that she suffered from pain down one side. She suspected the lying-in-maid of coming to her bed in the evening and lying on top of her—a fear strengthened by the maid's unorthodox suggested remedy for her backache that she should undress and lie on top of her in a kind of all over massage. Anna Maria Cramer believed a witch was coming to her at night and lying on her, pressing down on her pregnant body. Another woman heard a mysterious voice crying "druckdich Madelin, druckdich" (be pressed down, Maggie, be pressed down) and she felt something trying to bite her neck. Her lying-in-maid Euphrosina Endriss was finally brought to confess that she had "pressed" the baby she carried about with her, squashing its skull so that it died. The themes here do not appear to be directly sexual. Rather, what is described is a kind of heavy, deadly embrace, again typified by an ambiguous mixture of love and hatred which might kill the infant with a kind of excess of maternality. The mother's feelings have more to do with extreme depression, immobility and passivity. In all these cases, the mother seems to suffer from a kind of lassitude, unable to move or act to protect herself and her child beyond screaming for help—she cannot fight back, and the oppressive sensation of smothering symbolizes her inaction and the diffuse nature of the threat to herself and her child, causing harm not from within her own body but in a kind of anonymous pressure from without. As with the disturbances of nourishment, the violence is indirect, its source unclear and retaliation impossible.

Why should it have been motherhood which engendered these murderous antagonisms between women? Mothers in the early modern period spent the first few weeks of their child's life "lying in," recuperating from the birth. These six or so weeks were set apart from normal life as the woman retreated into the lying-in-room, resting in the bed from which the husband would be banished. There she was the center of the house, and there, lying in bed, she would entertain her female friends who had supported her during the birth, holding a women-only birth party with wine and delicacies to celebrate her delivery. If she could afford it, she would employ a lying-in-maid, whose job it was to care for both mother and child. During this period when her life was predominantly lived in the world of women, she could not leave the house and some believed her to be under the power of the Devil. Evil influences might make their presence felt; ghosts might appear. At the end of this time she would go to church for the ceremony of purification or churching, which marked her return to marital cohabitation and public life; and the lying-in-maid would be dismissed. Today the attendant psychic conflicts of this period of the mother's life might be described as relating to the loss of the pregnant state and the ending of the unity of mother and child. Together with the incessant demands on time and energy that the new infant makes, these might be related to maternal depression and to a mixture of feelings toward the infant which may extend to anger, envy or even to wishing harm to the child.

What seems to emerge from these cases, however, is a different set of historically formed psychic mechanisms for dealing with this predicament. . . . In the first few weeks of life the child was at its most delicate, as feeding had to be established, either with the mother, a wet nurse or else by hand. Interestingly, it was during this period or else immediately after the lying-in-maid's departure that the child began to ail. But instead of seeking the source of her ills in post-natal depression, within herself, as we would, the mother's anxieties about the child's fate and her own ability to nourish it were directed outwards, so that harm to either mother or baby was believed to have been caused by another. . . .

The lying-in-maid was almost over-determined as the culprit, should witchcraft be suspected. Old, no longer capable of bearing a child herself and widowed, she was a woman who housed alone and was a transitory member of the households of others. No longer at the heart of a bustling household of her own, she was a hired member of the family for whom she worked, privy to the most intimate physical secrets of the bodies of those she tended. An interloper, she was never accorded a real place of her own—one even had to share a cramped bed with a servant which was so narrow that she fell out of it in the night. The lying-in-maid undermined the settled hierarchies of the household at a time when the new baby's arrival overturned the workshop's rhythm. For the six to eight weeks after the mother had given birth, she alone carried out the duties of a mother, dandling, washing and swaddling the baby; and caring for its mother, giving her nourishing soups. Just as she had no place in the house she might call her own, so also her work life left her humiliatingly dependent on others: on the midwife, who trained her, recommended her, and from whom she might hear of her next job; on her employer, the mother, who might choose not to re-employ her and who could blacken or enhance her reputation by gossiping with other mothers about her. She lacked the midwife's qualifications and official status as an employee of the Council, nor did she have the luxury of the midwife's official retainer to tide her over slack periods. Often, it was her very insecurity which was turned against her. One woman who went down on her knees to plead with her accusers only made them the more convinced that something was amiss; frightened people were likely to be caught in the Devil's snares.

But she was also invested with awesome power. She had her particular recipes for strengthening soups, she had her methods for bringing up young infants, she "alone cared for the child, and it was in no-one's hand but hers" as one lying-in-maid accused of witchcraft put it. She was strong at a time when the new mother was ill and weakened, and she was fulfilling her tasks. The new mother, sleeping alone in the marital bed, was not "mistress of the household" in sexual terms: old, infertile and unhusbanded as the lying-in-maid was, she represented a double threat to the mother, standing both for the mother's own future and sometimes representing a sexual threat as well. If the husband were "up to no good," the lying-in-maid, who in many cases had borne illegitimate children, might be suspected.

The lying-in-maid dealt with the waste products of the body, she had access to the afterbirth and to cauls, and she had the care of the infant's body. One lying-in-maid was accused of purloining the afterbirth, burning it at night under her bed in a bid to harm mother and child; and it was only with great difficulty that she managed to persuade the judges that she had merely been attempting to clean a pewter bowl. Another was foolish enough to accuse the midwife of hiding a baby's caul. Taking the "little net" to the child's father in the hope of gaining a handsome tip for her trouble, she not only antagonized the midwife but led people to suspect that she had her own nefarious purposes for the caul. Through the waste products of the body, things invested with their owner's power—hair, nails, afterbirth—the sorcerer could control the individual to whom they had belonged. These substances could be used to direct the emotions, causing the bewitched person to fall in love; and they could be used to harm. In this cosmology, emotions were highly sensitive to manipulation of the body. Emotions, like physical pains, could be the result of external events and could readily be ascribed to other people, their source sought outside rather than in the self. . . .

Above all, it was the lying-in-maid's maternal role which placed her in the role of suspect. Sometimes this might lead to straightforward conflicts over upbringing—Euphrosina Endriss was blamed for mollycoddling a child, giving it too many warm cushions. Midwives and mothers suspected maids of bathing the child in water that was too hot, or of swaddling its limbs too tightly so that it might become deformed. Injuries inflicted in the first few weeks of the infant's life might not manifest themselves for years: the failure of one child to speak, harm to one girl's reproductive organs, were all blamed on the lying-in-maid. "Why must it always be the lying-in-maid who is to blame?" asked one accused woman. A woman who could not be trusted, a woman unable to bear children herself, she was tailor-made for the role of the ultimate evil mother. The very intensity of the bonds between her and the child, as the person who enjoyed a primary attachment to the baby in its first weeks of life, were also the reason to suspect her. As with all witchcraft, it was the powerful ambivalence of feeling which nourished witchery: witchcraft was to be feared not from those indifferent to you, but from those whose relationship was close and whose intimate knowledge of your secrets could be turned to harm. Consequently every good wish a suspected woman might make for the health and wellbeing of an infant was charged with its opposite. So one young mother feared the frequent visits the lying-in-maid made to her infant's cradle, standing over it. She later discovered a knife underneath its crib.

And the lying-in-maid had a motive: envy. Envy was the motor of witchcraft as seventeenth century people understood it. One of the seven deadly sins, it was a feeling which could have material force. . . . Envy involves wishing harm towards an object. In the logic of sorcery, where emotions might be externalized onto things outside the person and where feelings had active force, the emotion itself was the wellspring of injury. Circumstances conspired to make the lying-in-maid appear a likely sufferer from envy and hatred. As seventeenth century people saw it, she was poor and single; her employer had a workshop and was comfortably off. Infertile herself, she tended a mother who was surrounded by the love, attention and presents of other women; and who had a baby. By contrast her own children had been conceived illegitimately or had died in infancy. So Barbara Fischer had been raped by her stepfather twenty years before she found herself accused of witchcraft. The child of their relationship had died just a few days after birth. At the time, she had begged the Council to let her marry, blaming her stepfather's refusal to let her wed for her own fall into sin with him. But the Council had punished her by confining her inside the house for her shame; and, two decades later, she explained her fall into witchcraft as the consequence of not being allowed to marry and become a mother. Interestingly, her diabolic lover appeared to her in the form of a journeyman dyer, the trade her stepfather had followed. Admission of the envy she felt for the mother she tended was, in her case as in many others, the first step in her interrogation towards a full confession. The witch too fully believed that to feel envy for a woman was to wish to harm her, and in this emotional world, where things were invested with meaning, emotions could also act directly. Anna Schwayhofer explained she had summoned the Devil when, conscious of her own sins, she despaired of God's mercy: she had taken communion without confession, and she felt "great envy, resentment and enmity to various persons."

To this point I have been exploring the psychic world of those who made the accusation. . . .

But the witch herself had an understanding of her own behaviour. Its main element concerned her own admission of envy. This was the breaking point which then catapulted her into a range of other confessions about the Devil. These form a distinct layer of testimony, elicited under torture and often given with a considerable degree of reluctance. In other contexts, however, where children were not the target of malice, the Devil could be a dominant theme: so the young Regina Schiller baffled authorities all over southern Germany for over a decade with her bizarre physical contortions and extravagant confessions, telling the authorities about her lurid pacts with the Devil and showing the written contract for so many years and so many days, the number indicated with little strokes of blood because she could not count so far.

By contrast, the witches whose fates we have considered here were chary of admitting even to flying or attending the witches' Sabbath, and when they did so they presented themselves as outsiders, women who hung at the edges of the wild assemblies, without finding friends amongst the fellow witches. One witch recalled that the others came from elsewhere, they wore masks and spoke with accents she could not understand, and they were well dressed, not of her class. She did not dance, and at the feast, few people sat at her table. This was certainly a means of cutting down their involvement and guilt and yet the strong sense of being outsiders which their words convey suggest that the fantasies mirrored their current experience of isolation, socially marginal, and shorn of friends who might succour them. Their relations with the Devil were distant and unsatisfactory. Even when conviction was a certainty, these accused witches still tried to minimize the extent of their sexual involvement with the Devil. . . . Instead, dirt and degradation feature. This is most evident in the names of their diabolic lovers, which had names such as hen-dirt, gosseshit and the like, names which combine animality with excrement. Common to almost all is the acknowledgement of the feeling of hatred and the sense of being deserted by God, exiled from the community of fellow Christians. Yet their deeds are projected onto the Devil: he whispers what they should do, he gives them the powder, he forces them to harm the children. In this way their hostile emotions (apart from the first feelings of hatred) could be projected onto the Devil and dissociated from themselves, in a kind of splitting characteristic of witchcraft at every level.

But if I am right that witchcraft could involve conflicts between women that have to be understood in psychic terms, we still need to explain why such conflicts were open to expression through witchcraft at a particular historical moment. After all, even in the town we have been considering here, there were witchcraft cases which followed this pattern or drew on these motifs for only a little over a century; and they were concentrated in the years from 1650 to 1700. After 1700, we can notice a dramatic inversion of the pattern. Now, children rather than their mothers became the objects of suspicion. Between 1724 and 1730, thirty-one child witches were locked up, while after the death of one suspected witch in custody in 1699, no older women were condemned. This reversal suggests to me that the dynamics of much witch-hunting have to be sought in the relationship between mother and child which, after a certain point, switched to the child rather than its mother. I suspect that witch-hunting in the seventeenth century must in part be related to the idealisation of motherhood in baroque society. This is not simply a matter of misogyny: after all, it was because the state took the fears and accusations of suffering mothers seriously that cases could be prosecuted. Germany in the latter seventeenth century was a society recovering from the ravages of the Thirty Years' War. In Augsburg, the population had halved: small wonder that people feared attacks on fertility. Here the widow played a double role. On the one hand, attacks on old, postmenopausal women are a staple of misogynist tract from the late sixteenth century onwards. But on the other, the widow, I have been suggesting, was merely the mother's mirror image, a woman who could be the repository of all the fears about evil mothers. Maternal hostility and fears about evil mothers could not easily be expressed directly in a society where Mary was revered by both Catholics and Protestants, and where the image of the suffering Madonna was ubiquitous. Hence, too, the tendency in folk tale to populate a story with evil stepmothers who alone can represent the bad mother, keeping pure the image of the good, dead mother. Here it is not coincidence that this period also saw a dramatic increase in executions of the ultimate evil mother, the woman who commits infanticide: such women had to be executed. This rise occurred from the early seventeenth century onwards, even though the Imperial Law Code of 1532 had paved the way for such executions three generations before. Together with witchcraft, this accounted for the vast bulk of women executed in Augsburg in the seventeenth century. The themes of much witchcraft, I would argue, are to be found not in a simple sexual antagonism between men and women, but in deeply conflicted feelings about motherhood. . . .

Diane Purkiss

Women's Stories of Witchcraft in Early Modern England: The House, the Body, the Child

Despite feminism's fascination with the figure of the witch, there have been surprisingly few attempts to read women witnesses' depositions at witch trials as texts authored by early modern women, texts that illustrate women's ideas about witches and witchcraft. There are several reasons for this neglect. The depositions of women witnesses are often presented as impenetrable or unreadable, offering a tangled network of signs which point only into a disorderly mass of "primitive" superstition. For example, Clive Holmes compares the depositions of the possessed and midwives to "those who testified simply to their experience of the witch's *maleficium*." He writes dismissively that "this kind of testimony [i.e. to *maleficium*] is

Diane Purkiss, "Women's Stories of Witchcraft in Early Modern England: The House, the Body, the Child," *Gender and History* 7:3 (1995), by permission of Oxford University Press.

more inchoate than the other two categories; it lacks their conceptual clarity and sophistication." Some judges and intellectuals in the early modern period found women's stories as incomprehensible (and unbelievable) as Holmes does. For example, Reginald Scot's account of the trials at St Osyth, Essex of 1582 reduces women's testimonies to small-time malice rather than trying to understand their stories about witchcraft as part of a coherent system of popular belief. This illustrates the dangers of using the works of the learned to interpret the stories of village women, since there is nothing "simple" or "inchoate" about such testimonies. Careful reading of them shows that they depend on a set of assumptions and tropes which make sense on their own terms, reflecting and managing the fears and desires of village women. . . .

. . . [T]erms like "witch" and "witchcraft" were not single or fixed, but highly unstable terms, sites of conflict and contestation between diverse groups. The term "witch" was labile, sliding across a number of different and competing discourses. It figured in, and was refigured in, the discursive self-definitions of both absolutism and anti-tyranny, both Puritanism and Counter-Reformation Catholicism, both colonialism and resistance to colonialism. It could be appropriated by patriarchy, protofeminism, medicine, skeptical rationalism and radical religion. In villages, too, witchcraft could become a central signifier in debates about power, employment, norms, values, property rights and land ownership. None of this implies that the supernatural aspects of witchcraft did not matter; rather they mattered in a variety of ways in different contexts. As the term "witch" traversed these diverse spaces, its own meaning was revised silently or openly rewritten, redefined and reshaped. Women were one among many of the groups which could take up the term "witch" and negotiate with it in these ways.

In what follows, I argue that some women's stories of witchcraft constituted a powerful and useful *fantasy* which enabled village women to negotiate the fears and anxieties of housekeeping and motherhood. Throughout, I am using the term fantasy in its quasi-psychoanalytic sense. In psychoanalysis, a fantasy is a story in which people both express and relieve their unconscious (and sometimes their conscious) fears, conflicts and anxieties. This conception of fantasy does not imply a judgement about the truth or falsity of women's stories or their beliefs; I am not interested in determining whether supernatural events took place, still less in deciding what "natural" events underlay them. In reading women's stories as fantasies, I do not intend to offer an explanation for all witch-beliefs, or any other grand historical narrative. As a feminist literary critic, I wanted to see if anything could be gained from a close reading of various quite well-known texts, mostly trial reports and witnesses' depositions, as stories told by women. I wanted to explore the meanings which lay within their vividness, their poignancy, their tenderness, their exact and exacting metaphors. I focus on cases where the majority of witnesses were women, and look at those cases in the context of sixteenth- and seventeenth-century witchcraft depositions in general. When early modern women thought about witches and constructed their figurations of witchcraft, their shaping fantasies reflected the need to establish and/or maintain a social identity within the village community. Accusers and accused worked and lived within certain definitions of female identity which were not entirely of their making and over which they exercised little control; as well as shapers of culture, these women were also shaped by it. Both witches and the women who feared them moved in a world which defined a woman's role in terms of the household: woman was first a producer of children and secondly the one who organized and maintained the household economy. However, within this circumscribed space a rich and elaborate network of cultural meanings was assigned to productive tasks, and these meanings in turn defined female identity. Women's stories of witchcraft were caught in this network of meanings. For women, a witch was a figure who could be read against and within her own social identity as housewife and mother.

Agnes Heard was one of several women arraigned as witches at St Osyth, Essex, in 1582. The indictment reads: "Agnes Heard, of Little Oakley, spinster, . . . on 1 Jan 1582 she bewitched to death a cow, 10 sheep and 10 lambs (£4) belonging to John Wade." This indictment, which foregrounds a male witness and plaintiff speaking about male arenas of husbandry, conceals the role that women deponents played in accusing Agnes and providing depositions giving evidence against her. The women's depositions against Agnes Heard focus on a series of domestic and familial incidents, incidents in which housewifery goes awry or children sicken. One of the deponents was Bennet Lane, the wife of William Lane. Bennet tells of her encounters with Agnes: when Bennet was a widow, Agnes Heard is at her house, and she gives Agnes a pint of milk, also lending her a dish to take it home in. Agnes keeps the dish for two or three weeks, so Bennet sends Agnes's daughter home to get it, remarking tartly that "though I gave thy mother milk to make a posset, I gave her not my dish." Agnes duly sends the dish back, but no sooner is it returned but Bennet's spinning goes wrong:

> she could no longer spin nor make a thread to hold. Whereas she was so grieved that she could not spin, she took her spindle and went to the grindstone therewith once or twice, and ground it as smooth as she could, thinking it might be by some ruggedness of the spindle that did cause her thread to break; and so when she had ground it as well as she could, she went again to work therewith, thinking that then it would have done, but it would not do no better than it did before. Then she saith, that she remembered herself, and took her spindle and put it into the fire and made it red-hot, and then cooled it again and went to work, and then it wrought as well as ever it did at any time before.

Bennet first tries the everyday method of grinding the spindle. Then, having "remembered herself," she applies a very common type of countermagic, the heating of a betwitched object until red-hot or the application of a red-hot object to it.

However, Bennet is soon in trouble again. Agnes Heard owes her twopence, and Bennet sets out to collect it because her own church tithes are due. Rashly, she also tries to borrow some more money from Agnes, who explains that she hasn't any spare cash. Bennet tries to insist because church tithes are due that day, and Agnes eventually agrees to borrow the money from a neighbour. She gives the borrowed money to Bennet, who says: "Now I owe you a pint of milk, come for it when you will and you shall have it." Agnes collects her milk and some butter the next day, but Bennet now develops serious problems in the dairy: "the next day, she would have fleet [skimmed] her milk bowl, but it would not abide the fleeting, but would rope and roll as it were the white of an egg; also the milk being on the fire it did not so soon seethe as it would quail, burn by, and stink." At first Bennet thinks of natural causes: her animals' feeding may be the problem, or her vessels may not be clean. So, as before, she begins with natural remedies. She scalds all her vessels and scours them with salt, but this has no effect. Afraid of losing her entire stock of cream and milk, she recalls another countermagical remedy: "she took a horseshoe, and made it red-hot, and put it into the milk in her vessels, and so into her cream; and then, she saith, she could seethe her milk, fleet her cream, and make her butter in good sort as she had before." . . .

It would not be fair to describe this case as typical, but Bennet's story does reveal themes and issues which arise repeatedly in other stories.

In shaping their stories of witchcraft, women focused on an encounter with the suspected woman involving either an exchange, usually of food or food-related items, or a failed exchange of food, or sometimes merely a discussion about food. On other occasions, an exchange or failed exchange resulted in disrupted food production.

The preoccupation with food found in the depositions can be understood in the context of the crisis in the early modern rural economy in the late sixteenth and early seventeenth centuries. As a result of certain economic and political pressures, the situation of the rural poor worsened dramatically as the sixteenth century wore on, and they became increasingly dependent on a limited diet of pulses, grain and bread, chickens, pigs and "white meats" [dairy products]. The last were especially crucial since they provided the only ongoing sources of protein and fat, and in this context the strong association of bewitchment with the dairy is significant. Much of the pressure from this scarcity and marginality fell on the housewife, exhorted from every pulpit to manage frugally, and responsible for dairying and for the survival of herself and her household. Acute anxieties therefore developed around the disruption of dairying. When the butter failed to churn, or the milk to skim, the result might be starvation.

However, women's domestic responsibilities were heavily invested with symbolic as well as pragmatic significance. In the case of Bennet and Agnes, we have already seen that Bennet struggles to reassert the control over spinning and dairying which she believes Agnes has taken from her. Housewifely authority inheres in the ability to transform "natural" items into cultural items, to do a certain kind of cultural work whereby wool is transformed into thread and milk into cream and whey. . . . When this process is disrupted by witchcraft, the authority and identity of the housewife concerned are put in question; she as housewife can no longer predict or control the processes of transformation required. Instead, witchcraft characteristically produces an estranging and shaming effect or utter disorder, dirt and pollution: milk behaves like white of egg, ale turns sour and smells vile, cows produce blood instead of milk, and pease becomes stinking and uneatable. Since domestic labor is all about maintaining order by ensuring that matter does not become wrongly placed, these supernatural events directly threaten the housewife's self-image as authoritative and competent, as can be seen by Bennet's attempts to restore her authority by asserting her housewifely skill and attempting to transform the dirt of bewitchment into cleanness.

If we think of Bennet's description of the effects of Agnes's acts as her *fantasy* about what a witch was, we can see that, first, for Bennet the witch is a kind of antihousewife, her own dark Other who causes pollution where there should be order, who disrupts food supplies which must be ordered and preserved, who wastes what is necessary. Secondly, the witch is an antihousewife because she *usurps* Bennet's authority over the household in order to misuse it, to invert it. Bennet's power to order and transform is displaced and replaced by the witch's power to disorder and pollute. Thirdly, the witch "is" the identity that Bennet must reject, suppress, define herself against, in order to develop and fashion her own identity as a successful, empowered housewife. She is Bennet's dark twin, a housewife who is not a housewife, who is the dark shadow of Bennet's own existence. Whereas most historians see the witch as the Church's Other, or as man's Other, I'm suggesting here that early modern women could also represent the witch as their Other, that female anxieties, fears and self-fashioning could also shape the notion of "witch" at popular level. . . .

The same themes of domestic authority and the breach of boundaries recur and are amplified in another female fantasy of witchcraft which overlaps with the one I have sketched above. These are stories in which the identity of the deponent (and often the witch) as mother is central to understanding the stories that are told. As with the stories involving housewifery, food is a central issue. The role of mother and the role of food provider are linked even today, and this linkage was even more central to early modern notions of maternal identity. The mother's body provides the child with his or her first food needs, in the womb and/or at the breast, and as part of her cultural work the mother as housewife is responsible for producing and providing food for the household. Moreover, children were the principal economic and social products of women's labor. While richer parents might value children as a source of continuity in an inheritance system, poorer parents needed their labor. Food supplies had to be produced and maintained in order to produce and maintain children.

Anxieties about maternity began before the birth. Pregnancy was often a worrying time for early modern women, especially if the child was greatly desired. It was usually understood as a time of illness, and early modern medical texts by men and women alike focus on the problem of how to prevent miscarriage. Medical science argued that birth defects or even the death of the child might result from the expectant mother's own thoughts or feelings about the baby. In this anxious context, it is not surprising that some women came to believe that witches could cause miscarriage. Jennet Hargraves, for example, was said to have caused the death of a child in the womb, while another suspect's familiar had "nipped out the brains of an unborn child." Some of the patients of Richard Napier, the Buckinghamshire physician and astrologer, also believed that witches had caused their miscarriages or stillbirths: Mistress Underhill was said by Napier to "fear ill means" when she miscarried in March 1627, while Mistress Mason lost her baby, pined and wasted away after a suspected witch had threatened her for buying a hare. Mistress Woodward also suspected witchcraft when she had a succession of stillbirths after a property dispute with Alice Coleman. These events are explicable in the light of what we have already learned about the image of the witch as usurper of the authority of other women over the domestic realm. Medical and popular knowledge alike affirmed the power of the mother's thoughts and feelings to shape and injure the child *in utero*. By usurping her place, the witch or her familiar could do the same. Moreover, the thoughts to be avoided by the expectant mother are countermaternal: the mother must *avoid* unfeminine feelings of rage, frustration and fury if she is to avoid miscarriage. These feelings often characterise the witch in other accounts precisely because the witch is the opposite of what the early modern woman should be. Here again the witch plays the role of dark Other of the early modern woman, expressing and acting on feelings and desires that women must repress for the sake of others in order to construct their identities as mothers.

The notion of the witch as antimother plays an even more obvious role in the next group of stories I shall examine, cases involving childbirth and lying-in. As Adrian Wilson has recently demonstrated, childbirth was a female ceremony and festival for the early modern woman. The space of the birth was a collective female space, constituted by the presence of gossips and midwife and the absence of men. The gossips were responsible for physically and symbolically enclosing the birthing-room, which was done by blocking keyholes and hanging up heavy curtains. The gossips also prepared the mother's caudle, a hot drink containing ale or wine warmed with sugar and spices, symbolically mothering the mother by supplying her with this special food. Its specialness, like the enclosure of the room, marked the mother's separation from normal household affairs and from the outside world. . . .

Early modern childbirth was a woman's festival, and in this context it is not surprising that like other festivals, exclusion from it could become a signifier of witchcraft. No fewer than five of Richard Napier's female patients reported that they believed themselves to have been bewitched by women who had not been invited to be gossips. Though the birth itself was crucial for constituting a community of women and an enclosed space, its evident that these very processes created a category of notionally harmful outsiders who might act against the controls which they had not helped to set up. The witch's disorder and antimaternal destructiveness again appear as the dark Other and alien alternative to the strictly organised process of controlling nature and pollution on which the birthing ritual centres and which the women must control in order to prevent harm. On other occasions, the witch selected birth as the moment at which to assail a woman with whom she had fallen out in other circumstances. Sometimes she chose the opening of the house for the childbirth ceremony as a moment to enter it in order to harm the vulnerable woman. . . .

The process of attempting to safeguard the woman and child continued after the birth itself was complete, during the lying-in stage. The lying-in period involved a series of carefully marked stages through which both mother and baby pass. It is characterised by a mixture of anxiety about closure and an unexpected openness. The new mother remained in the closed-off birthing room, but the house became progressively more and more open to visitors who partake of household food supplies shared with the mother. This combination of openness and anxiety about boundaries sets the scene for witchcraft fears and stories to develop around the mother's lying-in. As well, during lying-in the mother's authority over the household is suspended; she is no longer up and about, patrolling its boundaries. Since witchcraft occurs when women lose control of the processes of housewifery to another woman, it is not surprising that a woman who has already renounced household control seems especially vulnerable.

One Yorkshire story involves the importance of the ceremony of childbirth and the lying-in period to women's fears of and fantasies about witchcraft. Joan Jurdie was presented twice for witchcraft. The second presentation involved numerous depositions from women about a series of events around the childbed and lying-in of Janet Murfin, who was dead by the time of the trial, allegedly owing to Jurdie's *maleficium*. Anne Judd deposed that:

> Joan Jurdie, wife of Leonard Jurdie of Rossington, being bidden to the labour of Peter Murfin's wife, of Rossington, did not come [for] three or

four days after she was delivered, and when she came she would neither eat nor drink with the said Murfin's wife, and because the said Peter Murfin did not come into the house to drink with her, and this examinate going home with her unto her own house, she said to this examinate that Peter Murfin would not come in and drink with her, but tell him that I say he had as good have come. And the day following this examinate, having occasion to go to the said John Jurdie's house, Jane Throughheare, servant to the said Jurdie, asked this examinate how her sister and child did, this examinate made answer again, very weakly, whereupon the said Joan Jurdie made answer again, abide her, she is not at the worst, she will be worse yet.

The first notable thing here is the interchange of bodies and persons around the events of childbed. Anne Judd and Joan Jurdie are both on the move, entering and leaving the houses of others. Secondly, there is Joan's behaviour in connection with those activities. She has been invited to attend the birth, probably as a gossip, but does not put in an appearance till after delivery, during the first week of lying-in. Just as Joan has not involved herself in the community of women around birth, so she rejects the symbolic involvement in that community provided by eating and drinking with the new mother during lying-in. Joan Jurdie marks her separateness from Janet's person and household by refusing her gestures of inclusion. The grounds for her refusal also imply a disorderly carelessness about rules; usually men were excluded from the ceremonies of childbed, and even from the lying-in room in the early stages, and presumably these rules explain Peter Murfin's refusal to come in and drink with Jurdie. Consequently it is not surprising that when Janet began to feel ill her thoughts turned to Jurdie's visit. "Woe worth her" she remarked to Anne Judd, "for I did well till Joan Jurdie wife came." Katherine Dolfin, another deponent, reported that she too called on Janet during the lying-in period, when Janet told her "I was never well since Saturday that Jurdie wife was here." Jurdie had refused to share food with Janet, and now Janet cannot eat at all: "I could never eat any meat but supping-meat [since Saturday]." Peter Murfin, the sole male deponent in this case remarked that his wife's milk had turned to blood before she died. Witches often had this effect on maternal lactation. This reflects not only the witch's usual power to disrupt both food and maternity, but also the acute anxieties about the maternal milk supply which beset early modern women.

As in the case of Agnes Heard, Joan Jurdie was constructed as a witch by Janet Murfin and other women in Rossington in that she evaded housewifely and ceremonial control and order. She refused the hospitality which symbolised those rules and controls, but she had nevertheless crossed the boundaries of the household. Since Jurdie had refused to help safeguard Janet's childbirth and to acknowledge her role as food provider, it's not surprising that the effect of her malevolence was to pollute Janet's body as a source of food for her infant. The turning of Janet's milk to blood symbolises the witch's transformation of the woman from mother into antimother, from giver of life to giver of death. At the same time, Janet came to resemble Joan in this: Joan refused symbolic oneness with Janet as mother, thus casting herself as an antimother who then also transforms Janet into an antimother. . . .

Another St Osyth story involves the moment when the lying-in period ended and mother and child were about to be welcomed back into the everyday life of the village community. Joan Smith deposed that she was met at the door of her house by a group of women; the occasion was that of her first churchgoing after the birth of her child. The women were at the door ready to draw the latch; this account may point to a ceremonious reception of the new mother and child by the other women of the community:

> Joan saith, that one holy day in the afternoon since Michaelmas last, she had made herself ready to go to church, and took in her arms her young child, and opening her door, her mother (grandmother to the child), one Redworth's wife, and Sellis his wife were at the said door ready to draw the latch, she this examinate telling her mother she was coming out of doors to churchward. Whereat the grandmother to the child took it by the hand and shook it, saying, "Ah, Mother Pugs, art thou coming to church?" And Redworth's wife looking on it said "Here is a jolly and likely child, God bless it." After which speech Sellis his wife said "She hath never the more children for that, but a little babe to play withal for a time."

Plainly, Joan saw Cicely Sellis's words as sinister; she shows too much knowledge of and interest in Joan's household in general, and the child in particular. Joan deposed that within a short time after that her child sickened and died, but she added an unusual disclaimer, saying that her conscience would not allow her to charge Cicely with the death of the child. It's significant that the encounter happens on the doorstep, the very threshold of the house and the village community, a threshold which Joan and her child were just about to cross for the first time, perhaps to seek the protection of churching or baptism. Their liminal location symbolises their liminal status, about to rejoin the normal life of the village, and therefore vulnerable to witchcraft.

Cases of witchcraft involving children occurred so frequently that even the learned noticed the phenomenon. These stories share common themes, presenting the perceived genesis of the bewitchment of the child and the fantasy-image of the witch that this suggests. Many cases involving the bewitchment of a child centred on a gift of food. Jane Brooks gave an apple to a small boy, stroked his right side and shook him by the hand; her touch alone sent him into a violent convulsion, but he became much worse when he unwisely ate the apple she had given him. Mary Wade, confessing to bewitching Elizabeth Mallory, a daughter of a gentry family, was pressed to recall whether the Mallory family had ever received food from her; eventually she remembered offering them a dish of nuts when they visited her. When Jane Watson brought an apple to the child of Jonas Cudworth, the child reported that "she was very earnest [for me to] have it." These two stories show the importance interrogators and witnesses attached to the gift of food as a means of child-bewitchment. These suspects used a gift of food to take control of a child's body in a manner resembling the methods of Snow White's wicked stepmother. The stepmother figure is not irrelevant to the discussion, since early modern women tended to see witches as inverted mothers or counter-mothers who unsurped control of the home and family.

Another way to understand these cases is presented by the following unusually detailed deposition from Yorkshire, which offers a reading of the meaning of food in the context of witchcraft. The deponent is Mary Moor, a self-appointed female witchfinder whose accusations were rejected by local officialdom. Nevertheless her words indicate a way of interpreting contact between witch and victim at odds with the sociological explanations of Thomas and Macfarlane. Moor deposed that:

> she heard Susan the wife of Joseph Hinchcliffe, and Ann the wife of Thomas Shillitoe, both of Denbigh, discoursing thus together. The said Susan said to Anne "if thou canst but get young Thomas Haigh to buy thee threepennyworth of indigo, and look him in the face when he gives it thee, and touch his locks, we shall have power enough to take his life . . . and if thou canst but bring nine bits of bread away, and nine bits of butter in thy mouth, we shall have power enough to take the life of their goods."

This deposition explains why other Yorkshire villagers became suspicious when Mary Wade demanded a piece of bread from Elizabeth

Mallory, and was insistent upon having it "though she was not in want." The exchange of an object, a look, a touch, gives the witch power over a child's life. Taking away food in the mouth, bringing it into contact with the witch's body, gives power over goods, over the household economy and wealth. This deponent interprets the witch as one point in a moving current of objects that can connect her body with those of other people and give her power over them. A gift of food breaches the boundaries of the body; it is taken in, by witch or victim. In the victim, it is an invader, the representative of a hostile power, and it carries that power into the victim. In the witch, the piece of bread is held, confined within her mouth; it is a small embodiment of the victim who will also be engulfed. Food can be the innocent-seeming Trojan horse through which the power of the witch can enter the defended citadel of the body. A gift of food to a witch can turn traitor and become the instrument of her power over the giver.

Food has significance for women because it represents their productive labour and their means of nourishing, sustaining and protecting the bodies into which it is instilled. The witch's food, however, reverses this positive charge; instead of sustaining, it destroys. At the same time, the witch's gift of food to a child shows her again standing in place of the mother. The mother is responsible for feeding and maintaining the child, overseeing it, stroking and caressing it. It is the mother who knows the child's foibles, whose identity is mixed with the child's. Witches adopt these protocols, behaving as if they were the mothers of the children they betwitch; they feed them, stroke them, take too much interest in them, know too much about them. In women's fantasies, the witch represents the threat of losing control of and authority over the child; the resulting chaos and disorder of the child's body mimics the disordering of housework when the housewife loses control of it to a witch. Bewitched children exhibited symptoms of horrifying vehemence: extravagant and uncontrollably violent convulsions and rigours, the body thrown about as if by unseen hands, twisted and trembling. "Strangely handled" is the early modern phrase for this, and the phrase implies that the child is being unnaturally controlled by someone else; not, as might be appropriate, a parent, but another unsurping figure who cannot be seen by the parents. This terrifying unsurpation is made especially clear in a Wiltshire deposition: Margaret Fowler describes the way a suspect named Joan Meriwether "tooke the said child in her armes and kissed the child." When Joan leaves, the child "did fall into a very great distemper, as if it had been ready to have flowne out of this informants armes after the said Joane." As if Joan were its mother, but a mother who wants to hurt her child; as if Joan represented Margaret's worst fears about herself, her worst fears about the steadfastness of her child's love for her, as if Margaret's arms were no longer a safe harbour for the child? This mixture of love and terror is painfully dramatised in such stories. The witch also acts as a metaphor for the experience of watching a child's illness and being able to do nothing as it suffers, an agonizingly common experience of early modern families. The body whose suffering one can normally relieve struggles against an unseen force, seemingly alone, beyond help, beyond love.

The bizarre vomiting associated with possession is a related metaphor, it signifies the child's removal from the family community of commensality and also the rejection of maternal nurturance; bewitched children vomit household objects, women's tools, such as pins and needles, as if they were physically signifying their violent rejection of their mothers. Often there are signs that the betwitched child is no longer socialised; the child may lose the power of speech, may make strange animal cries, or may utter curses, or may be unable to join family prayers, or may refuse food. The socialisation of children is the mother's responsibility, and the lapsing of bewitched children into the presocial signifies the failure of her power over them and their outright rejection of that power. Convulsions, food refusal, vomiting, cursing, shrieking; all are symbols of the rejection of the mother powerfully dramatized in Margaret Fowler's story of her child's wish to fly after the witch. Stories of child betwitchment express and manage mothers' fears that their children will not love them or will reject them, fears of their children's independence, uncontrolled animality, voracity, violence. The witch could become the bearer or carrier of the fear and violence that could not be acknowledged within early modern ideals of maternity, and as such she could help to define those ideals. At the same time, and for the same woman, the witch could represent the mother's passionate wish to shelter her helpless and needy child from harm.

In women's stories, the witch was a woman who sought to enter into an inappropriately close or quasi-maternal kind of relation with the housewife as well as with her children, rather than remaining an egalitarian neighbour. The fear of a too-close relation with the mother is not confined to men. French feminist critics of psychoanalysis have stressed the importance of unresolved conflicts around the inability of the girl-child to separate herself fully from the mother. The witch, like the smother-mother, denies the housewife any adult, open role as neighbour and tries instead to draw her (back) into a problematically close mother-child bond. Women's stories about witches might express and offer fantasy resolutions for the daughter's fear of the mother, as well as the mother's fears for and of the child. The witch's actions replicate those of the "real" mother, pointing to the ambiguity of maternal behaviour as a signifier of feelings or intentions. What seems like love can destroy.

Sally Scully

Marriage or a Career?: Witchcraft as an Alternative in Seventeenth-Century Venice

Despite significant changes in the historiography of European witchcraft, the figure of the witch seems to remain the inevitable center of such studies. It is, after all, for his, or most often, her "witchly" qualities that the person, initially and subsequently, is made visible. All other aspects of the individual's life drop from the historical record as she becomes a piece of data. Absorbed into the documents only because of witchly deeds, real or imagined, the accused is isolated from a personal context. The text upon which the historian depends presents a one-dimensional picture, if a picture at all. The defendant is more likely to become a number, with some court shorthand as to personal characteristics. Only occasionally is a subject troublesome enough to leave an atypical trail in the records. . . . [T]wo recalcitrant and recidivist women in seventeenth century Venice permit a rounded depiction [however].

The trials of these two half-sisters suggest that the witch's hat was one of many, taken off and put on at will, signifying a vocational choice rather than a permanently assumed role. Moreover, what emerges is that the witch is an identity constructed, not even by contemporaries, but by subsequent historians. In the last two decades, general surveys of European witchcraft, based on printed sources preselected for their shock value, have been superseded by sympathetic and non-sensational statistical and archival studies of particular, local trials. Nonetheless, with the witch a given, elements of volition are still lost; the role of personal choice remains elusive. While the terms "agency" and "empowerment" already threaten to become abused in the nineties, it may be useful to view those accused of witchcraft as active agents in their own destinies rather than passive victims of either social ills or their own marginal belief systems. This can be accomplished if the noun "witch" is retired and this classification considered not nominative, but adjectival, describing an act rather than a person.

The element of volition can be restored to witchcraft studies using the same records which the new historiography employs: the records of the Roman Inquisition. The Inquisition isolated the individual and treated him or her as a solitary integer, not as part of a social unit. Its painstaking trials can sometimes provide insights into the role that those practices labelled "witchcraft" played in the context of a suspect's life and can correct for the historian's neglect of motivation. While the plural of anecdote is not data, gingerly reconstructed biography catches the individual who otherwise falls through the statistical grid. A career option rather than a fate or destiny, witchcraft may be considered as having a place alongside labor and family studies, rather than being an exotic territory or aberrant growth on the social body.

Many current, local, statistical studies have isolated women accused as witches, considering them a discrete group rather than integrating them laterally with other working women. The survival strategies open to women, marriage among them, also included witchcraft. The Inquisition documents offer an alternative vertical axis to the inevitable dominance of marriage, a horizontal shaft which runs through practically all other documentary trails. In assessments of the choices or lack of choices open to women, that witchcraft may have been a real option, manipulated with varying degrees of skill by various women, merits consideration.

This tale of two sisters demonstrates that the type of witchcraft chosen and the success with which it was pursued were parallel with other decisions made by or for the two women. Witchcraft practice was an extension of their composite life-pattern. The success with which it was pursued could help determine the desirability of other vocational options. Rather than reflecting a malevolent or exploited life, the women might have seen their witchcraft as part of an economic strategy which could also include marriage and prostitution.

An examination of the trials of the seventeenth century Venetians Marietta Battaglia and Laura Malipiero—accused, one twice, one four times, of witchcraft—suggests that witchcraft was a role available to women for managing their lives, operating as individual players on the social stage. To call it a career option may not be anachronistic. Marriage was a mixed blessing, playing an ambiguous role in the lives of these two women, as well as in those of their mother and of their children. Witchcraft could offer an alternative: in the case of one sister, a negative alternative, a temporary expedient; for the other sister, a positive way of finally avoiding marriage. Their use of witchcraft and their success therein were in an important sense determined by the market and how well they played it.

The trials also show that magic could range from the non-specialized incidental to the highly-specialized for which training was, at least in appearance, required. The form which the trials took on reveals a diversity which indicates less commonality among witchcraft charges than most have assumed, which cautions against the practice of isolating and artificially unifying studies of witch trials. Again, the linguistic or epistemological clarity imposed by the category "witch" may obscure diversities and unobserved communalities among those so labeled.

Maria Battaglia used the most available, least specialized, of the possibilities offered by witchcraft. Laura Malipiero exploited the array of witchcraft practices, moving from the less to the more specialized and pseudo-legitimate types. Although ultimately Laura also fell into the hands of the Inquisition, she combined witchcraft with a diversified professional life and was able to mitigate her sentences. Several of her pursuits were dangerous, but they were also lucrative and in great demand. She died in her own bed, left a sizeable estate, and maintained her final unmarried state. Witchcraft provided her with an alternative to marrying the lover whom she mentioned in her will only should he still be with her when she died. He was.

Both sisters manipulated the alternatives offered by society. For one, witchcraft was negative, an alternative to a hoped-for marriage; for the other, witchcraft was one of a number of specialties which offered a positive alternative to three negatively-experienced marriages. The use of witchcraft as part of a professional package conforms to current observations of the probability of multiple occupations for working women in early modern Europe. It is time to consider witchcraft as part of labor studies, not of some mysterious realm where nothing is learned about women's choices and opportunities.

Marietta Battaglia was first tried for witchcraft in 1637. She was already a *moglia relitta* [widow] at age thirty-eight. In June of 1645, when she reappears on the stand in a second trial, she is betrothed to Dominico di Georgio of Rovigo. She plaintively says in this trial that charges have been brought against her to prevent her pending marriage. Despite the disadvantages of her first, it is clearly a desirable union for her, both in her eyes and in those of her enemies. Otherwise, her charge that they intended to damage her marital chances would be meaningless. When she is sentenced in 1649, after being named in a third proceeding, along with Laura Malipiero, their mother Isabella, and thirteen others, she is tried as a single woman and sentenced to jail and perpetual banishment.

In many respects, Marietta Battaglia's career in magic parallels other aspects of her life. Hers was the relatively nonskilled role of the fortune-teller: predicting the *piria* [winners in the next election], . . . and various types of love magic, all standard forms of divination. At no point does the plaintiff allude to her professional training or capacity, nor do her customers testify as to the efficacy of her magic, again typical of trials for divination. The extent to which Marietta thought she was in league with the devil is the issue; her only defense is to question the motives of her accusers and to indicate that she was, essentially, a fake. Hers is assumed to be an unskilled trade. She argues that a particular performance of magic was done for love rather than money, both acknowledging the possible profit motive and hoping that this was the only concern of the Inquisitors. This desired exoneration may have been a reflection of her values and those of her culture; it was not the concern of the tribunal. She was accused of giving the devil his undue worship.

Love, or at least lust, might lead men to Marietta's house for more than one reason. Not only was she sought after for love magic, she was identified as a *meretrice* [prostitute] several times, and as a woman of "mala vita." While one must guard against the possibility that such epithets were intended merely to defame or destroy, or were part of a standard perception of witchcraft practitioners, Marietta's own testimony confirms the allegations. It was not unusual for prostitutes to supplement their incomes with love magic, and/or vice-versa. Several others named in the sisters' common trial are identified as both *streghe* [witches] and as *meretrici*; a *casino* [brothel] is identified as located in S. Giovanni Bragora. This parish is specified elsewhere both as a center for magic and for general iniquity. The two professions may have been collated in perceptions of the district; they were combined in reality in Marietta's life.

Marietta's other professions were a reflection of the types of magic she chose. She was a non-specialist—a *meretrice*, never a *cortegiana* [courtesan]—who "serviced" a number of men. Three of these men were angry, according to her defense, that she had begun to deny them carnal relations because of a change in heart. In her testimony, she claims that her pending marriage led these men to denounce her to the Sant'Ufficio [Inquisition]. A witness identifies himself as having been a customer for seven years. He testifies for the defense that Giacomo Smirno had also been Marietta's "man" until two months before, and that when she terminated he beat her, demanded money, and, when it was not forthcoming, broke her nose. A stray document in this lengthy file, signed by a parish priest, indicates something never revealed in the trial: Marietta had been pregnant. On 11 September 1649 he was called because she had lost a baby. Her sexual practices and her magical practices, all aspects of economic survival, left her vulnerable in more than one respect.

Marietta's sexual and social roles were not unusual ones for a lower-class woman; she did not handle them particularly well. Multiple and undifferentiated magical and sexual activity were supplemented by cooking, as would be revealed when both of her sentences were commuted if she would cook for half-wages at the Arsenale. A marriage would have offered a traditional escape from these roles. She was, she claimed, to have been married the very day she had been taken prisoner. Marietta was condemned for a second time on August 31, 1649. Even her plea against being banned from the city had an eternal ring: she was so poor she had nothing to wear. She did not know how to survive outside Venice. The city offered her various means to survive, but she remained laterally in a fairly low niche. For her, marriage would have been an improvement.

Laura Malipiero, Marietta's half-sister, also had a negative experience of marriage. The first of four accusations of witchcraft was brought against her by Francesco Bonamin, her putative husband of seven years and the father of her only two children. Laura was officially charged with bigamy, polygamy, and witchcraft. Her first husband, Todoro d'Andro, had been taken as a slave by the Turks. Her second husband used both the Patriarchal and Inquisition courts to get rid of her. The latter also, by the testimony of his ex-brother-in-law, beat her and bragged about it, as he had previously beat his first wife. Laura's third husband, the Bolognese Andreas Salarol, also disappeared. Her daughter, Malipiera, was so maltreated by her own husband that her eye was permanently loose in its socket. Laura's mother, Isabella, was the illegitimate product of an illicit union; her father died, presumably when she was a child. Laura was his only heir.

Laura's experience of marriage was not romantic; she subsequently seemed to use her wits and skills to avoid it. Her final lover remained just that for twenty years. She was able to gain control over her life through a series of career choices of which witchcraft was one. Even within the options which witchcraft offered, she moved from the less-specialized toward a more seemingly normal, prestigious, and better-paid specialty. Here again, the type of witchcraft chosen is a lateral extension of the other facets of a woman's life.

The label of business woman may not be either extreme or anachronistic when applied to Laura. At an early date she managed her life, and those of others, as a woman of affairs (*affari* or business). Francesco Caimus, a lawyer and witness for the defense, informed the court that since 1635 he had been a friend and had represented Laura's affairs "at the [ducal] palace." She herself handled the interests of the daughter of patrician Almoro Zane, overlooking the affairs of this noblewoman who lived in a convent outside Venice. That she had business, otherwise not defined, and had a business sense seems indicated by these glimpses of her activity.

Asked by the Inquisitors to define her trade, Laura replied that her *professione* was that of managing a rooming house. That she chose this as her professional identity may have been because it was her most neutral role, but it also may have been her main source of support. She rented a building from the pastor of San Biagio, and many witnesses in her trials had lived in her *camere*, some for a period of years. As someone who dealt in *camere locante* [rented rooms], Laura could not have been a business innocent. She would have had to have been involved in finance, however low-level, and accustomed to state regulation and dealings with the government.

The renting of rooms, because of the high probability that the tenants would be foreigners, or *forestieri,* was under the control of Venice's *Giustizia Vecchia.* In the seventeenth century, there was a magistrate aided by a judge, or *giudice,* especially for foreigners. All innkeepers, "*Hosti, Albergatori e Albergatrice,*" were required to maintain an alphabetical list of the foreigners staying with them. The *Esecutori contra la Bestemmia* had fairly standard actions against operators of rooming houses who failed to register their foreign tenants; they might be fined and/or lose their licenses. The *camere locante* involved continual state surveillance and put the landlady in a fairly visible position.

Beyond this, however, her *camere locante* offered both a stage and the players for some of Laura's more legally marginal activities. These were also good business and offered relatively high potential profits. They, however, would involve her in areas that were of great importance to the Inquisition. While her business sense may have served her well, she took risks when she tapped both the current interest in magic and magic books and the current need for medical help. It was these aspects of her economic life which would involve her in the Inquisition trials through which she can be known. At one point, her lawyer argued that the trial was about money rather than about morality or orthodoxy.

When Laura's house was searched by the *Capitano* of the Sant'Ufficio in 1654, a number of manuscripts were found. Some were rather crudely written *scongiuri* [spells]; others were sophisticated herbals and copies of the *Clavicle of Solomon,* a magic book which had achieved popularity only in the previous decade. It is in this book that the Inquisitors were interested, as they had been especially since the late 1630's, when they first directed their attention to it. Laura says in her defense that a roomer had left the books and that, in any event, she cannot read. The presence of multiple copies in various stages of completion, however, indicated that a copying and production operation may have been going on in her house.

Booksellers had been dealing in copies of the *Clavicle,* and had been prosecuted for it in Inquisition trials for *libri prohibiti* [prohibited books], during the 1640s and 1650s. Those involved in the trials were as often bookdealers as they were practitioners of the occult arts; there was a market for these texts in Venice. Laura's business sense rather than her interest in the magical arts was probably responsible for the presence of the manuscripts in her house. The multiplication of editions of the *Clavicle of Solomon* had been a real concern of the Inquisitors. It was in the transmission, social and intellectual, not the mere possession, that they were interested. A defense of illiteracy was irrelevant to them.

Laura's traffic in magical manuscripts and in practices labelled *stregarie* [witchcraft], postdated her general involvement in business. Yet even within her career in witchcraft there was an evolution from the amateur to the professional, from the less-specialized to the more specialized, from non-lucrative to high-paying magic. In moving from superstitious domestic exercises to a practice which both aped and mirrored medicine, Laura moved through several realms of magical operations. Her final trial, in 1654, had a pattern unlike that of her earlier trials. This trial had more in common with those of other so-called healers, *guaratrice*, before and after the Inquisition. She seemed, finally, to have transcended the earlier categories of witchcraft. In an unrelated trial a witness said, gratuitously, that Laura Malipiero [is] the "strega famosissima" [the most famous witch] in Venice. She had plied her trade well, perhaps too well.

Laura's practices can be seen to change and evolve from trial to trial; this unusually lengthy record allows the historian to trace the professionalization of a specialist. Ironically, it was a husband who first began Laura on the road which would ultimately provide her with a citywide reputation and a possible alternative to marriage. In his attempt, in 1629, to dissolve their marriage, Francesco Bonamin added the charge of magic to more traditional grounds for annulment; before the tribunal of the Sant'Ufficio, he accused her of witchcraft. Labelled thus were acts of magic performed within her own household: a token in a shoe, a spell in a purse, holy water in the soup. One after another, in suspicious accord, five of Laura's step-children testify to the truth of these charges. Although Laura claims her intentions were beneficent, the abuse of sacred things was, in the eyes of the Inquisitors, a heresy. She was sentenced to one year in prison.

In 1630, Laura's witchcraft was of the domestic, private and amateur variety. When she surfaces in the historical record again, in her second trial in 1649, it is for public and professional acts of a variety of undifferentiated magic. Along with fourteen others, among them her mother and sister, she is accused of various standard types of love magic, divination and other of the practices which were clearly and frequently labelled "stregarie". Her magic has evolved, and she is part of a group which exchanges techniques and shares customers. One might speculate on the role which her year in prison played in her associations and professionalization. This could be the source of whatever training Laura had; she alludes to none other. And it is only now that she pursues publicly the role of *strega*.

In 1654, when Laura appeared for her third time before the Tribunal, she was alone and was tried for a more specific form of witchcraft. Her practice of magic had acquired focus and the appearance, if only through mimickry, of a profession. She was charged with using witchcraft to medicate, and her trial took a form which had more in common with other trials for medical offenses than with her earlier *processi* [trials]. Whether heard before the Sant'Ufficio, as actions against witches, or before other tribunals, as dealings with charlatans or healers, proceedings had certain similar features. In her third trial, Laura's defense differed from her previous two. Alvise Zane, her lawyer in this new trial, chose to cast the defense in the mold of a medical rather than a witchcraft trial. He argued that this was a trial about business concerns. Other Sant'Ufficio *processi* for medical offenses tended to follow similar outlines, indicating that this charge was handled differently. Again, the idea that all witchtrials, and by extension "witches", are essentially similar, may be more a perception of historians than of either the practitioners or their prosecutors.

The ways in which Laura's third trial differed from her previous ones, and from those of her sister, were several. She was presented as someone with a tradition of training behind her. The legitimacy of her methods was addressed and defended. Witnesses from the recognized health professions were called upon to testify to these matters. Also, testimonials from successful cases were forthcoming. All these intended to imply the legitimacy of her practices by analogy; the charge that she invoked the devil or abused the sacraments was not directly addressed. Rather she was covered with the garments of professionalism. In assuming the appearance of quasi- or pseudo-legitimacy, the trial appropriated the forms of earlier traditions. In the other witchcraft trials, the issues of training, validity of methods and efficacy of results had not been addressed; by implication they were meaningless categories. In the medical trials, they became relevant. The Inquisitors had to be convinced that "real" medicine, and not some misapplications of holy processes and procedures, had been practiced. Not incidently, these trials offer a view of official and lay perceptions of medicine's legal and spiritual boundaries.

In her third trial, initiated essentially as a malpractice suit, Laura was presented as someone trained in a legitimate, if marginal, field of healing. She had learned her trade from pharmacists and *barbieritonsori* [barbers], both *arte* [guilds] licensed and controlled by the state to perform medical functions. Laura herself indicated that she was licensed, a possibility which cannot be discounted. Her methods were presented as thereby supervised and professional. Again, this feature of her defense is analogous with other trials of those specifically accused of magical healing. Satisfied customers also attested to the normalcy of her treatments, as well as to their effectiveness.

Laura's customers would have been hard put to discern the difference between what she was doing and medical practice as they perceived it. Medicine as implemented in Venice, as distinct from that taught at the nearby University of Padua, had much more in common with the recipes in her handbooks and the treatments reported by her customers than might be now apparent. Both the Paracelsan treatments, which had become a competitor in the medical marketplace, and the more traditional medicine as popularized for a general audience, emphasized herbs, oils and potions. The most desirable herbs had always come from Crete and Corfu. Recipes given for diet and various mixtures were the standard feature of medical advice in popular manuals. The difference between these and those attributed to Laura and other *guaratrici* was one of degree rather than kind.

Pharmacists, who dispensed both the advice and the mixtures, were at the center of most patients' lives. During these plague-ridden years, pharmacies multiplied so greatly in Venice that a limit had to be placed on them: no pharmacy could be within 100 paces of another. The barbers performed what mechanical operations were necessary. Even the state, which requisitioned medical knowledge as part of its defensive arsenal of survival against both the plague and possible enemy tactics, referred to the information thus obtained as "secret recipes." Such medical lore was treated as a valuable political asset and maintained as a secret state. Whatever contrived mystery surrounded the cures of *streghe*, it would not have seemed remarkable in the environment of seventeenth century Venetian perceptions of medicine and medical legitimacy.

The Inquisitors were concerned only to see if any magic, implicit or explicit worship of the devil, had crept in the interstices of these treatments. It seems that it had; Laura, like her sister, faked the various divinatory aspects of her operations. The use of magic by both women tapped into the perceived credulity of their customers rather than any primal belief system which the women shared. Recent studies on witchcraft see women using love magic in an effort to control men, which assumes that they themselves believed in it. These two sisters knew it did not work; when they had an alternative source of control, they used it. The difference between the two sisters is that Laura found a lucrative trade which addressed the current universal concern with health and post-plague survival and therefore afforded her a degree of economic and social mobility unknown to her sister. Marietta Battaglia never performed medical magic; for this she herself turned to others. The sisters were equal in recognizing witchcraft as a survival strategy, unequal in their ability to use it to their advantage.

Marietta would have preferred marriage to the expedients which life otherwise offered her. Laura was able to die in her own bed, with her last and faithful lover of twenty years in final attendance on her body. The terms of her will indicate the control she had over her life; the amounts involved show that she was fairly successful at her pursuits. The practices labelled witchcraft were not the same, nor was the role they played in the two sisters' lives, and, by implication, in other practioners' lives.

The documentary trial which Marietta and, especially, Laura left is rare. The latter sister's record is the fourth longest in the Venetian Inquisition's records, the longest for witchcraft. Full biographies of accused witches are few, although historians who follow archival leads will surely find more. . . .

Until many more individuals' stories are found and evaluated, these unusual biographies permit speculation: the word "witch" was and is an interpretive category which may not be useful and could, in fact, obscure historical investigation and understanding. The acceptance, application and repetition of the word paves the way for a single-field theory, reducing many and perhaps irreconcilable phenomena through a false intellectual economy. The identification of "witches" by historians might mask real diversity, as well as important commonalities, among those accused. The label and the accusation itself played an undiscovered role in the social intercourse and discourse of the time; the lay rhetoric of accusation, admission and denial encodes a whole conversation to which we are not yet privy. . . .

"Witches" existed, then as occasional and diverse personifications of a category of offense, and now in the eye of the historian. Caught in the historical spotlight for only a moment, the accused subjects can present no more than that image of themselves which was deemed witchly. . . .

. . . The noun *strega* is rarely used in the trials surveyed and never by the prosecutor or the defendant; it designates a trade, like "baker" or "prostitute," not an identity. It is vocational, occasional and external, not an internal, dominant and determining characteristic. It has become the essence of these women only because they are frozen in a particular kind of historical document; they are isolated in the transcript of a witch trial.

The use of the noun by historians too often assumes an identity and reification which cannot be proved to exist. By retiring the nouns "witch" and "witchcraze" as remnants of an earlier marginalizing sensationalism, these categories can be integrated in a new and more socialized synthesis. Liberated from the isolation imposed, first by history and then by historians, these women can indeed be seen as agents, more or less successful, in their own destinies.

Suggestions for
Further Reading

There is a huge literature on witchcraft, which continues to grow every year. The best—and newest—place to start on any topic is the four-volume *Encyclopedia of Witchcraft: The Western Tradition*, edited by Richard Golden (New York: ABC-Clio, 2006). The following is only a select sampling of newer works specifically on the era of the witch hunts; it does not include books from which excerpts appear in this book.

General surveys of the witch hunts in all of Europe include Joseph Klaits, *Servants of Satan: The Age of the Witch Hunts* (Bloomington: Indiana University Press, 1985); Brian P. Levack, *The Witch-Hunt in Early Modern Europe*, 2nd ed. (London, Longman, 1995); and Bengt Ankarloo, Stuart Clark, and William Monter, *Witchcraft and Magic in Europe: The Period of the Witch Trials* (Philadelphia: University of Pennsylvania Press, 2003). The last is part of a six-volume series covering witchcraft and magic in Europe from Biblical and pagan societies through the twentieth century.

Brian Levack has edited two multi-volume collections of articles, *Articles on Witchcraft, Magic and Demonology*, 12 vols. (New York: Garland, 1992), and *New Perspectives on Witchcraft, Magic and Demonology*, 6 vols. (New York: Routledge, 2001). Other wide-ranging collections of articles include Bengt Ankarloo and Gustav Henningsen (eds.), *Early Modern European Witchcraft: Centers and Peripheries* (Oxford: Oxford University Press, 1989); Jonathan Barry, Marianne Hester, and Gareth Roberts, eds., *Witchcraft in Early Modern Europe: Studies in Culture and Belief* (Cambridge: Cambridge University Press, 1996); and Stuart Clark (ed.), *Languages of Witchcraft: Narrative, Ideology and Meaning in Early Modern Culture* (London: Palgrave Macmillan, 2000).

There are several good collections of original sources: Barbara Rosen (ed.), *Witchcraft in England 1558–1618* (Amherst: University of Massachusetts Press, 1991); P. G. Maxwell-Stuart (ed.), *The Occult in Early Modern Europe: A Documentary History* (New York: St. Martin's, 1999); Alan C. Kors and Edward Peters (eds.), *Witchcraft in Europe 400–1700: A Documentary History*, 2nd ed. (Philadelphia: University of Pennsylvania Press, 2001); and Brian Levack, *The Witchcraft Sourcebook* (New York:

Routledge, 2003). Marion Gibson has edited two collections of sources; *Early Modern Witchcraft: Witchcraft Cases in Contemporary Writing* (London: Routledge, 2001) includes scholarly editions of the surviving witchcraft pamphlets from Elizabethan and Jacobean England, sixteen in all, while *Witchcraft and Society in England and America, 1550–1750* (Ithaca, NY: Cornell University Press, 2003) includes many types of texts.

Recent work on witchcraft has stressed the fact that patterns of persecution differed widely in different areas of Europe, and many of the best studies are those that focus on a specific city, country, or region. See Christina Larner, *Enemies of God: The Witch Hunt in Scotland* (Baltimore: Johns Hopkins University Press, 1981); Ruth Martin, *Witchcraft and the Inquisition in Venice 1550–1650* (London: Blackwell, 1989); David Gentilcore, *From Bishop to Witch: The System of the Sacred in Early Modern Terra d'Otranto* (Manchester: Manchester University Press, 1992); James Sharpe, *Instruments of Darkness: Witchcraft in Early Modern England* (Philadelphia: University of Pennsylvania Press, 1997); and P. G. Maxwell-Stuart, *An Abundance of Witches: The Great Scottish Witch-hunt* (London: Tempus, 2005).

Single case studies provide fascinating details which general surveys cannot. Michael Kunze, *Highroad to the Stake: A Tale of Witchcraft*, trans. William E. Yuill (Chicago and London: University of Chicago Press, 1987), provides a gripping narrative of a single case of otherwise obscure people charged with witchcraft in Bavaria; this is a book that is impossible to put down, and, though slightly fictionalized in terms of details, is based on exhaustive archival research. Retha Warnicke, *The Rise and Fall of Anne Boleyn: Family Politics at the Court of Henry VIII* (Cambridge: Cambridge University Press, 1989), explores the case of one of the most prominent women ever accused of witchcraft. Gilbert Geis and Ivan Bunn, *A Trial of Witches: A Seventeenth-Century Witchcraft Persecution* (London: Routledge, 1997), trace an English case of two women hung for witchcraft, with in-depth analysis of the court proceedings. Wolfgang Behringer, *Shaman of Obertsdorf:Chonrad Stoeckhlin and the Phantoms of the Night*, trans. H. C. Erik Midelfort (Charlottesville: University of Virginia Press, 1998), examines in detail the case of a stableboy executed for witchcraft and communicating with the dead, mentioned in the extract by Behringer in this book. Despite the sensational subtitle, James A. Sharpe, *The Bewitching of Anne Gunter: A Horrible and True Story of Football, Witchcraft, Murder, and the King of England* (London: Routledge, 1999), provides careful reconstruction of a case involving a young woman who claimed to be bewitched, but was later tried for false accusations.

The newest studies often tie witchcraft to other intellectual and cultural issues. Ian Bostridge, *Witchcraft and its Transformations, c.1650–c.1750* (Oxford: Clarendon Press, 1997), explores the slow decline of witchcraft beliefs, paying special attention to the writers and officials who tried to prop them up. Gary K. Waite, *Heresy, Magic and Witchcraft in Early Modern Europe* (London: Palgrave, 2003), examines connections between the Reformation and witchcraft, while Michael D. Bailey, *Battling Demons: Witchcraft, Heresy, and Reform in the Late Middle Ages* (University Park, PA: Pennsylvania State University Press, 2003), examines those between fifteenth-century movements of reform and the development of demonology. Lyndal Roper, *Witchcraze: Terror and Fantasy in Baroque Germany* (New Haven: Yale University Press, 2004), analyzes witchcraft within the context of the post-Reformation world of religious conflict. She pays particular attention to the language of the witch trials, as do Jeanne Favret-Saada, *Deadly Words: Witchcraft in the Bocage* (Cambridge: Cambridge University Press, 1980), and Marion Gibson, *Reading Witchcraft: Stories of Early English Witches* (London: Routledge, 1999).

Some of the books that examine the issues of gender and witchcraft tend to emphasize misogyny and male control of female sexuality, such as Marianne Hester, *Lewd Women and Wicked Witches: A Study of the Dynamics of Male Domination* (London: Routledge and Kegan Paul, 1992); Anne Llewellyn Barstow, *Witchcraze: A New History of the European Witch Hunts* (New York: Pandora, 1994); and Sigrid Brauner, *Fearless Wives and Frightened Shrews: The Construction of the Witch in Early Modern Germany* (Amherst, MA: University of Massachusetts Press, 1995). Like the essays by Roper and Purkiss included in this volume, Deborah Willis, *Malevolent Nurture: Witch-Hunting and Maternal Power in Early Modern England* (Ithaca: Cornell University Press, 1995), examines the links between witchcraft and motherhood. Diane Purkiss, *The Witch in History: Early Modern and Twentieth-Century Representations* (London, Routledge, 1996), provides a thorough and often witty analysis of contemporary representations of witches and the academic study of witchcraft.